West Germany

An Introduction

West Germany

An Introduction

Günther Kloss

Department of European Studies and Modern Languages
University of Manchester Institute of Science and Technology

A HALSTED PRESS BOOK

JOHN WILEY & SONS
New York

First published in the United Kingdom 1976 by
The Macmillan Press Ltd

Published in the U.S.A. by
Halsted Press, a Division of
John Wiley & Sons, Inc.
New York

Printed in Great Britain

Library of Congress Cataloging in Publication Data

Kloss, Günther.
    West Germany.

    Bibliography: p.
    Includes index.
    1.   Germany, West.   I.   Title.
DD259.K55   1976   943.087   75–25564
ISBN 0 470–49357–7

To M. K. and D. K.

Contents

List of Maps, Figures and Tables

Preface

This book is intended to provide a comprehensive, up-to-date background to West Germany. I hope it will be of assistance to the student of the language, politics and culture of that country, as well as to the general reader.

The use of German names and terms throughout (explained in a German–English Glossary on pp. 168–74) has been deliberate: I feel the serious student of modern Germany needs to familiarise himself with this essential terminology. In spite of this my aim has been to make this study easily readable and relatively inexpensive. For this reason I have had to be brief in many areas where further explanation and analysis might have been helpful. Since I have also had to omit all references and footnotes from the text the bibliography is more comprehensive than the reader would expect in a short introductory work of this kind.

Much of the recent statistical material comes from newspapers and periodicals as well as from official sources, and I have made use of additional reports, journals, statistical publications and books, both in German and in English, not specifically cited. In accordance with current West German practice statistics usually include West Berlin; prior to 1958–9 the Saarland is mostly omitted and early figures up to 1962 also often exclude West Berlin. Some of the figures for 1973 and 1974 are provisional.

I must acknowledge the help and advice of my friends and colleagues, more particularly Lothar Fietz, Alan Milward, Frank Mullineaux, Margaret Geake, Anita Phebe, David Williams, Iain Bride, and above all Professor Spalding of Bangor, who first suggested the need for such a book to me. Many individuals, organisations and offices in Germany provided me readily with material and answered my queries—not least Sigrid Lanzrath from that irreplaceable institution, Inter Nationes. Of course, any errors or inconsistencies are my responsibility alone.

The manuscript would never have been completed without my wife's encouragement and assistance, and I am especially grateful to Sandy Simpson, Christine Clarke, Rosalind Southern and Janice Coppel for their patience and perseverance in deciphering my original text and translating it into legible form.

University of Manchester Günther Kloss
Institute of Science and Technology

Acknowledgements

The author and publisher express thanks for permission to reproduce the following maps.

Map 1: originally published in Gerhart Binder, *Deutschland seit 1945,* Stuttgart (1969), p. 21; permission of the publishers, Seewald Verlag, Stuttgart.

Map 2: originally published in *Statistisches Jahrbuch für die Bundesrepublik Deutschland 1974*, Stuttgart/Mainz (1974), p. xxix, by the Statistisches Bundesamt in association with Verlag W. Kohlhammer; permission of the Statistisches Bundesamt, Wiesbaden.

Map 3: originally published in F. J. Monkhouse, *The Countries of North Western Europe,* 2nd edn, London (1971), p. 162; by permission of the publishers, the Longman Group, London.

Maps 4, 5 and 6: originally published in *Jahresbericht der Bundesregierung 1973,* by the Presse-und Informationsamt der Bundesregierung, Bonn (1974), pp. 405, 435, 418; by permission of the Bundesminister für Verkehr, Bonn.

Map 7: originally published in T. H. Elkins, *Germany,* 2nd edn, London (1968), p. 147; by permission of the publishers, Chatto & Windus (Granada Publishing Ltd), London.

The publisher also wishes to thank the Embassy in London of The Federal Republic of Germany for help in preparing the dust-jacket and cover design.

1 Post-war History

The Immediate Post-war Period

On June 5, 1945 the Berlin Declaration of the four military commanders-in-chief completed the demise of the Third Reich and simultaneously became the formal basis for four-power government in Germany. The Berlin Declaration put into effect the plans that had been worked out by the European Advisory Commission in London in 1944 and had been sanctioned by the Crimea (Yalta) conference in February 1945. The Berlin Declaration stated that the Allies 'assume supreme authority with respect to Germany'. Germany, within the frontiers of 1937, was divided into three (later four) zones of occupation, a special Berlin area under joint Allied occupation, was formally established (see map 1), and the creation of a Control Council, consisting of the three (later four) commanders-in-chief, who exercised the supreme authority, and a separate inter-Allied *Kommandantura* (governing authority) for the Greater Berlin area, consisting of the military commandants in the city, was announced.

The report of the Tripartite Conference of Berlin—the famous Potsdam Declaration—which was the outcome of a meeting between Stalin, Truman, and Churchill (later Attlee), confirmed this approach. The Potsdam Conference marks the turning point in East–West relations in the post-war period. The three statesmen agreed on a general outline of policy—Germany, for example, was to be treated as a single economic unit—but failed to reach agreement on detailed measures. The stipulations in the Potsdam Agreement, particularly those relating to German economy and reparations, were only partially fulfilled, as the German situation developed according to an entirely different pattern from that foreseen in 1945. The Allies had announced that 'the German people have begun to atone for the terrible crimes committed under the leadership of those whom, in the hour of their success, they openly approved and blindly obeyed', and this time few Germans were able to deny the truth of this statement. However, the worsening international climate between East and West meant that Germany this time escaped much of the revenge of the Allies.

The borders of the original three zones of occupation and the special area of Greater Berlin had been defined in detail during the London conferences of 1944. Russia was allocated the eastern, Britain the north-western, and the U.S.A. the south-western part of Germany. Greater Berlin was similarly divided into sectors. France later acquired certain areas from the American zone adjacent to her own territory.

It was decided at Potsdam that the former German territories east of a line running along the rivers Oder and Neisse should be administered by Poland, pending a final delimitation at a peace settlement. The northern part of East Prussia, including the city of Königsberg, was handed over to Russia, again pending a peace treaty, but in this case Britain and the U.S.A. formally promised to support the Russian claim to a permanent transfer. The government of the *Deutsche Demokratische Republik* (DDR, German Democratic Republic), the state into which the Russian zone had been converted, recognised the Oder–Neisse line as the new border between the two countries in 1950. The western half of Germany,

American zone of occupation

French zone of occupation

British zone of occupation

Russian zone of occupation

under Polish administration

under Russian administration

Map 1   The division of Germany (1945).

the *Bundesrepublik* (Federal Republic), on the other hand, maintained that this frontier could only be finally determined in a peace treaty with Germany as a whole. While West Germany emphasised the right of self-determination it also stressed that West Germany had no intention of altering the eastern frontier by force.

A decisive shift of attitude and emphasis occurred in 1970, under Chancellor Brandt's new government, when West Germany opened negotiations both with the Soviet Union and Poland, as well as with East Germany, with a view to the conclusion of agreements. A treaty with the Soviet Union was signed in August 1970, and another with Poland in December of the same year. In an historic vote and against bitter opposition both were approved by the West German parliament in May 1972. These eastern treaties renounce any territorial claims and declare the borders of all states in Europe including those between the two German states and the Oder–Neisse line inviolable. Although peaceful, mutually agreed adjustments are not ruled out, a revision of the Polish western frontier seems remote and the West Germans have now at last realised this. It was a particularly painful process since, because of a further stipulation in the Potsdam Agreement, German people remaining in Eastern Europe including the areas immediately to the east of the Oder–Neisse line were transferred to the rest of Germany. Most of this expulsion took place, often under harsh conditions, between

1945 and 1947, and most of those expelled went to West Germany. Their total number amounted to over 9 million, among them over 5 million from the territories just mentioned.

The Potsdam Agreement listed as the main purposes of the occupation of Germany her demilitarisation, the elimination or control of armaments industries, denazification, and preparation for the eventual reconstruction of German political life on a democratic basis. But Potsdam demonstrated Allied unity for the last time, and it indicated to the shrewd observer that no more definite agreement could be expected within the next few years. On the international level, the newly established Council of Foreign Ministers soon reached deadlock on most problems concerning Germany. Inside Germany, the Allied Control Council began its operations on August 30, 1945. Since, however, all decisions required unanimity, this body, too, ran into difficulties. In the early years, differences of opinion divided the French as much as the Russians from the Americans and British. France, for example, was opposed to any centralisation and prevented the setting-up of the central agencies specified in the Potsdam Agreement. Russia wanted more reparation payments from the western zones of occupation than the Americans regarded as reasonable. The Allied Control Council functioned until March 1948, but was then indefinitely adjourned.

Each military commander-in-chief exercised supreme authority on behalf of his government in his respective zone of occupation. Since the Control Council as co-ordinating and policy-making body soon became ineffective the measures carried out in each zone varied a great deal. All four occupation powers, however, began their programme of democratisation systematically from below, on the local level, where the first elections were usually held. They later created *Länder* (states) within their respective zones, administrative units with initially very limited social and economic functions delegated to them by the military authorities. In the course of the year 1946 elections took place in all four zones for parliaments for these Länder, the so-called *Landtage*. Whereas the French allowed only rudimentary central institutions in their zone and their three *Ministerpräsidenten* (Prime Ministers) were not even allowed to meet jointly for discussions until spring of 1948, the three other powers soon established some kind of central administration. The British instituted a Zonal Advisory Council and later a permanent Conference of Prime Ministers. The Americans allowed the Prime Ministers of the Länder in their zone to set up a permanent secretariat in order to co-ordinate the administration in the Länder. This was extended in the spring of 1947 to include a parliamentary assembly with delegates from the Landtage.

Germany in 1945 has been described as a burnt-out crater of great power politics. She had not only suffered total military, political and even moral defeat, but lay physically in ruins as well. Twenty per cent of all residential units were destroyed by bombing or fighting. Communications were disrupted so that the easiest way to travel any distance in 1945 was on the buffers of goods trains. Vast sections of industry were destroyed or were being dismantled. On the level of production in 1946–7 every German would have been provided with a new suit every forty years and a new shirt every ten years. The food shortage was particularly acute during the severe winter of 1946–7, much worse even than during the last year of the war. In Köln in 1947 only 11.7 per cent of the children aged six to twelve years were of normal weight. The black market flourished. At the same time, the Americans and British began huge relief operations. The new German governments were thus chiefly concerned with creating acceptable conditions for the German civilian populations, the numbers of which were daily swollen by thousands of those expelled from other countries.

Towards a West German state

The unsatisfactory conditions in Germany itself, the lack of progress on the international level and the increasing tension between East and West, led to a gradual reorientation of the policy of the western states. Realising that the totally different approach of the Soviet Union towards her zone and the future of Germany as a whole would prevent a union of the four zones of occupation in the near future, the Americans were the first to adopt a more positive attitude towards their former enemy. Instead of a policy of decentralisation and dismantling, they now wished to put Germany, or at least part of it, on the way to economic recovery. The British and American zones of occupation were economically fused on January 1, 1947, and later in the same year a parliamentary body and a Council, consisting of representatives of the eight participating Länder, were created, to supplement the five already existing executive offices for economy, finance and transport. The remaining two occupation powers were invited to join this arrangement. The Russians declined, and the French were initially reluctant to attach their zone to the new *Bizone* in any way, since they were essentially in favour of decentralisation and hoped to preserve this by maintaining four-power control. The deepening East–West split, exemplified by the failure of the Moscow and London meetings of the four foreign ministers in 1947, the mounting danger of a possible Soviet infiltration of the political vacuum existing in West Germany, the Marshall Plan aid programme, which had to be administered jointly for the whole of western Germany, and the French fear of becoming isolated as the unification of the British and American zones progressed, finally determined the French governmentt to agree to fuse its zone with the United Economic Area.

It was clear that West Germany required a more thorough reorganisation. Representatives of the American, British and French governments, together with delegates from the Benelux countries met in London between February and June 1948. The progress of these negotiations was considerably assisted by the walkout of the Russians from the Allied Control Council and their hostile attitude to the entire project. The London negotiations were concluded with the issue of a communiqué, and on July 1 the military governors handed over to the Ministerpräsidenten (prime ministers) of the eleven West German states the so-called Frankfurt Documents. These determined the organisation and the shape of the new state that was to be created in the following months. Document One authorised the Ministerpräsidenten to convene a constituent assembly to draft a democratic constitution, but the West German heads of governments were initially very reluctant to do this. They knew that such a step would deepen the split in Germany, and wanted to avoid anything that would look like a 'state' until it could comprise the whole of Germany. The military governors had to apply considerable pressure before the Ministerpräsidenten agreed to proceed; as a compromise the constituent assembly was renamed *Parlamentarischer Rat* (parliamentary council), the new constitution was to be called the *Grundgesetz*

(basic law), to stress its provisional nature, and it was to be ratified not by popular referendum, which would have given it too high a status, but by the already
existing Länder parliaments. Document Four put forward in very general terms
the guiding criteria that the military governors were to adopt when they
examined the new constitution. Document Three set out in general terms the
powers that the Allied governments would reserve for themselves during the occupation period—the essential terms of the later Occupation Statute.

During the time of the preliminary negotiations further important events occurred which deepened the division of Germany and considerably increased international tension. The Western Powers decided to carry out a currency reform
unilaterally in the three western zones. Such a reform was as necessary a
prerequisite to the recovery of Germany as the thorough political reforms
previously initiated. A shortage of goods coincided, as a result of Nazi financial
policy, with an abundance of money. Prices soared, particularly on the black
market, and barter became a normal means of trading. In order to put the
economy back on a sound footing the currency had to be devalued. This was
done in June 1948, when all West Germans obtained forty new *Deutsche Mark*
(DM, German marks) in exchange for forty old *Reichsmark* (the previous
currency). Later measures made the effective internal rate of exchange one new
Deutsche Mark for fifteen old Reichsmark, which meant that, once again, most
Germans had lost most of their savings. On the other hand, the change brought
about by the new currency was immediately visible, for suddenly fresh food
appeared in the shop windows, the hens began to lay eggs for the general public,
and an abundance of other goods was available in the shops. The monetary
reform was 'the spectacular début of an economic renaissance in Western Germany' (A. Grosser). Followed by a determined economic policy, based on a free,
self-regulating market and introduced even before the formal establishment of
the West German state by the then administrative director of the United
Economic Region, Ludwig Erhardt, the currency reform prepared the way for
the astonishing recovery of Western Germany. Within a few years her economy
was booming and provided a stable base for her political development, precisely
the kind of foundation the Weimar experiment had lacked.

A new currency was introduced in the East three days after that in the West,
highlighting the growing gap between the two Germanys. The results in Berlin
were very painful, for here the West and the East introduced their own different
currencies in their respective sectors. This hastened the division of the city into
two separate administrative units. In September 1948 the non-communist
majority of the City Council moved into the British sector, because it was
threatened by a Communist-inspired mob, which had invaded the council
chamber. In November a separate Council meeting was held in the East and a
separate city administration set up.

The Berlin blockade

On 24 June 1948 there began the Soviet blockade of the vulnerable access
routes to West Berlin, which is surrounded by the Soviet-occupied Eastern zone
of Germany. The Soviets first harassed and later totally closed all overland
supply routes to the western garrisons and the German civilian population in
West Berlin. The purpose of the siege was to force the three Western Powers to

abandon their position in the former German capital. The Western Allies responded by establishing an airlift, which in just over ten months in almost 200 000 flights carried about 12 million tons of food, consumer goods and industrial equipment for the 2.2 million West Berliners into the beleaguered city. In May 1949 the Russians lifted the blockade, but from 1948 onwards Germany was inextricably involved in the Cold War; indeed, Germany had become its centre.

Although access from West Germany across East German territory, limited to two waterways, four roadlinks, and five railway lines, remained precarious, tension in Berlin slackened for a while after 1949. In 1958 the Soviets proposed in an ultimatum to convert West Berlin into a 'Free City'. From then onwards the crisis gradually moved to a climax on August 13, 1961, when the government of the Deutsche Demokratische Republik completely sealed off the eastern from the western sectors and began to build a wall along the total length of the sectorial border. The construction of such a physical barrier was probably inevitable, since the comparatively simple journey across this border provided an easy, and virtually the only, escape route for East Germans who wanted to flee to the West. 2.8 millions had left East Germany since 1948 and from 1955 the annual rate had usually exceeded 200 000. From 12 July 1961 more than 1000 people fled daily. East Germany could no longer tolerate this drain on her manpower. The measures she took meant, however, the almost total physical division of the city. The personal suffering inflicted on its inhabitants on both sides of the Wall was considerable. The Four-Power Agreement of September, 1971, which for the first time contains a Russian guarantee of the access routes to West Berlin, and the subsequent agreements between the Bundesrepublik and the Deutsche Demokratische Republik, and between West Berlin and the DDR, made travel between West Berlin and the Bundesrepublik easier and permitted West Berliners to visit relatives and friends in the other half of the divided city. Communications across the wall were also improved.

The Grundgesetz

The Grundgesetz, the constitution of the new Bundesrepublik Deutschland, was accepted by the Parlamentarischer Rat on May 8, 1949. The final version obtained Allied approval, with a number of reservations on specific points. The powers vested in the Federation were also subject to the provisions of the Occupation Statute, which came into force on September 21, 1949 and governed the relations between the new state and the Western Allies. It listed a number of reserved powers, for instance in the field of disarmament and demilitarisation, foreign affairs, protection and security of Allied forces, and control over foreign trade. The sovereignty of the Bundesrepublik was thus initially severely restricted. A German Foreign Office was only established in 1951 when the Occupation Statute was revised. Supreme Allied authority was exercised by an Allied High Commission, which controlled the Federal Government and exercised the powers reserved for the Allied authorities.

The first German *Bundestag* (lower house of the Federal Parliament) was elected in August 1949 and had its inaugural meeting on September 7 in Bonn, the new 'provisional' capital. Professor Heuss was elected *Bundespräsident*

(Federal President) a few days later, and Dr Adenauer *Bundeskanzler* (Federal Chancellor).

An almost parallel development took place in Eastern Germany. The Deutsche Demokratische Republik was founded in October, a provisional parliament constituted, a provisional government formed, and the first president of the DDR elected. Germany was once again divided.

The Development of the New Bundesrepublik

The first West German government was a coalition between the strongest parliamentary group, the *Christlich–Demokratische Union/Christlich–Soziale Union* (CDU/CSU, Christian Democratic Union/Christian Social Union) under its chairman Dr Adenauer (139 seats out of a total of 402), and two smaller parties, the *Freie Demokratische Partei* (FDP, Free Democratic Party), a liberal party and the *Deutsche Partei* (DP, German Party), a national-conservative group with 52 and 17 seats, respectively. The second strongest parliamentary party, the *Sozialdemokratische Partei Deutschlands* (SPD, Social Democratic Party of Germany) with 131 seats went into opposition. This pattern repeated itself after each federal election until the government crisis in 1966: the CDU/CSU headed a coalition with one or two smaller groups, chiefly the FDP, and the SPD, though gaining seats at each election, remained excluded from governmental responsibility. Adenauer's party became virtually identified inside and outside Germany with the Bundesrepublik—quite unlike any party during the Weimar Republic. Dr Adenauer, who was 73 when he first became Chancellor, held this office until October 1963 when he was succeeded by his Minister of Economics, Dr Erhardt, who was known as the architect of the 'Economic Miracle', the amazing economic recovery.

A slight economic recession was the chief cause of the breakup of the coalition of the CDU/CSU and FDP. In December 1966 CDU/CSU and SPD, the two strongest parliamentary groups in the Bundestag who together held 447 of the 496 seats, combined in a 'Grand Coalition'. It did not survive the federal elections of September 1969. In a surprise move SPD and FDP formed a coalition under Chancellor Brandt: the SPD was now the influential senior partner in the Bonn government for the first time in the history of the Bundesrepublik, and the formerly all-powerful CDU/CSU found itself in the entirely new role of opposition. The premature elections of November 1972 confirmed the socialist-led government in power, although a change of Chancellor occurred in 1974 when Schmidt replaced Brandt after a scandal over Brandt's employment of a man subsequently discovered to be an East German spy.

West Germany under Adenaeur

Adenauer's chief goal during his early years as German Chancellor was to achieve complete sovereignty for the Bundesrepublik while linking her more firmly with her Western Allies. The international situation assisted him here: the greater the tension between the two blocs the more authority would be handed over by each side to 'its' Germany. But the greater the independence of each half, the more it became integrated with its respective bloc. Thus the Bundesrepublik had very close associations with other West European states when the Occupation Statute was repealed, the Allied High Commission dissolved and the occupation régime officially terminated on May 5, 1955. This does not alter the fact that the Allies still retain overall responsibility for Germany as a whole. West Germany's relatively early independence is the direct outcome of Dr Adenauer's methods of 'give and take', which for many years were vigorously opposed by the SPD opposition. He inspired trust in the Western Allies by being flexible and supple whereas the SPD opposition wanted to be rigid and direct, and by giving pledges in advance of gaining concessions from them. In the *Petersberger Abkommen* (Petersberg Agreement) of November 1949 he accepted officially the international control of the Ruhr and in exchange obtained Allied concessions on the reparations issue and their permission to join certain European institutions. The question of German rearmament became very acute when the Korean War in the early 1950s raised widespread fears of a similar conflict in central Europe. In spite of outspoken opposition inside Germany—it was, after all, scarcely five years after the end of the war—Adenauer was willing to agree to this step if by this means the Bundesrepublik could gain equal rights with her Western neighbours. The outcome of the negotiations was the plan for a European Defence Community with a German contribution to a European army. This was coupled with a *Deutschlandvertrag* (Germany Treaty), which would liquidate the occupation régime. After a protracted debate France rejected the idea of a European army and the restoration of West German independence appeared to fall with it. However, an alternative was found by including West Germany in an enlarged Western European Union pact and by incorporating all the new German military units into NATO, the western defence alliance, and an only slightly revised Deutschlandvertrag came into force on May 5, 1955.

Adenauer's policy of European integration coupled with reconciliation with France found a popular and sincere response in Germany. Germany became a member of the Council of Europe. The *Ruhrstatut* was superseded by the European Coal and Steel Community, a project which the French Foreign Secretary Robert Schumann put forward in 1950 and which was warmly welcomed by the government of the Bundesrepublik. The European Economic Community and Euratom, in both of which Germany plays a leading part, followed in 1957.

Relations with East Germany

This Western policy, which since 1960 has had the support of all the major parties, has provided the young West Germany with the security and military guarantees she needed during the threat from the East. It has enabled her to expand her economy and increase her wealth beyond all expectations. It has not, however, brought reunification with the eastern half of Germany any nearer; in fact it has made it more unlikely. Adenauer pursued a 'policy of strength', arguing that a strong West Germany would, with the backing of her Western Allies, command greater respect from the Soviet Union and increase the chance of an eventual reunification. He was wrong. Integration with the West and reunification were alternatives and only a renunciation of the policy of integration and the acceptance of a status of neutrality would have given any chance of a united Germany. Though the real alternatives were never put to the German electorate in these terms, they instinctively approved Adenauer's European policy when they returned his Christian Democrats in one election after another.

The real consequences of this policy are only now beginning to be realised. The West Germans have to find a new attitude towards the other German state.

For many years successive West German governments did not recognise the *de facto* existence of a political entity in the other half of Germany. The Bundesrepublik held that legally the *Deutsches Reich* (German state) continued to exist. The Bundesrepublik and the DDR were neither successors nor parts of the Reich, and the four Allied powers retained responsibility for Germany as a whole. For many years the Bundesrepublik held that it alone was identical with the former German Reich. It therefore assumed all its rights and duties (including repayments of the debts of the Reich and of thousands of millions of marks' compensation to victims of the Nazi terror) but was limited in its sovereignty to the territory of the Bundesrepublik and West Berlin. It regarded the government of Eastern Germany as a foreign régime on German soil, which was not based on the self-determination of the German population there. One of the guiding principles of German foreign policy, the *Hallstein Doktrin*, was founded on this assumption: the Bundesrepublik would not entertain diplomatic relations with any state (apart from the Soviet Union, one of the four Allies) that maintained or assumed such relations with Eastern Germany.

Not only this rigid rule but the whole basic assumption has undergone a drastic reappraisal in recent years. The SPD-led coalition in particular made substantial progress towards the normalisation of relations between the two German states within a general East–West *détente*. Chancellor Brandt's concept of a 'special relationship', 'two German states within one German nation' opened the road to bilateral negotiations on government level, without discrimination and preconditions, and led to the signing of the *Grundvertrag* (basic treaty) between the two states in December 1972. The Treaty envisages substantial improvements in the relations between the two Germanys in a variety of areas, not least in travel. Indeed, it refers to 'normal, good-neighbourly relations on the basis of equality', and the intention of each government to apply for membership of the United Nations. Yet the heads of the new diplomatic missions at each other's capitals Bonn and East Berlin are only termed 'permanent representatives' and the overriding rights and responsibilities for Germany as a whole of the former four occupation powers are declared not to be impaired. The Grundvertrag was approved by the Bundestag in May 1973 and sanctioned by the *Bundesverfassungsgericht* (federal constitutional court). A host of other agreements between the two German states have been concluded since. Thus, the Bundesrepublik, while still withholding full recognition of the DDR as a foreign state, has accepted the fact that it is a reality and that there will be no reunification in the foreseeable future.

2 Government

Federal System

West German Länder

West Germany is a *Bund* (federation) of ten states or Länder (see map 2): the city states of *Hamburg* and *Bremen, Schleswig–Holstein* (capital Kiel) and *Niedersachsen* (capital Hannover) in the north; *Nordrhein–Westfalen* (capital Düsseldorf), the *Saarland* (capital Saarbrücken), *Rheinland–Pfalz* (capital Mainz) in the west; *Hessen* (capital Wiesbaden) in the centre; and *Baden–Württemberg* (capital Stuttgart) and *Bayern* (capital München) in the south. Most of the Länder are in turn subdivided into intermediate administrative units, the *Regierungsbezirke* (counties).

West Berlin is considered by the City authorities and by the West German government for all practical purposes to be the eleventh Land of the Federal Republic. This is contested by East Germany and the Soviet Union who refer to West (but not East) Berlin as an independent political unit which does not form part of either the BRD or the DDR. The three Western powers do not regard West Berlin as a Land of the Federal Republic maintaining that the *whole* of Berlin is still under four-power control. In fact, even the U.S.S.R. to a certain extent accepts the continuing rights and responsibilities of the four powers, as indicated by the Four Power Agreement of September 1971.

The twenty-two Berlin representatives in the Bundestag are not directly elected by the West Berlin population but indirectly chosen from the sitting members of the West Berlin city parliament. Their votes in any division of the Bundestag are recorded separately and federal acts of parliament do not automatically become law in Berlin but first have to be formally approved by the city parliament. While West Berlin is not a constituent part of the Federal Republic of Germany it is *de facto* almost fully integrated into the West German state. Bundestag committees have for years met regularly in the restored former *Reichstag* building; even the whole Bundestag used to hold sessions in Berlin prior to 1965, and several Bundespräsidenten have been elected there. Federal agencies operate in and from Berlin, and the Western Allies never raised any objection to the large financial subsidies (amounting to DM 5,320 m in 1974 alone) that are provided directly and indirectly by the Federal Republic in order to maintain West Berlin's economic viability and to retain its competitive position in West German, European and overseas markets.

The Soviet Union has now sanctioned these close ties in the 1971 Quadripartite Agreement, provided the Bundespräsident, the *Bundesregierung* (federal government), the Bundestag, and other political institutions of the Bundesrepublik do not perform in the western sectors of Berlin constitutional or other official acts that would indicate that it was part of the Bundesrepublik and governed by it. Indeed, the Soviet Union has agreed to a limited representation of the interests of West Berlin by the Bundesrepublik in international affairs.

It is, of course, true that the four-power status of Berlin is by and large operative in the three Western sectors only, because the Russians withdrew from the Allied Kommandantura in 1948 and gradually allowed East Berlin to become the capital of the DDR. The Western authorities rarely interfere in West Berlin's internal affairs, but the formal emphasis on the continued legal existence of an occupation régime gives them the right to station troops in Berlin and to claim free and unhindered access through the surrounding territory of East Germany at any time. The Allied presence in Berlin is necessary to guarantee the safety and freedom of over two million West Berliners who do not wish to be swallowed up by Communist East Germany. The Allied presence was, furthermore, regarded as one of the West's most valuable assets in any negotiations with the East.

The Saarland was not originally part of the Bundesrepublik. After both world wars the Allies yielded to French pressure and allowed the area to become

Map 2   The Bundesrepublik Deutschland: Länder and Regierungsbezirke (1974).

detached from the French zone of occupation. Under French tutelage it gradually gained an autonomous political status but developed close economic and
financial ties with France. The French franc was legal tender and the coal mines
were administered by French companies. Not unnaturally, the Saar provided a
constant source of friction between the Bundesrepublik and France. Eventually,
in 1954, the two states produced the *Saarstatut* which would have
'Europeanised' the area by placing it under the supervision of the West European
Union, while safeguarding French economic control. The Saar population
rejected this solution by a two-thirds majority. The French and German
governments then agreed to a phased return of the territory to West Germany.
On January 1 1957, the Saar officially became a Land of the Federal
Republic.

Most of the Länder were founded in 1945–6 and all are creations of the Allied
authorities. The Allies, who watched and directed the drafting of the
Grundgesetz, made it clear from the outset that the new West German State was
to be federal. Considerable differences of opinion existed among them as to the
precise distribution of powers between the central and the Länder governments.
Partly because of this discrepancy of view the latitude left to the Germans was
wide, though they, too, were divided among themselves about the degree of centralisation. The outcome of lengthy deliberations guaranteed the continued
existence and financial viability of the Länder, which had considerable residuary
powers.

The Allies had carved out the Länder from the territory of their respective
zones of occupation. Only three of the eleven Länder of 1948 had any historic
continuity: Hamburg, Bremen, and Bayern, although a strong pride in regional
traditions had survived Nazi rule in many parts of the country. Several of the
new Länder absorbed parts of Prussia, for the destruction of this overpowering
state and of what it stood for had been one of the chief objectives of the occupation powers. German politicians as well as Western Allies were alive to the need
to revise the boundaries of many Länder after the creation of the Federal
Republic, since the imbalances between them were too great (see table 1). They
thought that some of the Länder might have to be merged, in order to create
larger, better balanced, and economically and politically stronger units.
Provisions for the territorial rearrangements were, in fact, introduced into the
Grundgesetz.

The most anomalous situation existed in the south-west, where the century-old
states of Baden and Württemberg had been split by the boundary between the
American and French zones. Under the authority of a special Federal Act of
Parliament a referendum was held in 1951 which gave the voters the alternative
of either restoring the old separate states of Württemberg and Baden, or creating
a unified South-West State. Nearly 70 per cent of the electorate chose the second
solution and in April 1952 the new Land of Baden–Württemberg was created.
'Baden nationalists' contested this result before the Bundesverfassungsgericht,
which directed the federal government to hold a further referendum, this time in
Baden alone. This took place in June 1970 and clearly confirmed the earlier
decision.

So far no steps towards other boundary reforms have been taken because of
the obvious difficulties in carrying through such measures considering that a
future federal boundary law must have 'due regard to regional ties, historical and

Table 1   The Länder of the Bundesrepublik

Land	Area (Dec. 1972)		Population (Dec. 1973)		Density per sq. km	Gross domestic product (1973)	
	sq km	%	'000	%	(Dec. 1973)	DM '000m	%
Bayern	70 547	28.4	10 853	17.5	154	154 230	16.6
Niedersachsen	47 417	19.1	7259	11.7	153	91 154	9.8
Baden–Württemberg	35 751	14.4	9239	14.9	258	140 744	15.2
Nordrhein–Westfalen	34 054	13.7	17 246	27.8	506	262 052	28.3
Hessen	21 112	8.5	5584	9.0	264	86 992	9.4
Rheinland–Pfalz	19 835	8.0	3701	5.9	187	51 944	5.6
Schleswig–Holstein	15 678	6.3	2580	4.1	165	31 440	3.4
Saarland	2567	1.0	1112	1.8	433	14 775	1.6
Hamburg	753	0.3	1752	2.8	2326	44 805	4.8
Berlin (West)	480	0.2	2048	3.3	4267	33 866	3.7
Bremen	404	0.2	729	1.2	1804	14 499	1.6
Bundesrepublik	248 599	100	62 101	100	250	926 500	100

cultural connections, economic expediency, and social structure' [article 29]. In the interest of greater efficiency many people throughout the Federal Republic demand territorial reforms and early in 1973 an expert commission recommended the creation of five or six new Länder of approximately equal size and developed a number of models. However, all of the Länder are now firmly established and the procedure prescribed by article 29 is so complicated that a territorial reorganisation may never happen. Significantly, in plebiscites held in January 1975 voters in parts of Rheinland–Pfalz rejected a transfer of their districts to the neighbouring Länder Hessen and Nordrhein–Westfalen. On the other hand, because voters in two historic territories of Niedersachsen supported a demand to grant their areas independent Land status under article 29 the Bonn parliament is now obliged to make legal provision for some sort of boundary revision within a year.

Distribution of powers between Bund and Länder

A substantial territorial reform would influence federal domestic policy to a considerable degree for under the German federal system the member states of the Federation exercise considerable influence at federal level. The second chamber of the federal parliament, the *Bundesrat*, represents the Länder governments and actively participates in the federal legislative process. This is the most significant institutional expression of the federal principle of the German type. The principle hinges on the precise division of legislative and administrative powers between the Federation and the participating states. In West Germany, federal legislative powers do not necessarily mean that federal agencies exist to administer federal legislation. Largely for historical reasons many of the Länder execute federal laws on behalf of the Federation. Both Bund and Länder have legislative autonomy in certain areas, yet most of the executive functions, even in clearly federal matters, lie with the Länder.

The Grundgesetz defines the areas of legislative competence in considerable detail and the Federation's supremacy is very marked. Article 73 enumerates most of the matters that are exclusively under the Federation's jurisdiction, like foreign affairs, nationality and defence, railways, air traffic, postal and telecommunication services, currency, weights and measures, the economy and foreign trade.

Article 74 contains a much longer list of powers, which the Federation can exercise only if a need for federal legislation exists, if for instance 'the maintenance of legal or economic unity, especially the maintenance of uniformity of living conditions beyond the territory of a Land, necessitates it' [article 72 (3)]. In this field of so-called 'concurrent' legislative competence the Länder have authority to legislate 'as long as, and to the extent that, the Federation does not use its legislative powers' [article 72 (1)]. In effect, the need for federal legislation is usually established by the federal parliament itself, and the Federation has used its powers extensively. Federal legislation now covers such matters as the legal codes and the legal system, refugees and expellees, war damage, restitution and reparations, nuclear energy, promotion of scientific research, student grants, road traffic and motor vehicles, construction and maintenance of major roads, shipping, and public health. In a small number of matters the Bund is entitled to establish general rules only [article 75]. This applies, for instance, to higher education, the civil service, the press and films, to nature conservancy and to regional planning. Finally, a 1969 amendment to the Grundgesetz [article 91 (a)] defines three 'joint tasks' which are planned and undertaken jointly by the Federation and the Länder: expansion of institutions of higher education, including teaching hospitals; improvements in the economic structure of the regions; and improvements in the structure of agriculture and in the protection of the coastline.

In all these fields federal law overrides Land law [article 31] and any existing Land legislation is automatically invalidated. Also, if a Land fails to comply with its obligations under the Grundgesetz or other federal law, the federal government may take the necessary steps, with the consent of the Bundesrat, to compel a Land to carry out these duties—a direct and effective, though rarely used, control mechanism. Furthermore, German constitutional theory holds that the Federation has certain additional, unwritten, 'inherent' and 'implied' powers, for example in the choice of the federal capital or the declaration of general amnesties.

Taking all these together relatively little exclusive control remains for the Länder, despite article 70: 'The Länder shall have the power to legislate in so far as this Grundgesetz does not confer legislative powers on the Federation'. The residuary powers lie in the field of education, cultural and religious affairs, the police, and local government.

New financial and supraregional requirements have gradually led to an extension of federal competence and there is no doubt that the trend towards increased centralisation will continue. The Länder fight anxiously to safeguard their rights, but are powerless when faced, for example, by the astronomical cost of the expansion of higher education in the 1970s; not even the wealthiest of the Länder would be able to finance out of its own resources the planned increase in student numbers in higher education, from 510 000 in 1970 to approximately 850 000 in 1980 and one million in 1985. Total educational expenditure in the Bundesrepublik, which was DM 28 000m in 1970, is expected to reach DM 67 000m (at 1970 prices) by 1980. Federal involvement in this area did not begin until 1964, when Bonn began to provide an annual contribution to the university building programme. By 1973 two federal ministries were dealing with Cultural Affairs, Education, and Research, and federal expenditure for this purpose amounted to DM 7600m in 1974 (excluding defence research). Now the Bundesregierung has a say in educational planning, a long-term educational policy is being developed at federal level, a federal law may establish a general framework for university reform, and the Federation is constitutionally bound to finance 50 per cent of any agreed expansion in the institutions of higher education.

The interdependence of Bund and Länder is particularly marked in the distribution of executive powers. The emphasis here lies with the Länder, not the Federation. Executive agencies, controlled by the Federation, apart from the federal ministries themselves, include the foreign service, the postal and railway services, and the armed forces. There is also the *Bundesbank* (federal bank). Federal agencies, which are relatively independent, deal with restrictive practices, statistics, the investigation of serious criminal offences on a national level and criminal statistics. Public corporations, federally controlled, administer social insurance.

The Länder administer their own laws, that is acts passed by the Landtage within their areas of competence. In the field of education all teachers are servants of the Land and their conditions of employment and pay are determined by the appropriate Land government, subject to the Federation's 'general rules' competence. The police forces are under the control of the Länder.

The Länder also administer federal laws, either 'on their own behalf' [articles 83 and 84] with very little interference from the Federation, or 'as agents of the Federation' [article 85] with more direct responsibility to the federal government, which can give detailed directives. An example of the former is the administration of the nationality laws, of the latter control over main roads. This means that the Länder maintain existing roads and plan and build new ones according to the direction of and with the financial means provided by Bonn. In all cases the federal government retains some control.

A similar division prevails in the administration of justice. Only the highest courts—Bundesverfassungsgericht, Federal High Court, Federal Labour Court, for example—are federal institutions; the lower courts, although applying federal law, form part of the legal systems of individual Länder.

Financial relationship between Bund and Länder

Financial dependence or independence is obviously a vital matter. In West Germany the Grundgesetz divides the power to raise taxes between Bund and Länder, distributes the proceeds of taxation between them, but places the greater burden for the administration of the tax laws on the Länder. Articles 104–115 contain the financial provisions and provide, for instance, that the yield from customs duties and certain excise taxes, for example on salt, coffee, tea or tobacco, accrues to the Bund, that the income from property tax, death duty, road tax and beer tax goes to the Länder, and that the revenue from the three most lucrative sources—*Einkommensteuer* (income tax), *Körperschaftssteuer* (corporation tax) and turnover tax, levied as *Mehrwertsteuer* (VAT)—must be shared between the Federation and the Länder. *Gemeinden* (local authorities) receive 14 per cent of the Einkommensteuer as well as part of the local rates and local business tax. The precise distribution between the Federation and the Länder of Einkommensteuer (47 per cent of total tax revenue in 1974) and Körperschaftssteuer has for many years been a source of bitter dispute and caused several amendments to be made to the Grundgesetz. The financial reforms of 1969 established the principle of equal shares in these two important taxes, but also for the first time brought the Mehrwertsteuer (22 per cent of total tax revenue) into the pool. The percentage shares of the latter, going respectively to the Federation and the Länder, are determined from time to time by acts of the federal parliament; the percentages for 1974 were 63:37 and for 1975 and 1976 62:38. As for the overall distribution of the total tax revenue between Bund and Länder, in 1974 approximately 50 per cent accrued to the former and 35 per cent to the latter; the remainder went principally to local authorities.

For many years there was a lack of co-ordination between the financial policies of the Bund and the Länder. Long and medium-term financial and economic planning for the Bundesrepublik as a whole was difficult and the means were lacking to deal swiftly with a financial crisis. A constitutional amendment and the *Stabilitätsgesetz* (Act to Promote Stability and Growth of the Economy) of June 1967, passed at the height of the first slight depression in the West German economy after the founding of the Bundesrepublik, provided such an instrument.

There exist considerable differences in *per capita* tax revenue between individual Länder, depending on their natural resources and degree of industrialisation (see table 1.1). In order to put the poorer Länder on a sounder footing the Federation pays direct subsidies to certain of them (1.5 per cent of VAT revenue, an estimated DM 800m in 1974) and the richer Länder (Nordrhein–Westfalen, Baden–Württemberg, Hessen and Hamburg) are required to contribute to the revenue of the others under the so-called 'horizontal equalisation' system (a total of 1830m in 1974).

Federal Legislature

The federal legislature is divided into two chambers, the Bundestag (lower house) and the Bundesrat (upper house)—see figure 1. The Bundestag consists of deputies elected by the entire West German population above the age of eighteen 'in general, direct, free, equal, and secret elections' [article 38 (1)]. The members of the Bundesrat are appointed by the Länder governments; they are not elected but represent the interests of their individual Land governments. The deputies of the Bundestag are increasingly subject to pressure from outside groups like the trade unions, the farmers and industry. Often they quite openly represent outside interests. The emphasis on party discipline appears to be less pronounced than in

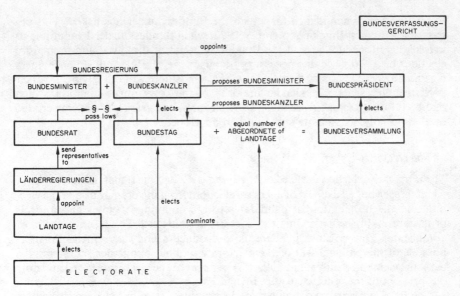

Figure 1   Constitution of the Bundesrepublik Deutschland.

Britain and pressure tends to be applied indirectly by not allocating interesting work to the disobedient member.

The members of the Bundesrat do not vote independently but have to vote together according to the instructions of their Land government. The number of seats for each Land varies from three to five, according to the size of their population (see table 2). Usually one delegate casts all the votes for his Land. This can lead to problems if a Land has a coalition government drawn from two or more parties. The Bundesrat is politically important because many bills need the approval of the second chamber before they can become law. Yet frequently the results of the elections to the Landtage do not coincide with those in the federal elections, and the composition of governments varies widely from one Land to another. As any change in a Land government is reflected in the composition of the Bundesrat it is quite possible that the majority in the Bundesrat differs from that in the Bundestag. This situation existed in 1975 when a SPD–FDP coalition was in power in Bonn, supported by quite a substantial majority in the lower house. In the Bundesrat, on the other hand, the SPD-led governments were in a minority and had only twenty votes, compared to the opposition's twenty-one (not counting the four Berlin votes). Under these circumstances party political considerations clearly influence decisions of the second chamber, and not infrequently bills which have already passed the first chamber are delayed by referring them to the *Vermittlungsausschuss* (mediation committee), a joint committee of both houses, for further consideration. They may eventually even be vetoed.

The Bundestag is elected every four years, usually in September, unless it has previously been dissolved. The Bundespräsident, the Head of State, not the Bundeskanzler, the Prime Minister, can dissolve parliament if the Bundestag fails to give a vote of confidence for which the Bundeskanzler has asked. This occurred for the first time in September 1972, when Bundeskanzler Brandt had to invoke this procedure so that the Bundestag could be dissolved and premature elections held. This became necessary because several FDP and SPD Members of Parliament had joined the CDU/CSU opposition without giving up their parliamentary seats. The slender majority of the government coalition, which had been formed after the 'regular' 1969 election, had gradually become eroded until eventually a stalemate situation had developed.

The electoral system

The form of the election is based on the *Bundeswahlgesetz* (federal electoral law), which prescribes all aspects of a federal election, from the preparation of the election and the nomination of candidates to the counting of votes and appeals procedures. Above all it defines the electoral system itself. This is one of the most complicated known, since it attempts to produce a body as representative as possible of the political will of the electorate without altogether sacrificing the personal element. And yet in 1972, 91.1 per cent of the electorate voted and only 0.8 per cent of the votes cast were invalid.

The law combines two fundamental principles. It is based on a system of proportional representation, but it retains the idea of one-member *Wahlkreise* (constituencies). This is indicated by giving two votes to each voter. One, his first vote, is for a candidate in his own Wahlkreis. Here the successful candidate has to obtain a simple relative majority, exactly as in Britain. Half of the 496 ordinary members of the Bundestag are elected in this manner. The whole country is divided into 248 Wahlkreise with an average population of approximately 240 000 (Britain: 630 constituencies with an average population of 60 000). As the law prescribes that the deviation from this figure must not exceed one-third a permanent *Wahlkreiskommission* (constituency boundary commission) recommends necessary changes reflecting movement in population. In Germany, as in Britain, a possibility of political manipulation exists here, and during the 1961–5 Parliament only a decision of the Bundesverfassungsgericht forced government and parliament to make the required substantial alterations. Although, generally speaking, the connection between a *Mitglied des Bundestags* (MdB, Member of Parliament) and his Wahlkreis is not so close as in Britain, most of the prominent West German politicians enter parliament through a constituency vote.

However, this is not the only way of obtaining a seat in the Bundestag. The remaining 248 members are chosen from candidates apearing on party lists, which are drawn up separately for each Land by every party that wishes to compete in the Land. The voter with his second vote declares his preference for a party list in the Land in which he is resident. As a kind of safeguard the names of most important politicians also appear in a prominent position on these Land party lists, so that even if they fail in their Wahlkreis they have a good chance of becoming elected. For it is the party lists alone that decide the number of Bundestag seats due to each party out of the predetermined total of 496. The results are shared out proportionally after all the votes cast for each individual party list in each Land where the party has submitted a list have been combined to form a federal total for that party. Thus, in the 1972 elections, proportional distribution gave the CDU/CSU a federal total of 225 seats. Since, however, each Land branch of the CDU had drawn up its own Land list—this is a concession to the federal element in the West German constitution—the federal total had to be shared out proportionately among the individual Länder, which yielded 61 CDU seats for the Land Nordrhein–Westfalen, 19 for Hessen, and so on.

Only at this stage are the two separate votes of the voter brought together, and only now the seats gained directly in the Wahlkreise assume importance in relation to the overall result. These seats are deducted from the total number of seats due to the respective party in each Land. In our example, CDU candidates were successful in 21 constituencies in Nordrhein–Westfalen and therefore only 61 − 21 (40 persons) on the CDU Land list joined the Bundestag—in fact, the first 40 names on the list. The greater the success of the Wahlkreis candidates the less chance have the candidates whose names appear on the Land party list only.

Since the actual distribution of seats is decided solely by the second or party list vote the electoral system of the Bundesrepublik is squarely based on proportional representation. In Britain, small parties have little chance of gaining representation in the House of Commons, and the British relative majority and single-member constituency system favours the two major parties. In Germany, smaller parties whose candidates fail to achieve a simple majority in a Wahlkreis can still gain representation in the Bundestag. In fact, apart from the CDU/CSU, the SPD and the FDP, four small parties or groups participated in the 1972 elections. In the Weimar Republic proportional representation led to a multiparty system, which contributed to the collapse of democracy. To prevent the recurrence of this tragedy the legislators put a most important hurdle in the way of splinter parties: in order to be represented a party must poll at least five per cent of valid votes cast in the whole of the Bundesrepublik. This proviso makes it difficult for new parties to enter the Bundestag (and the Landtage, where similar systems prevail) and strengthens the established parties. It has also been an effective means of reducing the number of parties represented in the Bundestag. That the trend in the Bundesrepublik is clearly towards an alternating party system with two major parties, despite the proportional basis of the electoral system, is partly due to this provision. It prevented the right-wing, nationalist *Nationaldemokratische Partei Deutschlands* (NPD, National Democratic Party of Germany), from gaining a foothold in the Bundestag in 1969 and in the same election almost excluded the 'third force' liberal FDP. In fact, since 1961 the FDP has not gained one single seat directly in a Wahlkreis.

There is, however, one loophole. Even though a party may not have overcome the five per cent obstacle it can still be proportionally represented if three of its candidates have been successful in Wahlkreise. This clause enables a large party to secure a small party as an ally and later possible coalition partner by not putting up candidates in three Wahlkreise itself and recommending its own prospective voters to vote for the candidates of the small party.

It is important to realise that under the German system the voter is able to make a distinction between party and candidate, that he is free to vote for a Wahlkreis candidate put up by one group and yet in his second, party list vote to choose the list of a different party. The FDP in particular profited from this splitting of votes in 1972: it obtained 4.8 per cent of Wahlkreis but 8.4 per cent of party votes.

The persistent growth of the two major parties CDU/CSU and SPD at the expense of all the other smaller groups has for many years provoked a debate about whether the British electoral system, with certain modifications, should be adopted in West Germany. The pressure for such a change was particularly strong during the 1966–9 *Grosse Koalition* of these two parties, but has receded since the 1969 election and the formation of the coalition between the SPD and the small FDP. Under a simple majority system the latter would almost certainly have been excluded from the legislature.

The social status of a German *Abgeordneter* (deputy) is lower than that of an English MP, but his pay and fringe benefits are better. His salary is as yet tax free, and there is even a contributory pension scheme. The leader of the opposition does not receive any remuneration from the State. Since 1969 a new type of Abgeordneter has emerged, keen to inform himself and to become an expert in one or more areas of parliamentary work. In fact, more people now look upon membership of the Bundestag as one stage in a career in politics. This is quite a revolutionary change for Germany, where for a long time parliamentary politics were not held in high esteem.

Parliamentary procedure

Once elected, the Abgeordneten of the Bundestag group themselves into *Fraktionen* (parliamentary parties). According to the standing orders of the Bundestag, which have to be approved afresh after each election, a Fraktion must have at least five per cent of the total Bundestag membership belonging to the same party in order to be officially recognised as such. A Fraktion is not only a forum for discussion, for it is through the parliamentary party that the officers of the Bundestag and the members of its numerous *Ausschüsse* (committees) are nominated. Parties are allowed with specific approval of the entire house to combine into one joint parliamentary party, which gives a small party a greater influence in Parliament. The CDU and its Bavarian branch, the CSU, have been given permission to form such a Fraktionsgemeinschaft at the beginning of each new parliament. This accounts for some of the considerable political influence of the CSU at the federal level, disproportionate to its size (48 CSU as compared to 177 CDU members).

The highest office in the Bundestag is that of *Bundestagspräsident* (President or Speaker), who is usually elected from among the members of the strongest party in the House, even if that party is in opposition. Thus the 1969 Bundestag had a CDU politician as Präsident, although the CDU was in opposition. He or she (the President of the 1972 Bundestag was a woman) is supported by a number of *Vize-Präsidenten* (deputy speakers) who are nominated from among the members of all the Fraktionen. The Bundestagspräsident does not only occupy a ceremonial office. He is the chairman of the very important *Ältestenrat* (council of elders), a kind of steering committee, composed of the Bundestagspräsident and his deputies and twenty Abgeordnete, including the *Fraktionsvorsitzenden* (parliamentary party chairmen) and whips. The Ältestenrat determines the agenda and other details of the Bundestag and its Ausschüsse and also arranges the distribution of the all-important chairmanships of the various Ausschüsse at the beginning of each new parliamentary term.

The proceedings of the full session of the Bundestag are stiff and stilted, despite repeated efforts to instil some of the spirit of the House of Commons into its German counterpart. The chamber is too large to enable an informal and lively exchange of views, in spite of the provision of microphones and procedural reforms like the introduction of a regular question hour and a limit on the length of speeches.

The first and third readings of a bill tend to be mere formalities. Most of the serious and detailed work of the Bundestag is done in the working groups of the Fraktionen and, above all, in the Bundestagsausschüsse, which consider each bill after its first reading in the full House. The 1969–72 Bundestag had only 199 plenary sessions, but its Ausschüsse held 1449 meetings and the Fraktionen 529. The Ausschüsse are reconstituted after each election and their chairmen and members are divided among the Fraktionen in proportion to their strength. The functions of each committee roughly correspond to that of one ministry. The 1972 Bundestag had 1 *ad hoc* and 19 standing committees. Two of these Ausschüsse are provided for in the Grundgesetz, those for foreign affairs and defence [article 45(a)]. In addition, there is a standing committee which safeguards the rights of the Bundestag against the federal government between two legislative terms [article 45] and the very important *Vermittlungsausschuss* (mediation committee), a joint committee with the Bundesrat [article 77 (2)]. Another committee that is composed of members of both houses is the so-called *Gemeinsamer Ausschuss* (joint committee), which becomes effective in a state of emergency caused by an attack from a foreign country (the so-called 'state of defence'); it then assumes the functions and duties of both houses [articles 115(a), 115(e), 53(a)]. In 1973, the *ad hoc* committee of the seventh Bundestag was charged with the reform of the criminal code.

The Bundestag has the specific right to appoint at the request of one-quarter of its members committees of investigation [article 44] to probe into government malpractice. Not many of these have been established—one inquired into a building contract awarded by the Defence Ministry, another into government wiretapping. In 1956 the Bundestag created the office of *Wehrbeauftragter* (Parliamentary Defence Commissioner). This is a kind of military *Ombudsman*, who is elected by the House. Following the long tradition of dominance by the military in Germany, this new office was designed to assist parliament in the control of the structure and development of the new German *Bundeswehr* (federal armed forces). The Wehrbeauftragter also receives in confidence individual complaints from members of the Bundeswehr. On several occasions the functions of the Wehrbeauftragter, and the attitude of individuals holding the office, have been the centre of public and parliamentary controversy, yet the very existence of such an institution has had a very salutary effect on the spirit and organisation of the Bundeswehr.

Matters are referred to the Ausschüsse by the full House for discussion. However, the Budget Committee is specifically empowered to act autonomously and even reach binding decisions on behalf of the whole House. It is here that the government's comprehensive budget proposals for both revenue and expenditure are most carefully scrutinised, whereas the whole House devotes comparatively little time to this and often uses the occasion of the reading of the annual budget for a debate on government policy.

An Ausschuss can alter a bill substantially; ministers or their representatives are often questioned by them. Committee members usually have expert knowledge in the particular field of the committee and often represent special interests.

Ministers, their parliamentary secretaries of state, or senior ministry officials (very rarely the Bundeskanzler himself) also answer questions in the question hour which is held at the beginning of almost all plenary sessions of the Bundestag. In spite of the power to ask supplementary questions from the floor of the House the German question hour is still considerably more formal than that of the House of Commons. The questions often concern local problems in constituencies but sometimes help to clarify a major point of government policy or lead to the discovery of a political scandal. In 1962, by means of many searching questions, the SPD opposition severely damaged the reputation of Defence Minister Strauss and caused a reshuffle of the CDU/CSU–FDP government coalition.

The *Bundesratspräsident*, the chairman of the second chamber, is elected for one year only from among the Ministerpräsidenten of the Länder and a fixed rota is observed in practice. The office is important insofar as its incumbent becomes the acting head of state should the Bundespräsident be unable to exercise his powers if, say, he is on a state visit abroad or dies or resigns in office [article 57]. Most of the legislative work of the Bundesrat is undertaken in its numerous committees where each Land has one vote. Here, the delegates of the Länder are often high-ranking civil servants, who act as alternates to their ministers and are experts in their particular field.

The Grundgesetz defines the powers and the functions of both the Bundestag and the Bundesrat. The main function of the Bundestag, as the elected representative assembly of the German people is obviously legislative, although it shares this power of law-making with the Bundesrat [article 77]. It elects (and dismisses) the Bundeskanzler as head of the government [articles 63, 67] and controls the executive administration. Together with an equal number of deputies from the ten Länder parliaments it elects the Bundespräsident [article 54]. It plays an important part in the election of the judges to the federal courts and the Bundesverfassungsgericht [article 94 (1) and 95 (2)] and has power to declare a state of emergency [articles 80 and 115(a)], although the executive has been given administrative powers to act without a formal state of emergency and without much control by the Bundestag.

The Bundesrat participates in the federal legislative process and no federal budget can be implemented without the consent of the second chamber. In addition, the Bundesrat has a share in the control of federal administration, which is unusual among constitutions of the federal type. It makes the Bundesrat a major focus of the co-operation between Bund and Länder. The Bundesrat is therefore the most direct expression and the chief guarantor of the federal character of the West German Republic, not least because any constitutional amendment requires a two-thirds majority in both houses [article 79]. The extensive powers of the Bundesrat thus give to the eleven Länder (including Berlin) an important voice in federal affairs and offset the gradual erosion of the residual powers of the Länder.

Since the Länder take such an active part in the implementation of federal legislation, the Bundesrat has been given an extensive say in the manner of implementation. *Rechtsverordnungen* (delegated legislation) are widely used in Germany by the executive to make detailed provisions supplementing the general acts by virtue of powers conferred by the legislature. The Bundesrat's approval is required for federal ordinances concerning some specially listed areas like the running of the federal railways and postal charges, for ordinances made under federal Acts that specifically require the consent of the Bundesrat before becoming law (now the vast majority of federal legislation) or that are executed by the Länder as agents of the Federation or as matter of their own concern [article 80 (2)], and for the issue of general administrative rules by the federal government [articles 84 and 85]. The second chamber's consent must be obtained by the federal government before it forces a Land to comply with its obligations under the Grundgesetz or another Act [article 37 (1)]. It has a role to play in a state of emergency and also in the quite different state of legislative emergency [article 81] which may arise when a bill is not passed by the Bundestag and when, despite a vote of no confidence in the Bundeskanzler, the Bundestag is not dissolved [article 68]. It may then fall on the Bundesrat alone to legislate for a period of up to six months. This situation has not yet occurred.

The legislative process at federal level is fairly cumbersome chiefly owing to the extensive involvement of the second chamber. Bills may be introduced into the Bundestag by the federal government (three-quarters of those that are ultimately enacted), the Bundesrat, or by at least fifteen members of the Bundestag. A legislative proposal emanating from the Government must first go to the Bundesrat for comment prior to the first reading in the federal lower house. This ensures close co-operation between Länder and Bund from the outset. It also makes the members of the Bundestag aware of the basic attitude of the Länder to the proposal, for the Bundesrat's comments must be forwarded with the government's draft to the lower house for the first reading, which usually takes the form of a broad debate on general principles. Detailed examination follows in one or more Bundestagsausschüsse to which the bill is immediately referred. Often government officials participate, public hearings are held, and political bargains between the party teams on each committee are struck here. An amended version of the bill with reports from all the committees concerned is now presented to the full House for the second and the third readings, which are consecutive. Generally, the Ausschuss members will have remained in close touch with their Fraktionen so that the Ausschuss version of a bill is usually accepted. However, the debate during the second reading is often detailed and individual sections are voted on. Amendments are also proposed and put to the vote.

When a bill has passed the Bundestag after its third reading it returns to the Bundesrat [article 77]. The procedure now depends on whether the bill requires the approval of the second chamber (*Zustimmungsgesetz*) or not (*einfaches Gesetz*). Approximately 50 per cent of all federal legislation falls into each category. The Bundesrat itself has interpreted its powers widely. It has an absolute veto in the case of bills that require its approval under the constitution. In all other cases the Bundesrat has a suspensive veto. The first chamber must then vote again and can overrule the Bundesrat by a vote of the majority of its members if the Bundesrat rejected the measure by a simple majority, or by a vote of two-thirds of the members present if the Bundesrat rejected the bill by a two-thirds majority. Normally in cases of disagreement the Vermittlungsausschuss is called into action—indeed, it must meet where the Bundesrat exercises its suspensive veto. Its eleven Bundesrat members are made up of one minister from each Land, who are not bound by instructions from their governments, while the eleven Bundestag members are chosen in proportion to the strength of the parliamentary parties in the House. The Vermittlungsausschuss concerns itself only with the clause of the bill which is under dispute. Its compromise recommendations have to be approved by the Bundestag without debate. The Bundesrat must vote within a fortnight of the lower House signifying its approval; if it still rejects the amended bill the Bundestag may override it. Most references to the Vermittlungsausschuss originate from the Bundesrat and objections arise more often than not because Land interests are affected. Eighty to 90 per cent of the bills referred to the Vermittlungsausschuss eventually become law, and it is even more astonishing that during the first four parliamentary terms (between 1949 and 1965) only nineteen bills failed ultimately because of a veto by the Bundesrat. After a bill has passed both Houses of the federal Parliament it has to be signed by the Bundespräsident and countersigned by the appropriate minister before it is promulgated in the *Bundesgesetzblatt* (Federal Gazette).

Land Legislatures

Each Land of the Bundesrepublik has its own regional parliament, called Landtag (except in the city states Hamburg and Bremen). The scope of the legislative powers of the Landtage is defined by the Grundgesetz, and they work within the framework of the constitutions of the respective Länder. The Landtage are generally considerably smaller in size than the Bundestag and tend to be more parochial and informal, certainly livelier and sometimes more interesting to an observer. Elections occur at various times between the federal elections and federal issues easily overshadow regional ones. Nevertheless, the results not infrequently differ from those of the Bundestag elections and account for the differences in the political make-up of the Länder and federal governments. Ever since 1946–47, for instance, the SPD has been the strongest single party in Hamburg, Bremen, and Hessen and quite often polled over 50 per cent of all votes cast there, although it was in opposition in Bonn from 1945 until 1966.

Federal President

The Bundespräsident is the West German Head of State. He is elected every five years, without prior debate, by a body convened solely for this purpose, the *Bundesversammlung* [article 54]. It consists of all members of the Bundestag and an equal number of representatives chosen, on a proportional basis, by each of the Landtage (see figure 1). This complicated formula assures proper representation of regional interests at the election, and, since the composition of the regional parliaments is by no means identical to that of the Bundestag, it is also designed to prevent the automatic election of a candidate favoured by the ruling party or coalition in Bonn.

The Bundesversammlung of 1972 had 1036 members (including the Berlin representatives). The CDU/CSU had 501, 470 belonged to the SPD and 65 to the FDP. A candidate requires the votes of the majority of members in order to be successful. Only one ballot was needed to elect Walter Scheel, then Chairman of the FDP, federal Foreign Minister and joint FDP/SPD candidate, as the

Table 2 Recent Landtag elections

Land	Date of election	Total number of seats	Distribution of seats				Government	Number of votes in Bundesrat
			SPD	CDU	FDP	Others		
Schleswig–Holstein	April 1974	73	32	40	—	1	CDU	4
Hamburg	March 1974	120	56	51	13	—	SPD/FDP	3
Niedersachsen	June 1974	155	67	77	11	—	SPD/FDP	5
Bremen	November 1971	100	59	34	7	—	SPD	3
Nordrhein–Westfalen	May 1975	200	91	95	14	—	SPD/FDP	5
Hessen	October 1974	110	49	53	8	—	SPD/FDP	4
Rheinland–Pfalz	March 1975	100	40	55	5	—	CDU	4
Baden–Württemberg	April 1972	120	45	65	10	—	CDU	5
Bayern	October 1974	204	64	132 (CSU)	8	—	CSU	5
Saarland	May 1975	50	22	25	3	—	CDU	3
Berlin (West)	March 1975	146	67	68	11	—	SPD/FDP	4

fourth German Bundespräsident. He obtained 530 votes out of 1033 and his CDU/CSU opponent 498.

In 1969 neither the CDU/CSU nominee Dr Schröder, Minister of Defence, nor the SPD/FDP candidate Dr Heinemann, Minister of Justice, obtained the required majority in the first or second ballots. In the third ballot a relative majority is sufficient and here the socialist Dr Heinemann was elected by 512 to 506 votes with five abstentions. The result of this particular ballot was significant for it became possible only when the group of FDP electors at the last minute pledged their support for the SPD candidate. In departing from its long and close association with the CDU/CSU the FDP moved to the left and prepared the ground for the SPD/FDP coalition government formed after the Bundestag elections later in the same year.

The office of the West German Head of State is fundamentally non-political. He has considerably less power than his counterpart in the Weimar Republic for in Weimar the popularly elected President was a political force independent of government and parliament while in the Bundesrepublik his functions are chiefly advisory and representative. His power to act independently is narrowly circumscribed by the Grundgesetz. After a federal election he alone proposes to the newly elected Bundestag a candidate for the Chancellorship [article 63 (1)], yet he will, of course, only put forward a candidate likely to obtain the required majority. Under normal circumstances he will therefore be very cautious in exercising this right of initiative and will be guided by the Fraktionen, with whom he will have consulted beforehand. If the Bundestag rejects his nominee but cannot agree by a majority of its members on another candidate and elects in a third ballot a Kanzler by a relative majority only, the Bundespräsident has again an independent rôle: it is his task to choose between appointing this 'minority Chancellor' or to dissolve the lower house altogether [articles 63, (2)–(4)]. This situation has not yet arisen. The only other provision for the Bundespräsident to act on his own is contained in article 39 (3), whereby on his request a meeting of the Bundestag must be called.

In certain other instances it is the duty of the Bundespräsident to make a decision in conjunction with other political bodies. Thus he may dissolve the Bundestag if a vote of confidence requested by the Bundeskanzler is unsuccessful, but only after the latter himself proposes such a step [article 68]. Again on the recommendation of the Bundeskanzler the Bundespräsident appoints and dismisses federal ministers and it is a matter of dispute whether he can refuse to appoint a candidate proposed by the Kanzler [article 64 (1)]. Similarly, his functions include the appointment and promotion of federal judges, high federal civil servants, and officers of the armed forces, and he can undoubtedly refuse to make such recommended appointments [article 60 (1)]. Several such instances are known.

The remaining duties of the Bundespräsident—they constitute the greater part of his activities—are chiefly of a ceremonial nature, in accordance with international custom and protocol. As Head of State he represents the Bundesrepublik in international law [article 59]. He receives and accredits foreign ambassadors and officially appoints West Germany's chief diplomatic representatives abroad. On behalf of the Bundesrepublik he enters into international agreements and treaties with other states after the appropriate constitutional processes are complete. Virtually all decrees and instructions issued by the

Bundespräsident, including those conferring decorations, require the counter-signature of the Kanzler or the appropriate minister. On the other hand, an act passed by both Houses of the federal Parliament becomes law only when the Bundespräsident promulgates it; he must examine whether it is constitutional and whether it has been passed in accordance with the proper legislative procedures. Only in a very few cases has his decision been challenged in the Bundesver-fassungsgericht. In practice, the influence of the German Bundespräsident is not founded on constitutional power but on the personality of the individual incumbent.

Federal Chancellor

Drawing on the unhappy experience of the Weimar constitution the makers of the Grundgesetz sought to weaken the legal position of the Head of State (who was popularly elected in Weimar) and strengthen that of the Kanzler still having a multiparty parliament in mind. The Bundeskanzler is elected by the Bundestag, initially on the proposal of the Bundespräsident [article 63], (see figure 1). The latter will naturally choose a candidate whom he expects to command a majority and in a multiparty system this involves careful consultation, for such a man is not necessarily the leader of the strongest party in the House. The opposition CDU/CSU group in the 1969 Bundestag was stronger than the main govern-ment party, the SPD, whose leader and chairman Willy Brandt was, nevertheless, proposed by Bundespräsident Heinemann and elected in the first ballot with a majority of two. Dr Adenauer, the first Bundeskanzler, was elected with a majority of one, on his admission of his own vote. It is clear that the parties themselves must negotiate extensively beforehand in order to present the Bundespräsident with a successful candidate. In October 1969 the two smaller parties SPD and FDP clearly outflanked their rival CDU/CSU and quickly presented the Bundespräsident with a workable coalition.

If his nominee fails to obtain the required majority of members the Bundestag may proceed to elect a candidate of its own, initially with a majority of members, and eventually, if a third ballot is reached, with only a majority of the votes cast. Once elected, a German Bundeskanzler occupies a very strong constitutional position, comparable with that of the British Prime Minister. To avoid any likelihood of a repetition of the innumerable government collapses during the Weimar Republic the Grundgesetz provides that a Kanzler cannot be defeated by simple vote of no confidence, which may easily bring down a government that has to rely on the support of several parties, but only by a 'constructive' vote of no confidence [article 67]. This means that the Bundestag can express its lack of confidence in a Bundeskanzler only by electing a successor by the majority of its members. The Bundespräsident is obliged to appoint the person elected. Should the Bundeskanzler himself ask specifically for a vote of confidence and not ob-tain it there is no constitutional necessity for him to resign. It is open to the Bundespräsident for twenty-one days to dissolve the Bundestag but even in this case the proposal needs to come from the Kanzler. The constructive vote of no confidence was tested at the federal level for the first time in April 1972, but the CDU candidate Rainer Barzel failed by two votes to obtain the required absolute majority. Brandt remained Kanzler.

Adenauer as Kanzler

The Bundeskanzler chooses his ministers, recommends their formal appointment to the Bundespräsident [article 64] and may dismiss them without interference from the Bundestag. Nor is there any limitation to the number of ministries: Adenauer cabinets have had more than twenty but the SPD/FDP coalition government included only fifteen in 1974. The Bundeskanzler 'determines, and is responsible for, general policy' [article 65]. Each minister conducts the business of his ministry independently but only within the limits of general policy. As these general policy decisions need not be collective cabinet decisions, the position of the Kanzler is further strengthened. Naturally he chairs meetings of the cabinet, which is composed of all federal ministers and parliamentary secretaries of state, and his voice is the dominant one, even if the standing orders of cabinet meetings prescribe a majority decision in the case of a difference of opinion. A great deal depends here on the personality of the Bundeskanzler. Dr Adenauer, who held office from 1949 to 1963 (see table 3), exploited to the full the freedom of manoeuvre given to him by the Grundgesetz. He had tremendous confidence in his own 'lonely decisions' and often acted independently, without prior consultation with, or the approval of, his government colleagues. No one doubted his tremendous capacity for work, his tactical skill and his political finesse, but throughout his term of office there was a lack of partnership between him and the leaders of the opposition, which gave rise to bitter feelings on both sides. At the same time Adenauer displayed an aloofness from, and an indifference to, his immediate cabinet colleagues, which made working under him difficult. Nevertheless, his early successes, his popularity, and his strong constitutional position enabled him to control his party and government. Only once did a minister resign because he disagreed with the Kanzler, when Dr Heinemann, the Minister of the Interior, left Adenauer's government in 1950 over the question of German rearmament. He later joined the SPD and was Bundespräsident from 1969 to 1974.

By 1961 Adenauer who by now was 85 years old had lost much of his earlier support, not least because of his irresponsible behaviour over the candidature for the Presidency in 1959 when he suddenly announced that he would stand for the office himself, hoping that he could get a protégé of his elected Kanzler. A few weeks later, however, he reversed his decision after a study of the constitution had convinced him that the powers of the Bundespräsident were very limited. Yet he was re-elected as head of a CDU/CSU/FDP coalition, even after the 1961 federal elections in which the FDP candidates had promised the voters not to join another cabinet under Adenauer's Chancellorship and had obtained a record 12.8 per cent of the votes as reward.

Adenauer's successors

Professor Erhardt, the political architect of the astonishing economic recovery of post-war Germany, was the obvious successor once Adenauer stepped down in 1963. The former Bundeskanzler disliked him and was dubious about his ability to lead the party, the government and the nation, but the party chose him as the man who would guarantee the continued support of the electorate. Erhardt endeavoured to be the 'Chancellor of the people' yet lacked the ability to make

Table 3   Federal governments since 1949

Bundestag	Total number of members	Bundeskanzler	Coalition partners	Number of coalition MPs*
First (1949–53)	402	Adenauer (CDU)	CDU/CSU FDP DP	208
Second (1953–7)	487	Adenauer (CDU)	CDU/CSU DP	333
			GB(BHE) [until Oct. 1955]	301
			FDP [until Feb. 1956]	281
Third (1957–61)	497	Adenauer (CDU)	CDU/CSU DP	287
Fourth (1961–5)	499	Adenauer (CDU) Erhardt (CDU) [from Oct. 1963]	CDU/CSU FDP	309
Fifth (1965–9)	496	Erhardt (CDU) Kiesinger (CDU) [from Dec. 1966]	CDU/CSU FDP CDU/CSU SPD	294 447
Sixth (1969–72)	496	Brandt (SPD)	SPD FDP	254
Seventh (1972–)	496	Brandt (SPD) Schmidt (SPD) [from April 1974]	SPD FDP	271

* At the beginning of a Bundestag term.

decisions and to stand firm in the face of attacks both from within his own party and from the FDP members in coalition with him. His popularity rapidly deteriorated when he proved unable to control the recession of 1966. After the FDP abandoned the coalition Erhardt eventually agreed to resign from the Chancellorship.

December 1966 marked the beginning of the Grosse Koalition between CDU/CSU and SPD and the Chancellorship of Dr Kiesinger, until then

Ministerpräsident of the Land Baden–Württemberg. The very nature of the new government combination required a different person to lead it. Kiesinger was a man of intellect and charm who saw himself more as chairman and coordinator than as an elected dictator. His government succeeded in restoring the economy and initiated some important reforms and policy changes, but the strain of pending elections in September 1969 and a cabinet split on financial and economic policy, made obvious shortly before polling day by differences about whether to revalue the Mark or not, resulted in stalemate and inactivity in the cabinet.

Brandt and Schmidt as Chancellors

The contrast between Dr Kiesinger and Willy Brandt who succeeded him in October 1969 could not have been more pronounced. This is in part due to their different political background: Kiesinger is an ex-Nazi who worked in Hitler's Foreign Office during the Second World War, whereas Brandt, who had been active in the socialist movement from an early age, emigrated to Scandinavia during the Nazi era and participated in the anti-German resistance movement. The two men represent different generations and in the 1961 elections Brandt's managers deliberately modelled the image of their young and active candidate on President Kennedy. Brandt's apparent sincerity, honesty and tolerance won him wide acclaim both at home and abroad. For the first time since the war the Sozialdemokraten had found a chairman of national stature whose personality was strong enough to compete with the image of Konrad Adenauer. Being a shrewd and experienced politician his realism commanded considerable respect from his government colleagues. He does not appear to have abused his authority—indeed, he was occasionally criticised for hesitating too long before taking a firm decision. He entered office on a programme of new ideas and far-reaching reforms and began by reshaping his own office; in addition to being the Chancellor's secretariat, the Chancellery became during the first Brandt government a powerful co-ordinating office for the work of the entire government. After the premature 1972 elections the SPD/FDP coalition under Brandt and his Foreign Minister Scheel was renewed and the government pledged to continue its existing policies.

Willy Brandt resigned in May 1974. He took the political responsibility for negligence in connection with the employment of an East German spy as his personal assistant, but he was also tired and had lost much of his former drive and political acumen. His tragic departure does not tarnish his international and domestic reputation which is at least equal to that of his great predecessor in the Chancellery, Dr Adenauer. It is mainly based on his *Ostpolitik* (Eastern Policy), his historic achievement in facing the German people with the real consequences of the Second World War, recognising the permanent division of Germany and establishing a new relationship with Eastern Europe. It won him the 1971 Nobel Peace Prize.

Helmut Schmidt, Brandt's Minister of Finance and formerly Federal Defence Minister and briefly Federal Minister of Economics, leader of the SPD parliamentary party between 1966 and 1969, formed a new government in less than a fortnight. Walter Scheel having departed to become Bundespräsident, Hans-Dietrich Genscher, the former FDP Minister of the Interior, became Foreign Minister and Deputy Chancellor. The cabinet had only fifteen members and substantial changes were carried out. Chancellor Schmidt did not only have to cope with a worsening economic situation, which made many of the costly reform projects of the coalition look decidedly illusionary and called for firm leadership from the top, but was also faced with internal wrangles in his own SPD party and a consequential decline in its fortunes in regional and local elections. In addition, the FDP coalition partner was worried about its own image so that the basis of the government, collaboration in an atmosphere of mutual trust, was in early 1975 in danger of being replaced by one of mutual distrust. Schmidt is a conscientious, hardworking, straightforward pragmatist, who grasps complex issues easily and is not afraid to make unpopular decisions. He quickly established himself in the eyes of many of his foreign colleagues as the political leader of Europe.

Federal and Land Ministries

Apart from the office of Bundeskanzler, which naturally always includes a special responsibility for foreign affairs (Adenauer was his own foreign minister from 1949 until 1955), the most important cabinet posts in post-war Germany were the *Bundesminister der Finanzen* (Federal Minister of Finance) and the *Bundesminister für Wirtschaft* (Federal Minister of Economics). Between 1971 and 1972 the two offices were combined and the new mammoth Ministry was thought to represent the most modern approach to the management of the economy and public finance, a vital task in Germany where the public has a special concern for economic stability.

The budget

It seems appropriate here to refer briefly to the annual budget. It is, of course, the task of the Bundesfinanzminister to prepare this, and in manner and procedure he is guided by Acts of Parliament. He attempts—usually unsuccessfully—to present his budget to the Bundestag well in advance of the beginning of the financial year, which in Germany is January 1. The budget covers the field of both the British Appropriation and Finance Acts and lists all expected revenue and expenditure. The annual *Finanzbericht* (financial report) provides the background to the budget and also, like the British public expenditure White Paper, outlines the government's intentions over the next four years. A calculation of assets and liabilities of the Federation is made separately. In drawing up the budget, the federal government is, in fact, bound by existing firm legal commitments, amounting to over 80 per cent of expenditure, and also by its own medium and long-term financial planning. The budget does not usually include new fiscal measures designed to influence consumer spending directly, like variations in the rate of tax or tax allowances. The annual budget is therefore of less immediate concern to the individual citizen than in Britain, and its presentation to the Bundestag is considerably less of an occasion. It is in any case first submitted to the Bundesrat before it reaches the Bundestag. The budget is discussed in considerable detail by the Bundestag, particularly by its budget subcommittee, before it is approved and quite frequently important political debates arise from the examination of the estimates. The *Bundesrechnungshof* (Federal Auditor General) scrutinises the accounts and reports back to Parliament.

Expenditure on the federal level was DM 20 400m in 1952 but by 1962 it reached DM 50 000m; in 1972 it exceeded DM 100 000m for the first time, and in 1974 it amounted to approximately DM 136 000m. The planned average increase in federal expenditure between 1974 and 1978 is 8.8 per cent, with an expected annual increase of approximately 9 per cent in the nominal gross national product. (This was, of course, before the 1974–5 recession.) The largest individual functional allocation in 1974 was for social security (DM 39 000m), followed by that for defence (DM 30 000m) and transport and communications (DM 20 000m).

In order to get an accurate overall picture of total expenditure and receipts the budget of the Bund must be considered together with the budgets of the individual Länder, which are prepared separately, and of the Gemeinden, as many executive functions are shared between the three. The breakdown of public expenditure in the Bundesrepublik in 1973 was as follows: Bund 38 per cent, Länder 34 per cent, Gemeinden 26 per cent, special funds (including EEC) 2 per cent. In 1950 the total expenditure was DM 28 000m or DM 590 per head of population, in 1962 DM 107 000m or DM 1883 *per capita*, and in 1971 DM 225 000m or DM 3673 *per capita*. The greatest *per capita* increases among the major headings of expenditure during the period 1962 to 1971 occurred in higher education and research, from DM 53 to DM 202, in public health and sports, from DM 77 to DM 206, and in transport and communications, from DM 148 to DM 324. Defence, on the other hand, increased from DM 300 to only DM 371. The most costly item per head of population is social security (DM 738 in 1971) and this accounted for 20 per cent of public expenditure in 1971.

Revenue obtained through taxation throughout the Bundesrepublik has risen steadily each year, except in 1967 when it only slightly exceeded the revenue of the previous year owing to economic difficulties at the time; in 1962 the total income from taxation amounted to DM 86 600m and in 1973 to 226 000m (or 24.8 per cent of the GNP, Britain 29·7 per cent in 1972). In 1970 55.7 per cent of the total revenue from taxation was raised from indirect taxes (Britain 50.7 per cent), the rest from direct taxes on corporations (7.4 per cent, Britain 9.6 per cent) and on households (36.9 per cent, Britain 39.7 per cent).

All ministers in the German federal cabinet are assisted by *Staatssekretäre* (secretaries of state), parliamentary and permanent. The institution of Parlamentarischer Staatssekretär is relatively new—it dates back to the Grosse Koalition of 1966–9—and is modelled on the British junior minister. A German Parlamentarischer Staatssekretär stands somewhere between government, parliament, and the civil service, and his relationship with his civil servant equivalent in the same ministry is ill defined. He is empowered to speak on behalf of his minister in the cabinet (most ministers have one, a few two such posts) and in both houses of the federal parliament, but he is not permitted to vote in the cabinet. Furthermore, within the ministry itself the *beamteter Staatssekretär* (permanent secretary) generally acts as his minister's deputy unless the minister makes other arrangements.

The Länder governments

Each of the ten Länder of the Bundesrepublik has its own government, which is elected by the Landtage. They are headed by Ministerpräsidenten, except in the city states Hamburg and Bremen, where they are called *Bürgermeister* (mayor), and Berlin, whose head of government is termed *Regierender Bürgermeister* (governing mayor). Their *Regierungen* (governments) or *Senate* in Hamburg, Bremen and Berlin consist of a varying number of ministers, but always fewer than in the federal cabinet. All the usual posts, with slight variations from one Land to another, can be found here, from the Ministries of the Interior, Justice and Finance to those of Economics, Agriculture, Regional Planning and Housing. No Land, of course, has a foreign minister nor a minister of defence, yet all have a *Kultusminister* (minister of education and cultural affairs) and several, like Nordrhein–Westfalen and Bayern, a minister for federal affairs.

Civil Service

The beamtete Staatssekretäre—some ministries have more than one—are the highest-ranking civil servants in the Bundesrepublik. Strictly speaking, they should be totally independent of political parties in accordance with the tradition of the German *Beamte* (professional civil servants). However, they are often political appointees and at least sympathetic to their minister's party—perhaps inevitable when the same political party led the government for almost 20 years. As a result of the first major change of government since the inception of the Bundesrepublik many of them had to leave their posts in 1969.

In 1973 almost half of the 3.4 million persons employed on a full-time basis directly or indirectly in the public service, excluding military personnel, had the special legal status of Beamter. Most school and university teachers and judges belong to this category, as do a substantial number of government and local authority employees, from manual workers and minor officials upwards to chief officers, and between 50 and 60 per cent of all employees of the *Bundesbahn* (federal railways) and the *Bundespost* (federal post office). The German civil service thus comprises employees at federal, state, and local level, but since most of the administration is delegated to the Länder and the Gemeinden it is they who employ the bulk of the Beamte (40 and 13 per cent respectively).

The origins of the German civil service go back to Prussia in the sixteenth and seventeenth centuries. Its members used to owe personal allegiance to the ruler and to the government, and they, together with the army, became the main pillar of the state, whose 'sovereign functions' they executed. Even today, on being formally admitted to the status of Beamter, a candidate must swear an oath 'to observe the Grundgesetz of the Bundesrepublik and all the laws in force in the Bundesrepublik and to carry out [his] duties in office conscientiously'.

A great deal of the German civil service's reputation of efficiency and incorruptibility has survived until the present day. Its prestige—at least inside Germany—is still high, although its once exalted social status has declined in recent years. This is partly because its members work side by side with *Angestellte* (ordinary white collar employees) who do the same jobs and are indistinguishable to the general public, partly because some top jobs that formerly used to be the preserve of career civil servants are filled by experts from outside the civil service. The old Prussian civil service virtues—duty, discipline, meticulousness, respect for the law—are today less universally encountered; nor is the civil service totally free from party-political influence. On the other hand, an attitude persists epitomised by a tendency to act strictly according to the book, a respect for a hierarchy, and the conviction of belonging to an élite, accompanied at times by a feeling of superiority towards lesser mortals. One explanation of this phenomenon is that the pattern of recruitment to the service and therefore its composition has changed remarkably little notwithstanding the political up-heavals of the past hundred years. New recruits still rarely come from the working class and half of the highest grade of civil servants themselves come from civil servant families. Thus the basic civil-service structure has not only sur-vived the Allies' attempts at reform in the early post-war years but has been assimilated remarkably well into a democratic form of government.

Unlike other monthly or weekly paid state employees, whose conditions of work and pay are determined by collective bargaining, the Beamte's special 'relationship of loyalty and service' with the state is regulated by special federal and Land legislation. In the case of the Federation this is the *Bundes-beamtengesetz* (Federal Civil Service Act) and a number of subsidiary acts. An additional federal act, under the Federation's 'general rules' competence, es-tablishes the general principles applicable to civil servants of the Länder and Gemeinden. These civil service acts define the qualifications and conditions of entry into, and the manner of resignation or dismissal from, the civil service. They describe in great detail the duties and the expected behaviour of a Beamter and also enumerate his rights. It is generally held, but disputed by the trade unions, that a Beamter is not permitted by law to strike. In return for his loyal service to the state a Beamter and his family enjoy an exceptional degree of material security, and he is entitled to the full support and protection of his employer, the state. He enjoys almost absolute security of tenure and has an ab-solute right to receive a salary and considerable supplementary benefits in accor-dance with provisions and scales laid down in yet further special legislation. Promotion is virtually automatic and since 1973 all Beamte like other public servants receive an extra month's salary annually. Often a German Beamter con-tinues to work and to receive his salary even when he is elected to membership of the regional Landtag. On becoming a member of the Bundestag his civil service status lapses only temporarily. No wonder that up to 55 per cent of members of the various parliaments are now Beamte. Good accident and illness insurance is provided and he receives a state pension, which after thirty-five years of service amounts to 75 per cent of his terminal salary. A widow receives 60 per cent of her husband's pension.

The career structure of the German civil service is rigidly stratified and again controlled by law. There are four grades, the ordinary, middle, executive and higher grade, each covering different types of jobs, from railway guards to Staatssekretäre in ministries, and there is no division into separate classes accor-ding to function, as in the British Civil Service. Although promotion within a grade is common transfer to a higher one is less so. The middle and executive grades have grown particularly rapidly, comprising 39 and 41 per cent, respective-ly, of all Beamte in 1974—one of the main reasons for the pay explosion in the public service. Training and selection are rigorous everywhere and a long probationary period has to be served until the status of Beamter is eventually con-ferred on an individual.

Law is still the most common degree subject for Beamte of the highest level working in federal, Länder or Gemeinde administration, regardless of their specific duties. In fact, as the higher grade is only a minority of the Beamte (16 per cent), it is a somewhat exclusive group, which commands high salaries and whose members enter it directly as a rule and not by promotion. Increasing thought is being given to reform of the German civil service, but relatively little has been achieved so far.

Local Government

The organisation of local government

Below the level of the Land governments we find a bewildering variety of local and district authorities whose administrative structure varies from one Land to the next but a general pattern, especially as far as the functions of these authorities is concerned, is clearly discernible. All local authorities, whatever their size or importance, whether a small village of a few hundred inhabitants, a *Dorf*, or a big city of several hundred thousand, a *Grosstadt*, have the same status in the eyes of the law: they are Gemeinden, corporations vested by the Basic Law with the right to 'regulate, under their own responsibility, all affairs of the local community, within the framework of the law' [article 28 (2)]. They can, therefore, claim universal competence; they can undertake all local responsibilities as of right, unlike their British counterparts, which are permitted to undertake only those tasks that have been specifically authorised by law. German Gemeinden set great store by their self government. However, as in most countries, central and regional governments have made considerable inroads into the autonomy of local authorities for administrative and financial reasons, so that the powers now exercised by the German Gemeinden do not differ as much as they used to from those of British local authorities. It can be argued that the German arrangement makes for greater flexibility—there is often a voluntary partnership between several Gemeinden or between Gemeinden and private enterprises, for example in the supply of housing and electricity, or Gemeinden are more involved in the promotion and finance of cultural activities than are British local authorities and are, generally speaking, more enterprising. Local pride and the active interest of citizens in the affairs of their local community is encouraged.

The Bundesrepublik, including West Berlin, comprised in January 1975 some 11 000 Gemeinden, among them sixty-four with more than 100 000 inhabitants, including Hamburg (1.8 million), München (1.3 million), and Köln (1.0 million). In 1973 there were just over 5000 Gemeinden with less than 500 inhabitants but only 2.3 per cent of the West German population lived in these small villages, whereas the sixty-two big towns housed 33 per cent and a further 22 per cent resided in the middle-sized towns with between 20 000 and 100 000 inhabitants. Local government reform, which like almost any legislation concerning local government has to be undertaken on a Land basis, is now in progress almost everywhere. It is, above all, designed to rationalise the administrative structure and to create larger and therefore more viable and effective local government units. The common pattern is one of either several small Gemeinden combining to form a bigger authority, or one or more small ones being absorbed into a neighbouring larger town. This reorganisation is often done on a voluntary basis and is substantially reducing the number of very small or 'gnome' Gemeinden.

Thus between 1968 and the beginning of 1975 the number of Gemeinden in the Bundesrepublik decreased by 13 000. Instead of 16 500 villages with less than 1000 inhabitants only 6500 were left in 1974, but the number of local authorities with a population of between 10 000 and 50 000 increased from 580 to 890. In Baden–Württemberg, for instance, the reform bill introducing voluntary, government-sponsored redrafting of Gemeinde boundaries was fought over in the Landtag in a debate lasting several days and broadcast live on the regional radio; some 1000 Gemeinden (out of a total of 3400) opted to combine in the first year. Later legislation compulsorily reduced the number of independent local authorities even further, to 1100.

The functions of local authorities

With regard to the exercise of local government functions the two-tier arrangement is normal: small Gemeinden cede those functions that they cannot exercise alone like the provision of hospitals, roads or schools, to a larger unit, the *Landkreis* (rural district). In January 1973 there were 283 of these, compared to 414 in 1968: another result of local government reform. One hundred and ten larger towns were *kreisfreie Städte*, all-purpose authorities not forming part of a Kreis. In a conurbation, large towns and surrounding Kreise are often combined in regional planning associations. Some very large towns are again internally divided into *Bezirke* (districts), with some delegated administration and advisory councils. Hamburg, Bremen and Berlin have the peculiarity of being at once Gemeinden (the two Nordsee ports are very proud of their tradition of democratic local government, dating back to the days when they counted among the most important towns with the Hanseatic League) and Länder within, or in the case of Berlin associated with, the Bundesrepublik.

The functions fulfilled by German local authorities are conveniently grouped under three broad headings:

(1) Those responsibilities that they have to exercise on behalf of the Federal government or the Land government. These include public health control, registration of population, issue of passports, organisation of elections, issue of building permits, licensing of various kinds and refugee relief. The state strictly controls the exercise of these delegated duties and pays for them. There exists, in fact, no Land administrative agency at local level: the local authority acts on behalf of the Land, as the Land administration on behalf of the Bund.

(2) Those responsibilities that are compulsory by law yet only to a limited extent regulated by the government. The Gemeinde itself has the discretion to decide as appropriate on the extent, the manner, and the timing of these operations, which extend to, for example, the provision of school buildings (teachers are generally appointed and paid for by the regional government), certain roads, housing (shared with the Land and the Bund), fire prevention, and the supply of water, gas, and electricity. The government usually gives grants but its control is restricted to ascertaining that the measures taken are within the law.

(3) Those functions in which a Gemeinde is autonomous. The government simply exercises general supervision to see that the Gemeinde keeps within the legal powers. The list of these voluntary duties is long and comprises, among others, parks, sport, recreation in general, baths and swimming pools, refuse

collection, certain means of communication, further education, museums, libraries, theatres, orchestras and many social services. It is in the cultural and leisure field that the difference in emphasis between the function of German and English local authorities is most striking. In 1973 they devoted DM 152 per inhabitant, or DM 3000m in all, to this function. Stuttgart (population 625 000) is a good example. It spent DM 41m on cultural activities in 1974; DM 16.7m of this went as a grant to the Württemberg State Opera and Theatre. There is, in fact, an abundance of municipal opera houses and theatres, and state theatres and opera houses, like the one in Stuttgart, also receive subsidies from the local authority. Hundreds of authorities, even quite small ones, have built and maintain superb open-air swimming pools, often supplemented by indoor pools. Gemeinden are also active in other fields: several large towns, including München, Stuttgart, Nürnberg, Frankfurt and Köln, are now either putting their trams underground or have begun to build an independent underground system.

In order to be truly autonomous a local authority must have sufficient independent revenue to enable it to fulfil adequately its non-delegated duties; this revenue must keep pace with the growing and justified demands made on local authorities by its citizens and must be sufficiently flexible to allow the communities a share in economic growth. German local government tax revenue, which is regulated by the Grundgesetz [article 107], is more elastic than most, yet in spite of a substantial reform in its allocation in favour of the Gemeinden in 1970 German Gemeinden complained bitterly of a financial crisis. In 1973 their total unadjusted income is estimated to have been DM 79 000m. Taxation was the source of approximately one-third of this, another third was direct income and includes charges for services, for example refuse collection and income from the many productive activities of the Gemeinden (transport, electricity, properties), and government allocations (chiefly for education, roads, and housing) accounted for about 29 per cent. The net borrowings reached 8.5 per cent. The tax income, in 1973 13.1 per cent of total tax receipts, is composed of a variety of taxes: those allotted to the local authorities *in toto*, like real-estate tax or entertainment tax as well as 60 per cent of the *Gewerbesteuer*, a trade tax levied by the local authorities on business activity, and 14 per cent of the local yield of the national Einkommensteuer.

Total expenditure (capital and recurrent) of all Gemeinden in 1973 is estimated to have amounted to DM 86 000m. An average of 28 per cent of this went on salaries and wages, the percentage being especially high in the larger towns. The unprecedented rise of salaries and wages coupled with a general cost increase resulted in greater borrowing in order to finance essential capital schemes. In absolute figures, and per head of population, the total debt of the Gemeinden was in 1973 higher than that of either the Federation or the Länder. This mounting debt, especially of the larger towns, in turn forced many authorities to cut back school and road building, provision of recreational facilities, etc., and gave rise to a demand for allocation of yet more tax revenue to the Gemeinden.

The most prominent institutions in German local government are an elected council, usually called *Gemeinderat* or *Stadtrat* or at district level *Kreisrat* presided over by a *Bürgermeister* (mayor) or in medium-size and large towns an *Oberbürgermeister* (lord mayor). Whereas the functions of the Gemeinderat are roughly comparable with those of the English local council, the role of the Bürgermeister differs in most parts of the Bundesrepublik from that of the English mayor, and it varies inside Germany according to the pattern of administration adopted.

Internal organisation of the Gemeinden

All details of local government structure and functions are defined in *Gemeindeordnungen* (local government acts) for each Land. German councils, as elsewhere, are both deliberative, legislative and executive bodies, for they themselves carry out a number of administrative functions (for example, allocation of building permits). Councils, whether Gemeinderat, Stadtrat, or Kreisrat, tend to be smaller than in Britain (Stuttgart: sixty) and meet, like their main committees, on average once a month. The entire council is elected every four, five or six years (depending on the Land) on a proportional basis from party lists. The big parties usually participate but there are often independent groups especially in the south-west. Co-opted members although permitted under some laws are rare, both on the main council and in its committees. There are fewer committees and subcommittees altogether than in Britain. No committee interferes in the routine work of the officials and in general councils concern themselves considerably less with administrative detail than in Britain.

German local authority administration is efficiently organised. It is divided into four to nine departments, each comprising several related services. The head of each group is usually a professional administrator, sometimes a technical expert, and his appointment by the council will usually be for a limited time during which he becomes a temporary Beamter. Departments can be effectively co-ordinated.

Small Gemeinden naturally will have a very simple organisation and often their officials will be honorary. They may act jointly with other authorities as in making joint appointments of technical staff. Many of the duties a small Gemeinde cannot carry out on its own are in any case transferred to the Kreis, whose organisation will be parallel to the organisation of the Gemeinden in the particular Land. They, too, will carry out functions on behalf of the Land as well as voluntarily assumed duties, but they are naturally more remote from the general public. In addition, their chief executive officers undertake extensive inspectoral duties on behalf of the Land, quite separate from their local government functions. In fact, the chief executive of the Kreis, the Landrat, is the inspector for all the lower tier Gemeinden in the Kreis and thus occupies a dual position which may be very helpful to the small local authorities. Overall control remains with the Ministry of the Interior of the Land but immediate supervision, leaving aside the Landrat, rests with the administrative Regierungsbezirk into which a Land may be divided. 'Self-government in the German sense means freedom within a tightly controlled framework of law' (Committee on the Management of Local Government). Government control, which may be quite detailed, will be concerned with investigating whether steps taken and decisions made, or about to be made, satisfy the law, and this relates to administrative structure as well as to budgeting.

Notwithstanding legislation introduced in 1971, German Gemeinden are still hampered by insufficient powers to control speculation with land needed for new development or redevelopment, and compulsory purchase powers are still insufficient. Familiar European problems like urban renewal, urban sprawl and traffic face German Gemeinden and call for greater powers and new solutions. Further federal legislation is now in preparation.

During the early years of the Bundesrepublik private enterprise was encouraged to rebuild without any noticeable local authority restriction or planning. In a remarkably short period most of the buildings ravaged by bombs and fighting were reconstructed, yet they were usually fitted into the old pre-war, not infrequently medieval, street pattern. In the 1960s the motor car brought a fundamental reorientation; as a result houses rebuilt ten years earlier, or those that had survived the war, were torn to the ground or mutilated to make way for wider streets, urban motorways and flashy office blocks. An unprecedented wave of 'modernisation' hit the country. The Gemeinden were infected by this fever and irreparable harm was done to the atmosphere and character of many a German village and town. Only in recent years has it been recognised in Germany that in the interest of preserving the general quality of the human environment the freedom of the individual local citizen must be curbed, and the powers of the Gemeinden increased. After 20 years of *laissez-faire* this proves to be a painful and slow process.

Political Parties

For the first time in the history of the German state, and in contrast to most other states with written constitutions, the political parties of the Bundesrepublik have been given official recognition in the constitution: article 21 of the Grundgesetz declares that 'parties participate in the development of the political will of the people. They may be freely founded'. In contrast, in the Weimar Republic political parties frequently acted outside the established political order and in opposition to the system of government. It was in order to eliminate the possibility of a recurrence of such practices that these and further provisions regarding the organisation and finance of political parties were included in the Grundgesetz. An additional *Parteiengesetz* (Act on Political Parties) was enacted in 1967 and amended in 1969. This new legislation has already given rise to numerous cases before the Bundesverfassungsgericht. In fact, the internal structure of political parties and their role in the political process is governed more by legal decisions than by informal practices.

The Parteiengesetz

Apart from spelling out in greater detail the nature of parties the purpose of the much-delayed Parteiengesetz, a first draft of which was prepared as early as 1951, was twofold: to secure a proper democratic structure in each party from the local level upwards by prescribing certain institutions, like regular party conferences and properly elected governing bodies and to bring party finances under public scrutiny. The second point caused most of the difficulties, for two of the three major parties, CDU and FDP, were reluctant to reveal the extent and the sources of their substantial private support (only the names of any supporter giving more than DM 20 000 to one party at any one time must be disclosed.) This is understandable, since this support provides a substantial part of their income as the figures for the year 1973 suggest: The CDU received DM 29.2m as donations but only DM 21.1m as membership dues. The FDP, too, obtained DM 6.3m from donations and only DM 2.2m from membership fees. SPD party members, on the other hand, paid DM 44.3m subscription in 1973, seven times as much as the party received from donations (5.9m). These figures reflect the higher subscription for SPD members but also the much higher membership of the SPD (995 000 in July 1974), as compared to CDU (500 000) and FDP (68 000). One detects a pronounced reluctance among the German electorate to identify itself actively with the cause of any political party, a situation that only lately shows signs of changing. From these figures the SPD emerges as the financially soundest of the three parties represented in the Bonn Parliament. It is also the richest, for it owns more shares, land and property than any other party and is the proprietor of a substantial number of papers and printing presses, among other publicity outlets.

The 1969 federal elections are estimated to have cost DM 115m. There is no legal limit on such expenditure, neither for an individual candidate nor a party. Apart from the SPD most parties finished the year of the election with substantial overdrafts, notwithstanding very heavy subsidies paid from taxpayers' money. One of the most controversial clauses of the Parteiengesetz provides for such payments to cover 'the necessary costs of an appropriate election campaign' of the participating parties both at the federal and Land level. Since 1974 the fixed rate of the federal election subsidy is DM 3.50 per registered voter, provided a party has at least 0.5 per cent of all second votes cast. The money is distributed among the parties in proportion to the (second) votes cast for each party and is paid over four years, beginning one year after an election, in annual instalments of 10, 15, 35, and 40 per cent of the total sum. Subsidies for the 1972 federal election amounted to approximately DM 140m. The 1972 payment to the SPD, for example (which consisted of two instalments because of the premature federal elections) was DM 44.7m, 39 per cent of its total income in that year. Decisions of the Bundesverfassungsgericht have established that regular subsidies to political parties out of the annual federal budget are not permissible and that an important principle of equality of opportunity would be violated if the repayment of election expenses was restricted to those parties that obtained in excess of 5 per cent of (second) votes cast. In 1969 even the NPD which obtained only 4.3 per cent of all votes cast and thus failed to gain representation in the Bundestag was still paid DM 4.5m federal election subsidies. Similar provisions exist in all the Länder.

The Grundgesetz envisages the possibility of banning a political party [article 21 (2)] if it endangers the constitutional order. The Bundesverfassungsgericht decides, and has so far declared two parties illegal—the right-wing *Sozialistische Reichspartei* (SRP, Socialist Reich Party) in 1952 and the *Kommunistische Partei Deutschlands* (KPD, Communist Party of Germany) in 1956.

In 1972, as in the previous three elections, only four political parties gained representation in the Bundestag—CDU, CSU, SPD and FDP—although eight parties had put up candidates. A similar situation exists in the Landtage and only on a local level can one find representatives of other political groups as councillors. The representation of only four parties in the Bundestag totally differs from the multiparty parliament of the Weimar days. This is a new departure in

Percentage Distribution of Party List (Second) Votes*

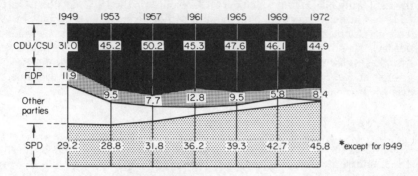

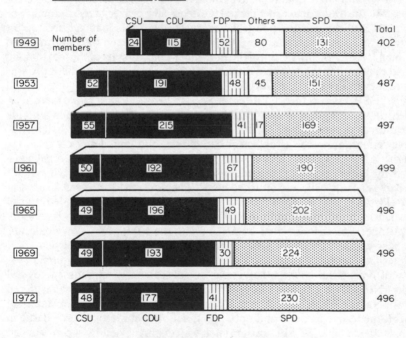

Figure 2   Federal elections since 1949.

German politics and has without any doubt resulted in greater political stability.

The integrating effect of the two major parties CDU/CSU and SPD is one of the most telling features of West German post-war politics (see figure 2). Between them they polled 60.2 per cent of all votes cast in 1949, 81.5 per cent in 1961 and 90.7 per cent in 1972. The post-1949 development shows that the smaller parties, of which there have been several, quickly lose the support of the electorate. These parties then tend to break up and their votes to be absorbed by one or the other of the big two. The latest case in point was the disappearance of the right-wing NPD from which the CDU profited in the 1972 elections. Only the FDP has hitherto survived, although not without a struggle, especially in 1969. This development has only been possible because the major West German parties have shed much of their former ideological rigidity and the German voter in turn has shown greater mobility and less allegiance to traditional political groupings. An analysis of the 1972 voting pattern revealed, for example, that every fourth elector cast his vote for a different party than in 1969.

The SPD

The SPD is the oldest of the existing parties and has a continuous history from 1863, interrupted only by the Nazi prohibition. As early as 1890 it was the strongest party in the Reichstag. However, it was excluded from participation in government since under the constitution the Imperial Chancellor was appointed by the Crown and not accountable to parliament. The Sozialdemokraten as chief opponents of the traditional order lacked the necessary degree of respectability to be accepted into the existing political framework, and this was aggravated by Bismarck's anti-socialist legislation. A rift developed between the party and the state which lasted well into the life of the Bundesrepublik, in spite of the fact that the SPD had proclaimed the Weimar Republic and shouldered government responsibility for several years during its life.

When the SPD was refounded after the Second World War, it could have been expected to stand a good chance of gaining sufficient support to make a major contribution to the emerging political system of the new Germany. It had an impeccable reputation in the struggle for democracy and unlike any other party, except the KPD, it was virtually able to resume where it had been compelled to leave off by Hitler. Some of its leaders had survived concentration camps and others had gone into exile and returned home. The SPD performed well in several Länder elections and led governments there, but power in Bonn eluded it until 1966 when it joined forces with the CDU/CSU to form the Grosse Koalition. Finally, since 1969 the party has combined with the FDP into a new coalition.

The post-war history of the SPD falls into two distinct periods, the year 1959 being the dividing line. The early years were dominated by the dynamic personality of Kurt Schumacher, the veteran socialist from Westpreussen beyond the Oder–Neisse line who was a courageous opponent of Hitler and had suffered terribly in Nazi concentration camps. He and Dr Adenauer differed substantially in temperament, background and upbringing and fought many a fierce battle in the Bundestag. The 1952 SPD programme was distinguished by a pronounced nationalist outlook, rather unusual for a socialist party. It found expression in violent opposition to Adenauer's policy of co-operation with the Western Allies and to Western integration. During this period the party stubbornly pursued a course of attempting to prevent any measure that might inhibit reunification. A bipartisan West German foreign policy did not emerge until the early 1960s.

The ideological basis of the Sozialdemokraten had always been more doctrinaire and less flexible than that of most other parties, and the same basic attitude can be seen from early pronouncements on domestic and especially economic policy. The party acknowledged changes in the social structure and attempted to appeal to sections of the electorate outside its traditional working-class supporters yet it failed to achieve this (as became obvious from the results in subsequent Bundestag elections). It continued to use some of the old Marxist–Socialist vocabulary in order to retain its traditional working-class vote and it advocated direction and planning of the economy, even nationalisation of some basic industries, at a time when the government's *Freie Marktwirtschaft* (free market economy) began to show obvious signs of success.

The 1959 Godesberg Programme marked a fundamental ideological rupture with the party's history and tradition. It recognised the success of Adenauer's foreign policy as well as the increased prosperity of all sections of the population and the changing situation in West Germany's industrial society. It sought a broader foundation than the former narrow class basis and declared that the SPD had developed from a party of the working class to a *Volkspartei* (mass party). The Godesberg Programme advocated an opening up towards the centre and deliberately catered for a plurality of views. The party's 'democratic socialism' accepted the existing essentially capitalist and private wealth-orientated social order, including the Freie Marktwirtschaft, but sought to improve it and achieve greater social justice through gradual pragmatic reforms of its internal structure. This remains the foundation of the party's policy although many younger party members, especially the *Jungsozialisten* or *Jusos* (Young Socialists), encouraged by the election victory in 1972, now advocate a return to a more ideologically committed Marxist–Socialist line of policy. They question many aspects of the SPD's (and therefore the government's) economic, social and education policy and have succeeded in creating a ferment inside the party.

Under the leadership of the popular Willy Brandt the party gained ground. After 1961 its vote increased steadily by about three per cent in each federal election, culminating in 1972 when for the first time the SPD became the strongest single party in the Bundestag. It still relied on its traditional working class vote but also drew support from a wide spectrum of the middle classes and the intelligentsia and even made headway in some Catholic rural areas, the traditional stronghold of the CDU/CSU. Since leading the government in 1969 the SPD has initiated a number of domestic reforms in, for example, education, defence, worker participation, social services, land speculation and planning, and divorce. Its greatest impact, both domestically and internationally, was made in foreign affairs through the improvement of relations with the East European states, particularly with the DDR.

Although the SPD lost Willy Brandt as Bundeskanzler in May 1974 he remained party chairman and therefore a uniting force of no mean importance inside the party. The SPD fared badly in a whole series of local and regional elections in 1974 and part of the blame must rest with the more radical party members. In 1975 the SPD will approve a new programme which will outline the party's goals up to 1985. This so-called 'Framework for Orientation '85' seeks to re-establish a consensus on crucial questions of social and economic policy. The final version will deal among other points with the extent of government planning, especially with respect to industrial investment. It pinpoints a number of priority areas, including vocational education, town-planning, and a reform of the social services and is expected to betray a slight move to the left, though firmly based on the principles of the Godesberg Programme.

The CDU

The CDU has a looser party organisation than the SPD and is a largely decentralised federation of Land associations. The federal party executive has a mainly co-ordinating function. Much of its influence depends on the quality and appeal of the party chairman, who until 1969 was also the Bundeskanzler, and the personality and skill of the party's general secretary, an office created in 1967. The CDU is not represented in Bayern for here the CSU, under its powerful chairman Josef Strauss, a national political figure in his own right, flourishes as an independent party with a membership of just under 120 000 (July 1974) and is especially closely associated with local and regional traditions. Ever since the first Bundestag, CDU and CSU have formed a joint Fraktion in Bonn although the partnership has not always been an easy one, especially since the disastrous 1972 elections.

The CDU was the outstanding new party to emerge after the collapse of the Third Reich. It was conceived as a Christian, interdenominational conservative party. This represented a major break with the past where the Centre Party had had a long political history through both the Empire and the Republic of representing Catholic interests. Nazi persecutions had brought both the major religious denominations closer together so that combination in a political movement seemed to many conservative-minded Germans a natural outcome after the war. Dr Adenauer established himself as chairman of the new party and it owed its rapid ascendancy and its long period of political power in Bonn chiefly to his personality. He combined the offices of Bundeskanzler and party chairman until his resignation from the chancellorship in 1963, but even then he retained the latter position for more than two years before handing it over to the party's economic expert Dr Ehrhardt. Neither Ehrhardt nor Dr Kiesinger, his successor and leader of the short-lived Grosse Koalition, nor Dr Barzel, the former Fraktionsvorsitzende and candidate for the Chancellorship in 1972, commanded the authority and respect that Dr Adenauer had enjoyed. This proved to be a severe handicap for the CDU, doubly so since in 1969 it was forced for the very first time into the role of opposition. It is symptomatic of the internal state of affairs of the CDU that it has been preoccupied for some time now with the leadership question almost to the exclusion of other issues. In 1973 Dr Barzel who was an excellent chairman of the Fraktion but did not have the same appeal as party leader and even less as a head of a future government, resigned from both offices and his party decided as a deliberate act of policy to separate the two. Helmut Kohl, the Ministerpräsident of the Land Rheinland–Pfalz, and Dr Carstens, a former senior civil servant, both younger and less well-known men, were elected to fill them. In early 1975 the question of the CDU/CSU candidate for the Chancellorship was far from having been solved.

This issue has detracted from the much more pressing need of leading an effective and constructive parliamentary opposition and of renewing the substance of the party's programme. One of the pillars on which the CDU/CSU's success was built was the political and economic recovery of the West German Republic. In foreign policy Dr Adenauer pursued a straightforward course of close alliance and integration with the West and hostility towards the East (without, however, achieving the supposedly overriding goal of a reunited Germany). Economically and socially the Freie Marktwirtschaft had stimulated the economy into persistent and remarkable growth. The CDU and its Bavarian sister party continued to live on past successes without attempting any fundamental reappraisal or adaptation to a changed environment, as the SPD had done in 1959. The CDU/CSU vote stagnated during the 1960s and both the 1969 and 1972 elections showed a slight decline in the percentage of the second votes cast for the party compared with previous elections. Indeed, in 1972 the CDU lost votes from all social groups, most in industrial and agricultural areas, least in urban districts from Beamte and salaried employees. In particular the younger voters turned away from the CDU/CSU whose supposedly Christian basis, its former *raison d'être*, had become difficult to maintain convincingly. After it broadened its base the SPD has come to rival the position of a political force of the centre, formerly held exclusively by the CDU/CSU.

The SPD under the leadership of its popular Chancellor Brandt had successfully carried through the improvement in the relations with Eastern Europe without losing the respect and support of Germany's Western allies. The CDU/CSU, on the other hand, was totally divided on the issue and the CSU in particular began to advocate a more nationalistic line. In the domestic field the SPD made a beginning with some social reforms, while the CDU/CSU suffered from an even more pronounced internal conflict (if less spectacularly paraded in public) between the two wings of the party, representing the interests of employers and enterprises on the one hand and the workers on the other. The rethinking process had in 1974–5 only just begun, and may affect the CDU/CSU's chances of taking advantage of the disillusionment of a substantial section of the electorate with the SPD/FDP coalition.

The FDP

When the new FDP was founded after the war it purported to continue the liberal traditions of the nineteenth century and of the liberal parties of the Weimar Republic. The new beginning was not easy; many former liberals had already joined either the CDU or the SPD, many of the traditional liberal ideas had been incorporated in their programmes, and in any case the concept of freedom of the individual, the fundamental premise on which the FDP rests, does not provide a strong basis for an organised party.

Right from the beginning the FDP had to cope with the old tensions between the conservative nationalist right wing, with strong roots in the west and the north of the Bundesrepublik, and the progressive left wing, centred in the southern half of the country. The first party chairman, Professor Heuss, who later became the first Bundespräsident, managed to reconcile many differences. However, this uneasy compromise did not last very long and the history of the FDP from 1949 to 1969 is full of dramatic conflicts and turnabouts. Since the party was poorly organised these usually centred on personalities and groups. Having become, with fifty-two seats, the third strongest party in the Bundestag the FDP was the CDU/CSU's main partner in government between 1949 and 1956. It returned to the cabinet in 1961, again under Dr Adenauer, after it had achieved a record poll of 12.8 per cent and returned 67 Abgeordnete on an anti-Adenauer platform! This hardly increased its credibility.

The turning point came in 1967 when the progressive Walter Scheel, who two years later became Foreign Minister and Deputy Bundeskanzler, replaced the national–liberal Mende as party chairman. The event took place at a time when the small FDP with a mere 49 out of 242 seats was the only opposition party in Bonn. It was then confronted with the necessity of producing a coherent alternative policy and this situation gave it a chance to free itself from the fetters of the CDU/CSU. The final break occurred in 1969 when the FDP delegates supported the SPD candidate Heinemann for the office of Bundespräsident. Later in the same year, having just managed to scrape through into the Bundestag, it formed a coalition with the SPD. Subsequently, several of its MPs defected to the opposition without relinquishing their seats so that the government majority became very precarious. The coalition was renewed after the substantial 8.2 per cent FDP vote in 1972. FDP supporters are predominantly to be found in the middle classes especially among the intellectuals, white-collar workers and civil servants but also among small industrialists, shopkeepers, etc.

Since its inception the FDP has fulfilled a precarious yet valuable role as a third force and has attracted liberal-minded voters from both the big parties. One of its important contributions to the political life of the Bundesrepublik has been to assist the process of softening the often rigid policies of the CDU and SPD. The FDP occupies a place slightly to the left of centre but distinctly between the two big parties. It is clear that in 1972 many voters who split their two votes between a SPD constituency candidate and a FDP party list wanted the renewal of the leftish liberal coalition and expected the FDP to keep socialism in check. Indeed, the FDP's social–liberal views, formulated in the 1971 Freiburg Theses, by no means coincide totally with the SPD's democratic socialism although there is a broad area of agreement. Differences exist, for example, over co-determination and the accumulation of private wealth. Its most original and substantial contributions have been in the field of foreign policy, where it was among the first to advocate the *de facto* recognition of the DDR and a general opening up towards the East, and in education reforms.

The party strives to remain an independent political force and to be recognised as such by the electorate. This proved to be a particularly difficult task in 1974 and 1975 when its popular chairman and ex-Foreign Minister Walter Scheel moved to the nonpolitical office of Head of State; forces within the party once again pulled in different directions and because of the Bonn coalition its fortunes were inextricably linked with those of the SPD. Since the latter party was going through a trough the FDP was pulled down as well and had a struggle to survive. Once again party strategists at Land level were making overtures to the CDU.

Other parties

Ever since political parties began to be licensed by the Allies after 1945, numerous other parties have been founded without much success. The short history of the neo-Nazi *Nationaldemokratische Partei* (NPD, National Democratic Party), which was founded in 1964, illustrates the point. It was by no means the first right-wing nationalist party in West Germany, as one would scarcely expect a total disappearance of any radical nationalist thinking after twelve years of intensive Nazi rule. In all cases the support for these groups centred on a few, usually rural, areas—particularly those with a high proportion of refugees (Niedersachsen, Schleswig–Holstein, Franken).

One or two of the antecedents of the NPD were very extreme right wing, like the *Sozialistische Reichspartei* (SRP, Socialist Reich Party), which was eventually prohibited by the Bundesverfassungsgericht. Another, the *Gesamtdeutscher Block/Bund der Heimatvertriebenen und Entrechteten* (GB/BHE, All German Block/Association of Expellees and those Deprived of their Rights) catered especially for the interests of refugees and all those who had suffered through the war. It attracted a not inconsiderable following, gained twenty-seven seats in the 1953 Bundestag, and was even invited to join the second Adenauer coalition government. Yet once again its fortunes declined relatively quickly. The moderate national conservative *Deutsche Partei* (DP, German party) has been described as the 'little brother' of the ruling CDU with whom it collaborated in three successive federal governments. It was only kept alive by the generosity of that party, and in the end thought to prevent extinction by combining with the GB/BHE. The new group turned more nationalist and in 1961 polled only 2.8 per cent of the second votes cast.

The NPD, the majority of whose leaders were ex-Nazis, sought to unite what was left of previous right-wing groups. To everybody's surprise it scored some success in late 1965 and early 1966 and caused serious alarm when it polled between 5.8 and 7.9 per cent of votes in four Landtag elections in 1966 and 1967. Fears were expressed that it might attract an even greater following, overcome the five per cent obstacle federally, and send delegates to the Bonn Parliament. This did not happen—the party achieved only 4.3 per cent in 1969. Very little is heard of the party today. The NPD had its major impact when the Bundesrepublik was going through its first economic recession, which the government seemed unable to master. The NPD vote, again stronger in areas with a concentration of refugees and in rural districts, appears to have been a protest vote from the stability-conscious Germans in favour of an organisation that promised to do something to remedy the situation. When the Grosse Koalition came into being with the specific aim of tackling the economic situation the ground was pulled from under the NPD's feet.

The *Deutsche Kommunistische Partei* (DKP, German Communist Party) is a case apart. It is the successor to the old *Kommunistische Partei Deutschlands* (KPD, Communist Party of Germany), which was proscribed in 1956. The KPD vote in the immediate post-war period had been in the order of 5 to 10 per cent but quickly declined when the communists took total control over East Germany. No communist was returned to the second Bundestag and by 1954 the party had seats in only three Landtage. The ban in 1956 seemed hardly necessary and with West Germany's improved relations with the East it became something of an embarrassment. A way was eventually found to legalise a communist party once again. The DKP now anxiously seeks to remain within the constitution yet its impact has been small: it had 40 000 members in 1973 and obtained a mere 0.3 per cent of votes in the 1972 federal election.

The Legal System

German law differs in many important respects from Anglo-American jurisprudence. In common with most other continental countries it is based on a code rather than a series of statutes and precedents. Another distinction, at least with reference to English Law, is that the West German written constitution includes [articles 1–19] a Bill of Rights guaranteeing certain 'inviolable and inalienable' human rights to every citizen. These include the right to life and liberty, freedom of expression, freedom of assembly, freedom of association, the inviolability of the home, the protection of property and the secrecy of the mail and of postal services and telecommunications. In the Bundesrepublik these are not just statements 'of the basis of every community, of peace and of justice in the world' [article 1 (2)], not a mere declaration of intent as during the Weimar Republic, but are binding on the legislature, the executive, and the judiciary 'as immediately enforceable law' [article 1 (3)]. In addition, the 1950 European Convention of Human Rights and the 1952 Protocol have been made part of German municipal law.

Each individual German citizen thus has the right to go to court if he feels that any of these rights have been infringed, even if by the legislature. And if no remedy is available in the ordinary courts he has the right to bring a 'constitutional complaint' to the Bundesverfassungsgericht in Karlsruhe [article 94 (4a)]. Many thousands of such complaints have been received and investigated. This direct enforcement of the constitution by the citizen is a procedure that is not usually found in written constitutions, even those containing a Bill of Rights. The Bundesverfassungsgericht has declared, for example, that article 3 of the Grundgesetz ('no one may be prejudiced or favoured because of . . . his religious or political opinions') would be violated if public radio corporations were to exclude any political party that had submitted Land party lists in the election from making election broadcasts. On the other hand, the Court denied to a group of prostitutes a declaration that regulations against loitering infringed their constitutionally guaranteed right of freedom of occupation and of choosing a place of work.

However, even basic rights cannot be unlimited in extent. The Grundgesetz permits, for example, the prosecution and punishment of criminals, even though this involves restrictions on the inviolability of the person and the freedom of the individual. Here, and in similar cases, parliament is specially empowered to legislate as long as the 'essential content' of the basic right is not violated [article 19 (2)]. Any amendment of the Grundgesetz requires a two-thirds majority of both houses of the federal parliament [article 79]. Article 1, which declares the dignity of man inviolable and establishes this as the basic principle of the constitution, cannot be amended, though the basic rights themselves may be redefined.

It is probably true that, despite the lack of a written constitution or of any constitutionally guaranteed human rights in English law, the general attitude of the Englishman is that he is free to do whatever the law does not specifically forbid, whereas the German assumes that anything not specifically permitted by the law is forbidden. After Germany's experience of National Socialist rule, when the basic rights in the constitution were suspended by presidential decree, it is not surprising that the Parlamentarischer Rat in 1948–9 dedicated themselves to founding a new, rigid constitution where human rights could not be easily taken away. The system has worked reasonably well, and both individual citizens and organisations are well aware of the important guarantees that these rights give. Significantly it took almost ten years, until 1968, for the federal parliament to pass legislation to provide for extraordinary powers in a state of emergency during which the restriction of a number of fundamental rights, for instance the secrecy of mail and telecommunications, might become necessary.

The Bundesverfassungsgericht

The Bundesverfassungsgericht is generally regarded as the Supreme Court of Law in the Bundesrepublik. The jurisdiction of this court is set out chiefly in articles 21, 93 and 100 of the Grundgesetz and more fully in the Federal Constitutional Court Act 1951. Generally speaking the court is called upon—it cannot act on its own initiative—when constitutional provisions are thought to be violated or are in dispute. The court has extensive jurisdiction and has over the years considerably widened its influence as the supreme guardian of democracy in the Bundesrepublik. It has dealt with well over 20 000 cases since its creation, and its decisions are binding on all governments, legislatures, courts and public authorities at both federal and Land level.

The Bundesverfassungsgericht undertakes the judicial review of legislation. It can investigate whether federal or Land legislation is compatible with the Grundgesetz and whether Land legislation is compatible with federal legislation. It may be asked to make a declaration by a lower court when a constitutional question has arisen in an actual case, or by the federal government, a Land government or a third of the members of the Bundestag, on an 'abstract' level, for instance when a question arises as to whether a whole law is unconstitutional. In 1951 the Land government of the former Land Baden unsuccessfully challenged federal legislation that provided for the reorganisation of the region and for a referendum on whether or not to merge the three states in south-west Germany into one. It won a second case against another federal law which extended the life of the parliaments in the existing states prior to the expected fusion in order to avoid a surfeit of elections. The court ruled that the Bundestag had no power to limit such right to vote of any citizen of these states as was provided for by their own constitutions and electoral laws. In another case the SPD opposition complained that the Petersberger Abkommen of November 1949 was an international treaty rather than an administrative agreement and therefore required Bundestag approval. The Court decided in favour of the federal government, holding that in this case the treaty was not with the three Allied governments but with the Allied High Commission as a collective agency of the occupation powers. In 1975 the Court was asked to rule whether an important reform of the Criminal Code, the new 1974 legislation on abortion, under which the termination of pregnancy within the first 12 weeks ceased to be a crime, was constitutional or not. It had issued an injunction soon after the Bundestag had accepted the changes, suspending part of the law.

The Court also deals with disputes between constitutional institutions, for example the Bundestag and the federal government, or the federal government and the Länder governments. In 1961 the Court decided the following famous case. The federal government attempted to create a nationwide television service, although only the technical aspects of broadcasting had up till then been regarded as within the concurrent power given by article 73 of the constitution, and the administration of radio and television stations and the production of programmes had been left to the Länder. Some Länder governments successfully argued that the federal government had acted unconstitutionally by invading the territory reserved to the Länder by the constitution.

Of the remaining powers of the Bundesverfassungsgericht, two need special mention here. The Court may be called upon to decide that one or more specified basic rights have been forfeited by abuse. Thus an application may be made to restrict the freedom of expression of the author of a newspaper article, on the grounds that he advocates the overthrow of the state, but not merely that he embarrasses the government, as under the Nazis. Finally the Bundesverfassungsgericht may declare a political party an illegal organisation, if by reason of its aims or the behaviour of its members it seeks to impair or destroy the free democratic basic order, or to endanger the existence of the Bundesrepublik Deutschlands [article 21 (2)]. In 1951 the federal government petitioned the Court to declare two parties illegal. After a year the Court decided to outlaw the extreme right-wing SRP and after a further four years it reached the same decision in the case of the KPD. In both instances the Court found that these parties rejected the fundamental principles of a free democracy, as evidenced by their political aims and their internal structure and organisation. There is no doubt that article 21 of the Grundgesetz was drawn up not with left-wing but with right-wing parties in mind, as the direct result of Germany's experience of totalitarian Nazi rule, but the words used did not limit the power of the Court to the control of Fascism. The Court itself has been anxious not to become too much involved in day-to-day political controversy yet the very nature of its task makes this inevitable. With the advantage of hindsight it is easy to see that the Adenauer government committed a major blunder in making the KPD application in the first place, and in a changing political climate the outlawing of the KPD became a source of embarrassment.

Codified law

The fundamental principle of the *Rechtsstaat* (rule of law) as the basis of the political and social order of the Bundesrepublik is constantly emphasised. It finds expression, in addition to the Grundgesetz, in a vast, complicated, and exhaustive body of codes and statutes, which are designed 'to constitute a key capable of deciding all problems that come before the courts' (Heidenheimer). Whereas in England the courts to a considerable, if diminishing, extent base their decisions on precedent, German courts see their chief task to be the administration of law by the application of written rules to specific facts. It has been said that the rigidity of the German system and the legalistic approach of German judges has produced 'a certain neutrality towards social values and political realities' (Neumann). During the Nazi era, for instance, many judges unflinchingly applied the Nürnberg racial laws which totally offended against basic moral values.

Most of German law is based on Roman law. With the exception of commercial law it first began to be unified after the creation of the German Empire in 1871. The two most important codes, still in force today but frequently amended, are the *Strafgesetzbuch* (criminal code) of 1871 most recently amended in 1969 and 1975, and the *Bürgerliches Gesetzbuch* (civil code) of 1900. Both are valid throughout the Bundesrepublik and they and other codes, including the codes of criminal and civil procedure of 1877, are listed in the Grundgesetz among the areas of concurrent legislative power. By tradition, German law is divided into

Privatrecht (private law) and *Öffentliches Recht* (public law). The former concerns the relationship of individuals to each other and comprises among other matters family law, the law of inheritance, the law of contract, and the *Handelsrecht* (commercial and company law). Part of it is codified in the Civil Code, part is found in the *Handelsgesetzbuch* (Commercial Code), and several statutes deal with, for example, copyright and patent law. Public law governs the relationship of the individual to the state and comprises criminal law, administrative law, constitutional law, the law of procedure, among other laws.

The personnel of the law

There are over 13 000 judges in Germany (in 1973), more than 800 in Berlin alone. This is because the term *Richter* (judge) is not restricted as in England to the relatively small number of High Court and Circuit Court judges but covers judges in all courts. All are legally qualified and state-employed. The German judicial hierarchy extends from the judge at a local court to the judge of the *Bundesgericht* (Supreme Federal Court). Germany has no direct equivalent of the English lay magistrates who decide 95 per cent of criminal cases, although in Germany in several courts the professional judge is in certain cases accompanied by lay assessors who assist him in deciding the case.

Only a lawyer who is qualified to be a Richter can become a practising lawyer of any kind. All lawyers receive the same training and there is no division between barristers and solicitors; after approximately three-and-a-half years of study at university, followed by a degree examination, they are given three years' further practical training in various courts at all levels before taking a second examination which qualifies them to become a Richter. If a lawyer then decides to enter the judiciary he embarks on a civil service career and soon is given lifetime appointment. A Richter is not allowed to be politically active, not even to belong to a political party. The Grundgesetz prescribes that 'the Richter is independent and subject only to the law' [article 97 (1)]. On the other hand, promotion within the judiciary is in most cases decided by the Land governments or ministers of justice—a possible source of conflict, which, however, does not appear to have impaired the impartiality of the Richter in post-war Germany to any notable extent. The German Richter dominates a trial. He is not merely an impartial chairman but actively participates in the interrogation of witnesses. He is dominant even when accompanied by lay assessors in the lower courts.

Apart from one or more Richter every German criminal court has a *Staatsanwalt* (public prosecutor) of whom there are over 100 in Berlin alone. The German Staatsanwalt must act when a crime is reasonably suspected. He acts on his own initiative or, more commonly, on the basis of a complaint received by the police or by his own office. The police investigate on his behalf and must gather as much evidence as possible both for and against the suspect. The prosecutor alone decides, after having scrutinised the evidence and possibly after a preliminary hearing, whether there are sufficient grounds to proceed with the case and whether it is in the public interest to prosecute. He may then draw up a formal indictment and transmit this with the entire dossier to the appropriate court which finally decides whether to commit the suspect for trial. Partly because of the important role of the public prosecutor in the preparation of a trial in criminal cases a long time elapses between the first report of a suspected crime and the final hearing, on average three to four months. Bail is virtually unknown and often the person accused of a serious crime is detained in custody for several months. The Staatsanwalt functions as an impartial investigating magistrate before a case actually goes to court. During the trial itself, however, he presents the case for the state but only after the examination of the accused and the witnesses by the Richter. The Staatsanwalt's submission precedes that of the defence lawyer. It asks for a specific sentence. After the defence lawyer's plea the public prosecutor has a further opportunity to speak before the accused is allowed the final say.

The courts

The Bundesrepublik has a unified system of courts, which are divided into ordinary and special administrative courts. All ordinary courts deal with both civil and criminal cases. At the lowest level there are 638 (in 1974) *Amtsgerichte* (local courts), many of which consist of only one Richter. They correspond to the new circuit courts in the English system and deal with criminal and civil cases of minor importance. Generally the Richter sits on his own but in certain criminal cases the court consists of one professional and two lay judges. Special provision is made in the *Jugendgericht* (youth court) for offences involving minors. The second tier of courts, corresponding to Crown courts, are the ninety-three *Landgerichte* (regional courts). They hear appeals from the decisions of the Amtsgerichte (every person found guilty has the right of appeal), as well as being courts of first instance. In civil cases three Richter sit on their own; in criminal cases one or three Richter are joined by two lay judges. Very serious crimes, especially murder, are tried before the *Schwurgericht*, a court composed of three Richter and six lay judges. Here, as in all other courts where several judges sit together, a simple majority is sufficient for a conviction. The *Oberlandesgerichte*, of which there are twenty, have chiefly appellate jurisdiction and are comparable to the English Court of Appeal. These courts have civil and criminal divisions with three Richter each. There is a further appeal from the regional courts to the Bundesgerichtshof. This sits in Karlsruhe, except for one of its fourteen divisions, which meets in Berlin. This court is the top of the pyramid of ordinary courts and one of five federal courts in Germany. It attempts to maintain uniformity among the hundreds of lower courts in the Länder. It is specially mentioned in the Grundgesetz, as is the manner of electing its over 100 federal judges [article 95 (2)]; they are chosen jointly by the federal Minister of Justice and a committee of all the Land Ministers of Justice and an equal number of members of the Bundestag.

Special administrative courts are particularly well developed in Germany. *Arbeitsgerichte* (labour courts) deal with questions of contracts of employment and other labour questions, *Sozialgerichte* (social courts) with social security problems, *Finanzgerichte* (finance courts) with fiscal problems, and a *Patentgericht* (patent court) with rival patent claims. With the exception of the patent court, they all sit at three levels and lay judges participate widely. The lower levels of the labour courts, for instance, consist of a chairman (a qualified Richter), one employer and one employee. Many of the Richter in these courts have previous administrative experience in their respective field and so possess a better insight into the problems involved. These courts work quickly and smoothly. The *Bundesarbeitsgericht* and *Bundessozialgericht*, the final courts of appeal for their areas of jurisdiction, are situated in Kassel, and the *Bundesfinanzgericht* and the Patentgericht in München. In order to co-ordinate their decisions and ensure 'uniformity of jurisdiction' [article 95 (3)] a joint division of all the federal courts was set up in 1968.

Perhaps the most important of the special courts are the *Verwaltungsgerichte* (administrative courts), again having a three-level structure, with the final court of appeal, the *Bundesverwaltungsgericht*, sitting in Berlin. Administrative courts are of great importance in a country where the civil service still occupies an exalted and authoritative position. The citizen must be protected and must be able to challenge administrative decisions. Verwaltungsgerichte 'deal with controversies over rights which have been allegedly infringed by an act of public authority' (Neumann), whether of a Gemeinde, or a Land or the federal government. A typical case arose some time ago in the Land of Baden–Württemberg. Here an Education Act provided that a child had to be six years old not later than December 31 of any year in order to be admitted to school in the autumn of that year. If his sixth birthday fell after that date, even only one day, he had to wait until the following autumn, regardless of whether he was ready for school or not. The father of a child adversely affected by this legislation took legal proceedings in the appropriate Verwaltungsgericht. He claimed that the action of the educational authority and the provision in the Act on which it was based were contrary to article 11 of the Land constitution, which stipulates that 'each young person, regardless of his background or his financial circumstances, has the right to an education commensurate with his abilities. The state school system has to be organised on the basis of this principle'. The father further argued that it was well established by educational psychologists that the ability to learn is not related to age but to mental development. Damage might therefore be caused to a child if he were excluded from school until he approached his seventh birthday and the rule therefore constituted an infringement of articles 2 (free development of personality) and 6 (natural right of parents to provide for the care and upbringing of their children) of the Grundgesetz.

The father won his case, though the final decision was made not by an administrative court but by the Verfassungsgericht of the Land Baden–Württemberg, to which the case had been transferred, since it involved interpretation of the Constitution. Most of the Länder of the Bundesrepublik have such courts, which decide on the compatibility of Land laws with the Land Constitution.

The central role of the Bundesverfassungsgericht (Federal Constitutional Court) in the constitutional system of the Bundesrepublik has previously been described. The Court has two divisions, each consisting of eight Richter. Half are elected by the Bundestag and half by the Bundesrat. Three Richter from each division come from other federal courts and remain in office until their normal age of retirement. The other five Richter are elected for a limited term of eight years but may be re-elected. They may not hold any other appointment, except that of university professor. Decisions of the divisions of the Court are again by majority; a Richter may, however, have his dissenting opinion entered in the records.

Police and Armed Forces

The police service

West Germany does not have a federal police force. The police are largely decentralised and organised on a Land level, although the Grundgesetz empowers the federal government to issue instructions to the police forces in one or several Länder to avert any imminent danger to the existence or the free democratic basic order of the Federation or of a Land [article 91]. Local forces that used to exist in some towns have now disappeared almost everywhere and have been absorbed into Land forces. Thus there exists one central police organisation for each Land under the control of the Minister of the Interior. Supervision at lower levels is exercised by the Regierungspräsident, the Landrat and the Bürgermeister. In each Land a Police Act defines the areas of competence of the various authorities and regulates the organisation of the police forces.

In all acts the police are charged with maintaining public safety and order. The presumption is that of a universal and general police power, restricted only by specific laws (the Grundgesetz, the Code of Criminal Procedure, and certain industrial and trade legislation). Such a general clause places a duty on the police to act in the public interest and to prevent real danger to an individual or to the general public. The police also help the public prosecutor's office to investigate crime and apprehend suspected criminals. Serious crimes are dealt with by the non-uniformed *Kriminalpolizei* (criminal investigation police).

River police and *Bereitschaftspolizei* (police reserve) are separate police forces on a Land level. The latter numbers some 18 500 men. Although a non-military force it is housed in barracks and, on the basis of an administrative agreement between the Federation and the Länder, is largely financed and equipped by Bonn. The Bereitschaftspolizei assists the ordinary police in large-scale operations and in handling unusual situations. It also undertakes the training and instruction of ordinary police officers.

A small number of specific police tasks are allocated to federal agencies. The uniformed railway police, for example, safeguards the equipment and operation of the Bundesbahn and protects its users. The *Bundesgrenzschutz* (frontier police) is a paramilitary police organisation, numbering 22 000 men, whose role has been considerably extended since it came into existence at the height of the Cold War in 1951. Its main task is to protect the borders of the Bundesrepublik and in this capacity it examines travellers' passports. It also protects official installations and organisations—airports, federal ministries, foreign embassies—and finally it is a potential reserve in emergency situations.

The *Bundeskriminalamt* (Federal Criminal Office), situated in Wiesbaden, attempts to co-ordinate the work of the independent *Landeskriminalämter*, which in turn centralise crime fighting and prevention in each Land. Although its powers were strengthened in 1969 and 1973 its efficiency still depends very much on voluntary co-operation agreements between the Federation and the Länder. The Bundeskriminalamt can intervene (usually only on the specific request of one or more Land administrations), in fighting crime beyond the boundary of an individual Land, yet crime prevention is a matter for the Länder alone. Scientific research, on the other hand, falls within its scope. The Bundeskriminalamt is primarily the central information agency for the Kriminalpolizei throughout the country and it is also the central national office of Interpol. After a modernisation programme it now has sufficient staff and modern equipment to fulfil this increasingly important function more effectively. It holds, for example, a collection of 2.5m fingerprints and contains in its files details of every car reported missing in the Bundesrepublik.

Finally, the *Bundesamt für Verfassungsschutz* (Federal Office for the Protection of the Constitution) under the federal Minister of the Interior keeps an eye on political extremists who might endanger or undermine the constitutional order of the Bundesrepublik. It is also the counterespionage service of the federal government and collaborates with the appropriate Land offices where necessary. Like the other main secret service organisation, the *Bundesnachrichtendienst* (Federal Information Service), which collects secret political, economic, technological and military information abroad, it was under critical scrutiny in 1974. Both had failed to uncover early enough an East German spy in a trusted position in the immediate entourage of Bundeskanzler Brandt.

Since the end of the war the German police has endeavoured to polish up its image, and the long campaign aiming to portray the police force as the citizens' 'friend and helper' has succeeded in improving relations between the public and the police force. There is no doubt that it now generally stays within the law, which allows it a great deal more latitude than in Britain, even if policemen, who are often armed appear at times somewhat 'trigger-happy'. However, the Kriminalpolizei is no more successful in the fighting of crime than the police forces in other countries: the overall rate of crime detection in 1973 was a mere 50 per cent and only seven per cent of car thieves and 31 per cent of other thieves were caught.

The Bundeswehr

The West German *Bundeswehr* (federal armed forces) is the largest national force within NATO. It is a mixture of long-term servicemen and conscripts (at a ratio of 53:47 in 1973) and in December 1973 had a strength of 483 000 military personnel. The defence forces also employed 176 000 civilians. Virtually all German units are assigned to NATO and form part of its integrated military organisation and command structure. West Germany was admitted to NATO in 1955 after the failure of the European Defence Community which had been conceived at the height of the Cold War in order to strengthen the Western Military Alliance by means of a German defence contribution. The EDC avoided the creation of an independent national German army that might have led to an undesirable revival of the century-old militaristic spirit. As it was, after 1945 many Germans were opposed to rearmament a bare half a dozen years after their country's total defeat, in spite of the obvious threat from the East. While Dr Adenauer's policy sought to increase the security of the new state and simultaneously to achieve West Germany's acceptance as an equal partner of the other Western nations, a widespread wave of protest, supported by the SPD opposition, swept through the Bundesrepublik. Yet it did not prevent the first units of the new Bundeswehr from moving into their barracks in 1955 and receded surprisingly quickly.

No doubt a partial explanation is provided by the new idea of the 'citizen in uniform' which was to be the basis of the ethos and structure of the armed forces, breaking with German military tradition. The Bundesrepublik was especially concerned to place the Bundeswehr and its leadership firmly under the control of parliament and government and to create a thoroughly democratic force. Supreme responsibility for the Bundeswehr rests with the Minister of Defence, but in wartime the Bundeskanzler assumes the supreme command. The highest representative of the Bundeswehr and military advisor to the government, the *Generalinspekteur* (Inspector General), and the chiefs of staff of the three services who have the actual command authority, are responsible to the Minister, and the powerful Defence Committee of the Bundestag and its special commissioner, the Wehrbeauftragter, guarantee a fair measure of parliamentary control. The latter office was especially established to ensure the development of the Bundeswehr as a democratic organisation. Initially the idea of the armed forces' complete integration into the state and society was greeted with some scepticism, by for example, some members of the old officer corps who had to be recruited to the new force and who had not only been brought up under the former code of absolute obedience but had also become accustomed to be treated as members of a class apart and above the rest of society.

The reformers conceived the new West German Bundeswehr as a kind of service industry, no different from, say, the Bundesbahn. According to the current 1969 Soldiers' Act the young men serving in the Bundeswehr enjoy the same constitutional rights as ordinary citizens (with only minor restrictions imposed by the nature of the job) and are not bound to obey a military order that infringes human dignity. This concept provides the basis for the instruction of the West German soldier. The Bundeswehr is one of the most liberal of all western armed forces. There is a minimum of drill and an astonishing degree of freedom for all ranks: they have the right to belong to a trade union and are permitted to wear their hair quite long. Conscientious objectors whose right to refuse military service under arms is guaranteed by the Grundgesetz [article 4 (3)] are exempt, but must perform alternative service in social work. The number of conscientious objectors has grown considerably since 1968. It may be said in conclusion that the West German armed forces appear to be well integrated into society so that this new 'citizen in uniform' approach has on the whole been successful. It does not appear to have made the German any worse a soldier than his colleagues in other NATO forces. It has certainly prevented the rebirth of militarism, and has eliminated the former special social status of the military. In fact, the Bundeswehr and particularly its officers are very much concerned about its low public prestige. Recruitment, which was difficult for many years, is now adequate.

This does not mean that the Bundeswehr is without problems. For one, the military and political climate in Europe has changed, as exemplified by the Strategic Arms Limitation Talks (SALT) and West Germany's own Ostpolitik. The Bundesrepublik is most closely affected by this transition from an era of confrontation to an era of negotiation as it shares a very long border with two major Warsaw Pact countries and in case of a possible attack by land or air is likely to be among the first countries invaded. For her security she has to rely on the presence on her soil of the troops of other NATO nations.

The Bundeswehr has always been defensive in character [Grundgesetz, article 87(a)] and the Grundgesetz expressly declares the preparation of a war of aggression unconstitutional [article 26 (1)]. The Bundesrepublik as early as 1954 undertook not to produce nuclear, chemical or biological weapons and does not even possess these. As the NATO strategy became modified into one of 'flexible response', based on a policy of credible deterrence yet also one of negotiated mutual balanced force reduction the role of the Bundeswehr changed likewise, entailing substantial alterations in military structure and organisation. Since 1969 the federal government has initiated an independent and critical review of the Bundeswehr. A whole series of White Papers, the first in 1970, the latest in January 1974, have outlined West Germany's security policy, described the development and state of the Bundeswehr, and set forth the government's proposed reforms. Several independent commissions have also delivered reports on such topics as the inherent injustice in the call-up system (which can absorb only a certain percentage of conscripts), on the structure of the Bundeswehr generally, and on the training and education of long-service personnel.

One recommendation was to continue the present mixed system of long-service volunteers and conscripts. The federal government has decided to retain compulsory military service and not to reduce the length of the call-up period below the present fifteen months. The 1973–4 White Paper pays particular attention to the new structure of the Bundeswehr, which is to be progressively introduced up to 1978. The purpose of this change is to contain the defence budget at the present level (DM 27 300m, or 22 per cent of government expenditure in 1973) or reduce it even further without imparing the combative strength of the Bundeswehr. The problem arises because the share of capital expenditure in the defence allocation—that is, the cost of buying new equipment—must be increased, to keep pace with rising prices. The only saving can come from personnel expenses. The intention, which affects the army in particular, is to maintain the overall official peacetime strength of 495 000 but to leave 30 000 non-essential positions vacant. Thirty thousand former regular soldiers and conscripts will constitute a trained reserve, which is able at short notice to augment the regular forces.

Many other measures which have been proposed or already introduced are designed to consolidate the Bundeswehr internally as well as to modernise it. In order to make military service more attractive—the Bundeswehr is particularly short of N.C.O.s—better pay, improved accommodation and social facilities are suggested. The substantial reform of the training and instruction programme for long-service soldiers will offer a wide choice of extensive specialised training which will lead to qualifications recognised in civilian life. Since 1973 two Bundeswehr universities provide the basis for the training of commissioned officers.

3 Economic Geography

Physical Regions and Climate

Geographically Germany is totally integrated with the continent of Europe and includes parts of the three physical regions into which central Europe is divided. There are no definite geographical frontiers especially in the east and west. Germany's borders are open and have varied considerably throughout her history.

The northernmost part of Germany, the *Norddeutsche Tiefebene* (North German Plain), is some 160 km broad in the west and widens considerably eastwards. Bounded in the north by the *Nordsee* and *Ostsee* (North Sea and Baltic) and in the south by the Central Uplands, it is covered by ice-age deposits of sand, gravel, clay and boulders, while the Nordsee coastline is a zone of marshy land. The *Mittelgebirge* (Central Uplands, the largest region) presents an exceptionally varied and complex landscape, a mixture of shattered old rock basins filled with deposits, and depressions. The *Alpenvorland* (Alpine Foreland), roughly south of the river *Donau* (Danube), and the *Alpen* (Alps), of which only the outer ranges are in Germany, form the third principal geographical region. The Alpenvorland was filled by sandstone, conglomerates and clays swept down from the Alpen during the ice age, and many lake basins were left by the retreating ice.

West Germany falls, with the rest of north-west Europe, in the Temperate Oceanic Climatic Region, yet its climate is transitional. It is subject, on the one hand, to maritime influences, especially westerly winds, owing to its position on the eastern side of the North Atlantic, and on the other to continental influences, or easterly air built up over the continental land mass. Southerly influences are mostly excluded by the barrier of the Alpen, but the position is further complicated by Germany's varied relief.

In winter the cold stable continental air predominates and covers most of Germany, only occasionally interrupted by an advance of warmer air from the west. When this happens stormy conditions prevail near the coasts, and rain falls on the coast and as snow inland and on higher ground. Winters are milder in western than in southern parts of Germany and snow lies much longer on the plateau of the Mittelgebirge and the Alpen. Precipitation generally is remarkably evenly distributed throughout the whole of the year. It is generally somewhat lower in winter than in summer. The wettest months tend to be June, July and August, when much of the rainfall occurs in thunderstorms.

In summer the continental air mass becomes very hot and conflicts with the now cooler air from the Atlantic. The result is an almost permanent low-pressure condition with shallow depressions, bringing sudden rainfall. Extensions of the Azores high pressure belt often stretch to Germany in July and August and bring prolonged very hot spells.

Generally speaking, the climate of the Tiefebene is not very different from that of most of the British Isles: damp, mild winters, followed by long springs, but summer temperatures tend to be higher. The climate of the Mittelgebirge varies greatly depending on relief. Sheltered areas have cold winters and hot summers, while at higher levels spring comes later and the growing period is shorter. The Alpenvorland, being rather high, has cold winters and a considerable amount of rain and snow, rather like the Alpen themselves. Valleys in the Alpen may, however, be quite sheltered.

Agriculture

In 1973 13.4 million ha, or 54.2 per cent of the total area of the Bundesrepublik, was used for agricultural purposes. This compares with 79 per cent in Britain, which is almost identical in size. The difference is explained by the much larger woodland area of West Germany, 7.2 million ha or 29 per cent of the total land area (Britain: 1.9 million ha or a mere 8.5 per cent of the total). Yet in Roman times and during the settlement period of the Germanic tribes some three-quarters of the total land was covered by forests. These were cleared in medieval times, and the typical German village settlement and layout of farms and fields date originally from this period.

Agricultural use depends on surface features, climate and quality of soil. While in Britain, with its moist climate, grassland farming is common and 61.4 per cent of the agricultural area is permanent meadowland and pastures, only 5.3 million ha or 39.8 per cent of the agricultural area was classified as permanent grassland in West Germany, but 7.6 million ha or 56.3 per cent as arable land and 529 000 ha as gardens, vineyards and orchards.

With a few exceptions the soils of West Germany are not naturally very fertile. They are variable, particularly so in the Mittelgebirge owing to the differing surface and rock details. This is reflected in the different land uses—wood, crop, pasture or heath.

Agricultural regions

The Bundesrepublik can be divided into five main agricultural regions.

The grassland region

This includes both the damp and mild marshland grassbelt near the Nordsee and the grass belt in the Alpen and the Alpenvorland with cool summers and cold winters. In the north, livestock rearing (cattle remain outdoors most of the year) and milk production are important, while in the Alpen milk, turned into cheese, butter, or other milk products, is the main produce.

The grass–arable region

Most of the remainder of north-west Germany is a mixture of grass, forest, and heath (amounting, between them, to more than half) and arable land. Cattle and pig rearing and dairying, the latter especially near the Rhein and Ruhr conurbation, are widespread. The fields produce grain and crops, mostly for animal feeding.

On the Ostsee coast of Schleswig–Holstein there is a narrow strip of potentially very fertile land, continued eastwards into the DDR. It grows rye and wheat, and also grass, potatoes and fodder crops to feed pigs, beef cattle and dairy cows.

The general arable-farming region

This describes, first of all, the country east of the river Weser as far as the boundary between the two Germanys. The climate is drier and more severe and the soil poor and sandy. We find predominantly cropland with rye and potatoes, used chiefly to fatten the large pig population, but also a few forests and meadows.

Under this heading also comes West Germany's most typical mixed farming land, extending over the basins and low plateaux of the entire Mittelgebirge. Farms are small and the open, almost exclusively arable fields are divided into tiny strips, each belonging to a different farm. Crops grown vary, depending on soil, slope and drainage; wheat as well as rye, oats and potatoes are common.

The grass–forest region

Chiefly grass and forests are found in the higher parts of the Mittelgebirge, for instance in the *Eifel* (north of the river Mosel), the *Bayerischer Wald* (on the Bavarian–Czech border), and the *Schwarzwald* (Black Forest, in south west Germany), interspersed with an occasional field again growing rye, potatoes and fodder crops.

The Alpenvorland and the adjoining higher parts of the south-west Mittelgebirge have a similar mixture of grass, arable, and forest, although grass is increasingly replacing arable in this region.

Specialised arable regions

The *Kölner Bucht* (Cologne Bay) and the foreland of the Harz (east of Hannover), transitional regions from the Mittelgebirge to the Tiefland and covered by very fertile soil, are West Germany's most valuable agricultural regions. Villages are prosperous and farming is efficient. Wheat, sugar beet and potatoes are grown. Sugar beet residues and potatoes are fed to stall-kept cattle and pigs.

The upper and middle Rhein valley, from the Swiss border northwards as far as Köln, and the valleys of its tributaries Neckar, Main, Nahe and Mosel form an elongated, climatically privileged area with good soils, especially in the Rhein valley. Vines and fruit are grown with vegetables and about one-quarter of West Germany's tobacco consumption.

Current trends in German agriculture

The total acreage of agricultural and forest areas has changed only very slightly since 1950, and the balance between them has also remained the same. However, within the agricultural sector, the percentage of arable land and land for fruit orchards, tree-nurseries, vineyards, etc., has grown at the expense chiefly of permanent grassland. Throughout, the yield per hectare has increased steadily. Harvested quantities, however, show variations, as the distribution between individual crops is changing. This reflects, above all, changing consumer habits and also shows the influence of the Common Agricultural Policy (CAP). The marked overall rise in the grain harvest, from 13.8 million tonnes in 1957–61 to 21.1 million tonnes in 1973, is particularly great in cereals used for animal feed. The increase in bread grains is chiefly in wheat at the expense of rye. One reason is that Germans are now eating more (white) wheat bread instead of (brown) rye bread. Although potatoes still occupy the largest area after the cereal crops this has declined markedly (reflecting a 32 per cent drop in consumption between 1957–62 and 1972–3), in spite of their use as industrial raw material. The sugar beet area, after rising sharply in the 1950s, increased only marginally during the 1960s but is now expanding once more.

The prevailing trend in German agriculture appears to be away from bread crops and potatoes towards fodder crops and livestock produce, especially meat and milk; more refined and specialised products are imported from abroad. The livestock industry is especially subject to market fluctuations. The general trend is for the number of pigs, cattle and poultry to rise, but there was a drop in the total number of pigs and cattle in 1971 and 1972. There are only about half the number of sheep now compared with 1950 (although a slight upward trend was visible recently) and only 320 000 horses were counted in 1973, compared to 1.58 million in 1950.

Harvested quantities of both vegetables and fruit have increased, with only slight changes in the cultivated areas and numbers of trees. Competition, chiefly from the other Common Market countries, has resulted in greater specialisation and a notable improvement in quality. Most of the wine produced in Germany is white. In 1970–71 over half of West Germany's wine consumption was imported. Germany specialises in good quality wines, for which it has an international reputation.

The spruce, the characteristic tree of the higher parts of the Mittelgebirge, is the most common tree in West Germany, occupying some 40 per cent of the forest area. Baden–Württemberg and Bayern between them have approximately half of West Germany's entire forest area. Most of it belongs to the Gemeinden or Länder and is skilfully managed by their own forestry services. The tendency now is to plant mixed forests instead of fast-growing conifers exclusively. West Germany is Europe's fourth largest producer of timber, yet still needs substantial imports to satisfy her needs.

Germany's degree of self-sufficiency, like that of the original Common Market countries but unlike Britain, is relatively high. In 1972–3 it produced 73 per cent of its total needs of wheat (Britain 1970–71: 45 per cent), 89 per cent of its sugar (30 per cent), 77 per cent of its meat (73 per cent), 100 per cent of its milk (100 per cent), and 90 per cent of its butter (14 per cent). Despite this, imports of foodstuffs were in 1971 valued at DM 28 000m, or 19.3 per cent of total imports, whereas exports reached 8000 million, only 4.5 per cent of all exports.

Germany's agriculture is, of course, firmly integrated with the European Economic Community, which controls a single market for agricultural produce. It is subject to E.E.C. controls, price fixing, price support and, on a more long-term basis, structural reform. Although the CAP, by guaranteeing minimum prices to farmers, has met their basic needs for security, it has so far failed to solve the fundamental problems of European agriculture, nor have the governments of the member states succeeded in their own countries with their individual measures. Agriculture is the 'sick man of the Community', and Germany is no exception.

The plight of the German farmer

The structural deficiencies of German agriculture are glaring. Farms are too small: in 1973 the average size of an agricultural holding was 13.02 ha, fairly close to the Common Market average of around 11 ha (Britain: approximately 60 ha), and in 1973 56 per cent of all farms were still of less than 10 ha. Many of these small farms are family concerns where all members of the household work either full-time or part-time, without any additional hired labour. This type of farm predominates in southern Germany but is also found elsewhere, for instance in the Eifel. It is the result of repeated subdivision of the land among all the children on the death of the farmer. Today, many of these farmers, in spite of a considerable degree of mechanisation, cannot make an adequate living from their land and are forced to seek employment in industry. In 1973 only 43 per cent of all farms were worked on a full-time basis, with no additional income from outside agriculture.

In addition, this very small acreage of land per unit is often further fragmented into numerous isolated plots, so that wide stretches of the German landscape are divided into innumerable strips, all with different crops. Under these circumstances it is difficult for a German farmer not to make a loss, and the wages he can afford to pay his agricultural workers are low. Not surprisingly the number of persons employed in agriculture has sunk steadily; while in 1950 there were still 5.02 million and 1960 3.62 million, their number had fallen to 1.87 million in 1973. Although 6.8 per cent of economically active persons were employed in agriculture, forestry, animal raising and fishing (Britain: 3.1 per cent in 1972), their share of the gross domestic product amounted to only 2.9 per cent.

The farmers are often deeply in debt. The advice given by the *Landwirtschaftskammern* (Chambers of Agriculture), to which the government has delegated certain duties and the credits granted by the *Raiffeisenkassen* (credit cooperatives) have not always been given on the basis of sound information and evaluation. Very few German farms, for example, keep proper accounts.

Inevitably the number of enterprises has diminished. In 1949 there were 1.94 million of one hectare and over. Their number had dropped to 1.62 million in 1960 and 1.14 million in 1973 (Britain: about 280 000), 28 800 less than in 1972. This tendency is welcomed by the government, provided it is the small, uneconomic units that are abandoned or combined. In the 1950s German governments desired above all to maintain the level of agricultural prices. In recent years the federal agricultural support programmes, formerly known as Green Plans and now published as annual *Agrarberichte* (Reports on Agriculture), and parallel measures by the Länder (including those under the 'joint task') have sought to improve the structure and efficiency of agriculture. In 1973 the Federation alone allocated a total of DM 5400m for this purpose and grants were provided for the improvement of the infrastructure (new roads, drainage, electricity), better education, *Flurbereinigung* (consolidation of holdings) and farm modernisation. Germany's agriculture was by far the most highly mechanised in the E.E.C. with (in 1970) ten tractors per 100 ha of land used for farming and 3.1

combine harvesters per 100 ha of cereal-producing land.

In spite of the increase in productivity, which was higher than in manufacturing industry, the government measures could not be fully effective since there were still too many small enterprises and grants were given indiscriminately, irrespective of size. The farming industry through its powerful lobby, the *Deutscher Bauernverband* (German Farmers Association), claims that the crisis is, if anything, worse than before, although the gross income per employed person rose more between 1963–4 and 1973–4 than that of the rest of the economy. The European Community has begun to initiate more effective sociostructural measures. They include pensions to help farmers to retire, facilities for training or retraining for people working on the land, and financial incentives for the creation of jobs outside agriculture in depressed areas. The German government on a national level is now more selective in its assistance, which envisages, for example, better old-age pensions and accident insurance for farmers and the improvement of educational opportunities in rural areas, apart from direct assistance to individual farms. It will take a long time to put German agriculture on a sounder basis and the painful process of adaptation is expected to continue at least until 1980.

Fisheries

Germany's most important fishing port is Bremerhaven where approximately half of West Germany's landings are made. Other ports for German deep-sea trawlers, which mainly fish off Iceland, are Cuxhaven, Hamburg and Kiel. By European standards the Bundesrepublik is only a medium size fishing country. Fish consumption per head of population has declined by 22 per cent since 1963, while the consumption of meat and especially poultry has steadily risen. This may be the result of comparatively steep price increases over the last few years but is probably also due to the long distance between most towns in Germany and the sea. Total landings in 1973 amounted to 956 000 tonnes (Britain 997 000 tonnes) and for the first time in several years showed a slight rise over the preceding year. Catches were mostly obtained from the Nordsee and consisted chiefly of cod and herring.

Carp and trout are the most popular freshwater fish. The consumption of trout is increasing and imports of both fresh and frozen fish cater for well over half of Germany's needs.

Mineral Resources and Energy

Coal

Bituminous coal, together with brown coal, Germany's most important indigenous source of power, laid the foundation of her rapid industrial growth in the nineteenth century and her powerful position on the continent of Europe. The lifting of controls imposed on coal production by the Allied occupation powers in 1945 and the inclusion of the coal, iron and steel industry into the European Coal and Steel Community (E.C.S.C.) enabled West Germany to rebuild her industry quickly. The Ruhr district, where Germany's most important coalfield is located, grew to be Europe's most important industrial region. Industries of other European countries, especially in France, Belgium, and Luxembourg, depended heavily on German coke and coking coal, which is now supplied within a European market free from exclusively national control. Since about 1958 the importance of coal declined as other cheaper fuels became available, and this process will continue, in spite of the oil crisis.

West Germany's main deposits of bituminous coal are found in the small Aachen field, in the Saar coalfield, and in the Ruhr coalfield (see map 3). The total output was 103 million tonnes in 1972 (Britain, the largest coal producer of the Community: 109 million tonnes). The Aachen and Saar fields are continuous with those across the Belgian and French borders, and the Saar in particular, as the base for important industries, has suffered from this position through a century and a half of Franco-German hostility. Whereas these two fields mostly produce low-grade coal, the Ruhr field has a wide range of available types, including the high-grade coking coal, and contains some 85 per cent (or 50 000 million tonnes) of West Germany's estimated reserves. Its share of total coal

Map 3   Mineral resources.

output amounted to 82 per cent in 1973. The exploited areas have gradually moved north and north-eastwards, towards the rivers Emscher and Lippe. As the seams dip down to the south mines have had to be driven deeper and deeper, some to over 900 m. Now, however, physical expansion of the mined area has virtually ceased and many uneconomic mines have had to be shut down, at a rate of one every three months.

German hard-coal production reached its zenith in 1956 with an output of 151 million tonnes. By 1973 output had dropped to 97 million tonnes, and several million tonnes had to be put on stockpile. The reason for this decline was competition from other sources of energy, notably oil and natural gas. There was also a recession in the steel industry, a prime consumer of coal. The number of miners has fallen steadily, from over 600 000 in 1957 to 210 000 in 1973 (110 000 working underground and 154 000 in the Ruhr alone), not only as a result of pit closures but also through increased output per man per shift over the past 15 years, from 1.6 tonnes to 4.07 tonnes (the highest in Europe), largely due to mechanisation.

There are, however, limits to mechanisation in the Ruhr because of the narrow seams. The social impact on the whole urban region, which was largely coal-oriented, has been tremendous. The town of Essen, for instance, lost 59 000 inhabitants between 1961 and 1973 and Duisburg 68 000. In 1969 those mines which until then had belonged to the big steel companies were detached, and virtually all Ruhr mines were merged, with the help of federal guarantees, into the giant Ruhrkohle A.G., a joint company operating forty-nine mines and twenty-eight coking plants in 1972. It is now the largest energy combine in West Germany, supplying in excess of 70 per cent of the country's coal needs. Yet, in spite of the advantage of large-scale planning and selling, further government aid was required in 1972 and 1973 to save the company from bankruptcy. 30 000 miners became redundant in 1972 and, notwithstanding improved sales prospects, one in every five pits is expected to be closed by 1975, while the output of those remaining is expected to increase.

The chief use of coal is coke-making in plants situated in the immediate neighbourhood of the pits. The byproduct, coal-gas, is piped to industry throughout the district and is fed into an extensive gas grid covering large parts of West Germany. In other parts of the field non-coking coal is turned into briquettes or supplies pithead power stations. Tar from coking plants is supplied to the chemical works on the river Rhein.

Brown coal (lignite) comes from later deposits and is of lower quality. While East Germany has vast deposits and is the largest producer in the world West Germany has only a relatively small field west of Köln and a few scattered deposits in other parts of the country. Brown coal is cheap to produce by opencast mining since the seams are usually thick, sometimes up to 100 metres. This compensates for the low calorific value and makes brown coal an efficient source of energy (in 1973 80 per cent of the 119 million tonnes of brown coal mined was used for this purpose) and raw material for briquettes, which are produced at the pithead. Hence the industry has suffered less of a decline than that of the Ruhr.

Oil

Germany's oil consumption increased fourfold between 1960 and 1970 and reached 209 million tonnes hard-coal equivalent in 1973. Only 6.6 million tonnes came from Germany herself, from the small fields in the Norddeutsche Tiefebene, near Hannover, Hamburg and the Nordsee coast of Schleswig–Holstein. As home production is declining and there have only been negligible finds in the German sectors of the Nordsee, West Germany grows even more dependent on imports from Libya, Saudi Arabia, Algeria, Nigeria and Iran.

Imported crude petroleum reaches German refineries from oil terminals on the Nordsee and Mediterranean through an elaborate system of pipelines of a total length of 1600 km, which carried 94 million tonnes in 1973. Wilhelmshaven on the Nordsee and Rotterdam supply refineries in the Ruhr and around Köln and Frankfurt. A pipeline running from Marseilles ends in Mannheim, Karlsruhe and Speyer. A branch extends into the Saarland and towards the most recent refinery centre, Ingolstadt in Bayern, half-way between Nürnberg and München. The latter is also connected by two transalpine pipelines to Genoa and Trieste.

Gas

Until comparatively recently most of West Germany's gas was derived from coal and was either produced by numerous small municipally owned gas works or by the coke ovens of the Ruhr and the Saar, where it was fed into extensive grids. This source is rapidly being overtaken by natural gas, whose share of total consumption increased from 57.4 per cent in 1972 to 61.5 per cent in 1973. The German inland gas fields are located in the Emsland and near Hannover and also near Karlsruhe and München. Considerable quantities (44 per cent of total natural gas) were imported from Holland and Algeria and distributed through a system of trunk mains. By 1975 a gas main 400 km long will connect the Eskofisk field in the Nordsee with the German coast at Emden. The refineries are also a source of gas but their output increased only marginally between 1968 and 1973.

Electricity

Like gas, the output of electricity is constantly rising as demands increase. It doubled between 1963 and 1973 to 299 000 million kW with a particularly marked increase in the domestic sector. In line with that of other sources of energy its growth rate is subject to the fluctuation in the economic situation since industry is its main consumer (more than 75 per cent).

Electricity production in Germany uses coal, brown coal, water, and atomic energy, but—owing to government restrictions in favour of coal—in 1973 only 15 per cent was obtained from oil; this percentage will decline, since under the government's energy programme the share of coal will increase. Over 90 per cent of Germany's electricity is produced by thermal power stations and it is here that the main expansion in power generation has taken place. There are several atomic power stations in operation, mostly in the southern half of the country where coal is more expensive, and more are planned. Apart from brown coal the cheapest source of electricity is water and the Bundesrepublik has a substantial number of hydroelectric power stations with storage reservoirs in the Alpen (the Walchensee plant south of München is Germany's largest), in southern Germany and in the greater Ruhr area. Several southern German power stations are operated jointly with Austria and Switzerland. A national network of transmission lines and exchange facilities with neighbouring countries enables Germany to consume electricity in the most economic way: the base load is provided by power derived from brown coal-fired stations and hydrostations while the more expensive coal-fired stations are only called upon at times of peak demand. In summer when the snow melts on the mountains, electricity is imported from Austria and Switzerland.

West Germany's consumption of primary energy of 379 million tonnes hard coal equivalent in 1973 (see table 4) was higher than that of any other member state of the European Community. The federal government's energy programme announced in 1973 was revised towards the end of 1974 to take account of the oil crisis. The government now intends to lessen West Germany's dependence on oil as an energy source by maintaining the present level of coal output of approximately 95 million tonnes and increasing the share of natural gas and nuclear energy.

Table 4   Consumption of primary energy in the Bundesrepublik

	1960	1970	1973	1980 (estimate)	1985 (estimate)
Total (million tonnes hard coal equivalent)	211	337	379	475	555
Percentages of totals (rounded off)	100	100	100	100	100
crude petroleum	21	53	55	47	44
coal	61	29	22	17	14
lignite	14	9	9	7	7
natural gas	0.4	5	10	18	18
nuclear energy	} 4	} 4	1	9	15
hydro power					
others			} 3	} 2	} 2

Iron ore and non-ferrous metals

The small German deposits of iron ore have been worked for centuries. In the Middle Ages Germany was the foremost mining country in the world and many miners from the Harz and the Erzgebirge took their skill to other regions and countries. Local iron-smelting industries flourished, especially in the eighteenth and nineteenth centuries, and the earliest mining college in the world was established at Freiburg in Saxony.

Today West Germany satisfies 95 per cent of her needs through imports, especially of trans-shipped Swedish ore with a high iron content, which is preferred for the Ruhr furnaces. Ore is also imported from Latin America, Africa and France (for the Saar). Home production, amounting to only 6.4 million tonnes in 1973 compared to 13.5 million tonnes in 1960, is on the decline, although not long ago large deposits of moderately rich ore were discovered in the Norddeutsche Tiefebene. The old deposits in the Westerwald near Siegen and in the Lahn and Dill river valleys are practically exhausted, so that mining is now virtually confined to the fields near Salzgitter and Peine in Niedersachsen and to a few other small fields. The Salzgitter ore, with only 25 to 30 per cent iron and a high phosphorous content, is used in iron and steel plant located at the field itself.

At one time silver, lead, zinc and copper mines flourished in the Harz. Now most of these are exhausted, although West Germany still obtains small amounts of lead and zinc from here and the Eifel, and East Germany is able to satisfy her entire needs of copper from the Harz mountains. Pyrite ores, worked primarily for sulphur, come from the Sauerland.

Potash and common salt

In 1973 the Bundesrepublik produced 2.6 million tonnes of potash (in terms of K_2O content) and 7.8 million tonnes of common and other salt. The output of both these minerals from rocks to the west of the *Harz* and also from small salt deposits in the *Niederrheingebiet* (lower Rheinlands), the Neckar valley and Berchtesgaden in Bayern, has consistently risen and large quantities (1973, 48 per cent of the potash mined) were exported.

Other minerals

In the Mittelgebirge, West Germany possesses a great variety of building stone, which contributes to the varied character of buildings throughout the country. Limestone, the basis of cement, is exploited in the northwest of the *Oberrheingraben* (Rhein rift valley) and in the Münster basin. Industries based on this and other raw materials needed for building have flourished and expanded greatly with Germany's building boom since the early 1950s.

Graphite comes from Passau in Bayern, kaolin from the *Oberpfalz* (Upper Palatinate) and pottery clays from a variety of locations.

Transport and Communications

The federal government's transport policy is outlined in the document *Der Mensch hat Vorfahrt* (People Have the Right of Way) of January 1973 and in a later Traffic Route Plan, which represents the first stage of a more detailed goal-orientated development programme for an integrated inland transport system. In the past investments in the transport sector were made in response to private demand. The government's rather belated intention is to reverse this trend by developing a coherent national transport policy covering the years 1976 to 1985 which will, through planned investment, put greater stress on public than on private transport, with special emphasis on commuter traffic in conurbations. Public passenger traffic is to be made more attractive in these urban areas by further improvements in the infrastructure, by revised subsidy arrangements, by creating regional transport authorities and by comprehensive town and transport planning. The Deutsche Bundesbahn was given high priority, without neglecting road construction in rural areas, and a host of measures was proposed to increase road, rail, air and shipping safety.

The Transport Route Plan envisages capital expenditure in the order of DM 120 000m (1972 prices) for the period 1976 to 1985, with the railway's share increasing from 30.5 per cent (1972) to 34.9 per cent (average 1976 to 1985) and that of the roads declining from 58.6 per cent to 53.8 per cent. The oil crisis and the Bundesrepublik's economic difficulties in 1974 have made imperative a drastic downward revision of these figures; indeed, the transport estimates in the 1975 draft federal budget are half a per cent down on 1974 while the overall expenditure is expected to grow by 8 per cent. A slowing down of the road-building programme, a critical examination of the Bundesbahn's development programme, and a realistic reappraisal of the urban area public transport concept is inevitable and perhaps not entirely undesirable. The federal government has, however, declared that it still adheres to its priority for extra measures (beyond the current 60 per cent capital-investment grants, rebate of road-fund licence and fuel tax, etc.) to improve suburban and local public transport.

Railways

Germany's first railway line, between Nürnberg and Fürth, was opened in 1835. Britain not only provided the first two steam engines for Germany but also the crews to run them. Germany, however, very quickly caught up with her European neighbours; by 1855 she had 8290 km of railway, by 1895 45 560 km and by 1915 62 410 km, one of the densest rail networks in Europe, equal to that of Britain. It is important to remember that in Germany the building of the railways had a revolutionary effect for, while in Britain and in France considerable traffic existed before railways were built, in Germany this was not the case and there was no strong desire to accelerate and develop the exchange of goods and people; the country was divided into many virtually independent and often very small political units, which kept most of their business within their state frontiers. Furthermore, German roads at that time were very primitive and waterways were undeveloped. The coming of the railways, although originally built with a view to passenger traffic, provided the opportunity for economic expansion. They made Germany's industrialisation possible. 'It was the railways which first dragged the nation from its economic stagnation; they completed what the *Zollverein* (Customs Union) had begun' (Treitschke).

In Britain, railways were constructed privately and in intense competition between rival companies. In Germany construction was either undertaken by the government of the individual states themselves or by private speculators under close supervision and even with assistance from governments (for example in Prussia). This avoided the building of parallel lines and allowed early technical unification. Progressively, the erstwhile private companies were nationalised and by 1918–19 all companies owned by the individual states were transferred to the Reich.

The West German Deutsche Bundesbahn is, like the waterways, telecommunications and major roads, a federal responsibility. Its network had in 1973 a length of 29 022 km (see map 4). The pruning of unremunerative branch lines has hitherto been less drastic than in Britain, and relatively few lines have been closed and replaced by bus services, usually operated by the railways themselves. Besides the Bundesbahn there are a few privately owned companies; but the length of line operated by them amounted to no more than 3410 km in 1973.

In 1945 destruction and later dismantling of parts of the railway network (one-seventh of all bridges in West Germany were destroyed as were some 100 000 engines and carriages) left the railways virtually in ruins. In addition, the Russian zonal boundary cut the predominantly east–west oriented system into half. In 1973 railway links with the DDR were still restricted to only eleven crossing points when there had been dozens before 1945. Within the Bundesrepublik the main flow of both passenger and goods traffic is now from north to south and a new main line pattern developed in the post-war period. One of West Germany's

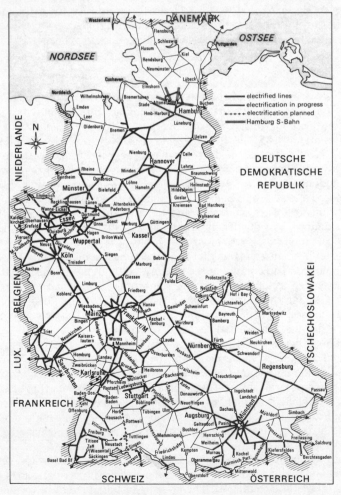

Map 4   Bundesbahn network (1974)

principal rail routes now links the Nordsee ports with Hannover, Frankfurt and southern Germany, while the frequency of traffic on the lines from the ports to the Ruhr and thence to Frankfurt, Basel, Stuttgart and München has greatly intensified. The line from Essen via Hamm to Hannover and Braunschweig is the only east–west connection with really heavy traffic.

This new pattern governed the large-scale electrification programme, which concentrated on the most heavily used main and suburban routes. At the end of 1973 approximately one-third of the total length of track was electrified, carrying 78 per cent of all tonne kilometres performed. Electrification is still progressing, assisted by loans from the Länder within whose borders the lines to be modernised fall, and by the Federation. Instead of the near 10 000 steam locomotives operated in 1958 the Bundesbahn in 1973 had only 829 but the number of electric units had increased from 980 to over 3500 and diesel units from 532 to 5400.

The Bundesbahn has been modernised in other respects too: modern signalling, track and rolling stock were introduced, services were speeded up and an aggressive and imaginative selling policy has attempted to attract more customers both for passenger and freight services. In conjunction with other European railways the luxury TEE express trains and fast goods trains were introduced, and in 1971 the Bundesbahn began to develop a regular-interval intercity passenger express network.

These and many other measures have not, however, prevented a steady fall in the railways' share of traffic. In 1950 their share of tonne km performed was 66 per cent; by 1960 it had dropped to 49 per cent and by 1973 to 41 per cent. Road haulage and pipelines benefited most from this loss. Similarly, the share of passengers carried per year declined from 1950 onwards and now only amounts to 14 per cent of the total. However, in obsolute figures a slight upward trend has occurred recently, both in the freight and passenger sectors. In the latter case this was largely attributable to increased fast suburban traffic.

Under the Railways Act 1951 the Bundesbahn is required both to provide a public service and to be run as a commercial enterprise. Its President and Board are politically controlled by the federal Minister of Transport; they have, for instance, only limited freedom to fix tariffs, they cannot close lines without the Minister's approval, and the Minister decides on the implementation of investment programmes. The deficit of the Bundesbahn has risen steadily year by year and the Bundesregierung had to subsidise it to the tune of almost DM 10 000m in 1974. The Bundesbahn reduced its staff between 1952 and 1973 from 529 000 to around 400 000, notwithstanding a progressive reduction in the working week, and increased its productivity in the four years 1967 to 1971 by 28 per cent. But 70 per cent of the total expenditure of the Bundesbahn goes on salaries and wages so that each wage increase immediately swallows up any rise in productivity. Also, the Bundesbahn has to pay for track maintenance and renewal out of revenue, while the German taxpayer pays about two-thirds of this cost in the case of road transport and nine-tenths in the case of inland water transport. Finally, the German railways are, for social reasons, obliged to provide certain services at far below cost price, for instance for commuters, schoolchildren and students, and small parcels. The Bundesbahn has insisted on fuller compensation for unremunerative local services run on social grounds and plans to close 600 freight sundries depots. It had hoped, with help from the federal government, to build four new high-speed lines and increase productivity by other capital investment. Instead, the government in late 1974 cut down the Bundesbahn's requested subsidies, prescribed harsh economies and blamed the undertaking for not having followed an elastic enough policy.

Local passenger transport

Electric trams and trolley buses, which used to be the common means of local transport in Germany, are now often being replaced by buses or—an outstanding development in over half-a-dozen urban centres—by various forms of rapid-transit systems. In several towns, among them Nürnberg, underground systems are under construction, which will eventually replace tram routes and will be equipped with interchange facilities for passengers from feeder bus routes. Other municipalities, like Bonn, Stuttgart, Frankfurt, and Köln, are putting their trams underground in the central urban area and seek to separate as far as possible their track from the remainder of the traffic in the outskirts. All these measures are designed to speed up public transport and make it more attractive for the public.

It is government policy to encourage the integration of public transport on a regional level, but only a few forward-looking schemes have been implemented hitherto. The most imaginative became operational in München in 1972 for the Olympic games. The construction of an underground system was considerably accelerated and the Bundesbahn built a 3 km-long tunnel under the centre of the city, linking its two main stations. This now carries most of the suburban electric trains and allows interchange with the underground. As the Gemeinden would never be able to plan and finance such comprehensive projects on their own, government grants of up to 80 per cent of the capital cost are being made.

Roads

Today the Deutsche Bundesrepublik boasts Europe's largest *Autobahn* (motorway) network, with a total length of 5481 km in January 1974, linking, often by parallel routes, all major industrial centres (see map 5). This very heavily used system, the construction of which was begun in the early 1930s and pushed ahead by the Nazis, must not only cater for German domestic traffic, but, in view of Germany's geographical position and the absence of effective expressways in most of her neighbouring countries, must also carry a very heavy load of international through traffic.

The number of vehicles licensed in the Bundesrepublik almost doubled between 1962 and 1972. The total number of vehicles licensed was 21.4 million in July 1973, 286 per 1000 inhabitants (Britain: 265). The density of passenger cars per 1000 inhabitants was 265, the same as in France and Sweden but greater than in Britain. In spite of efforts to improve the road network, which comprises in addition to the Autobahnen some 32 700 km of major *Bundesstrassen* (federal roads), some 65 500 km of secondary *Landstrassen* (roads that are the responsibility of the Länder), and some 63 800 km of country roads, the overall quality of these roads (excepting most motorways) is inferior to those in Britain and the average density of road length per unit of area is far below that of Britain. The federal government, in conjunction with the Länder governments, extends and improves the system on a basis of successive plans. In

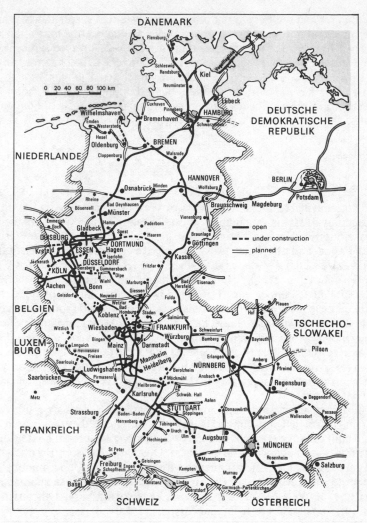

Map 5 Autobahn network (1974).

1971 the Bundestag approved the Minister of Transport's first five year programme, covering the period 1971 to 1975. The Autobahn network is shown as being extended by 1900 km up to 1975, and approximately 1500 km of new Bundesstrassen are to be built. In spite of the budget cuts the federal Ministry of Transport still had DM 5800m available for road construction in 1975 and intended to complete 500 km of motorway in that year. According to the road-building programme for the following ten years, which is now incorporated in the Federal Route Plan, a further substantial extension to approximately 10 000 km was envisaged. Only a proportion of the revenue from fuel tax and road tax is earmarked for road improvement.

All roads within a Gemeinde area have to be maintained by the local authority but the Länder and the Federation often give substantial grants to assist in their maintenance and improvement. Every traveller will notice the many new urban motorways, flyovers and underpasses that have been constructed in recent years, yet none of these measures has succeeded in solving the universal problem of the urban environment. A welcome step in improving the environment of many German city centres is the closing of certain busy shopping streets to motor traffic and the establishment of pedestrian areas. München and Köln are outstanding examples.

Waterways

Inland waterways

In 1973, the navigable inland waterways of West Germany had a total length of approximately 4350 km (see map 6). West Germany's main rivers are the Rhein with its tributaries Neckar, Main, Mosel and Ruhr, the Donau, the Weser, the Ems, the Elbe and the Saar. All of these are navigable and constitute the backbone of an inland waterways system. The Rhein is navigable for 719 km within German territory, almost its entire length up to Basel, using the French lateral canal at its upper end. Further downstream, barges of 6000 tonnes capacity can use the river as far as Duisburg but only 2000 tonne barges can go to Basel. The Rhein handles almost three-quarters of West Germany's waterway freight, which reached 246 million tonnes in 1973, just over a quarter of all the goods carried by any means of transport. The importance of Germany's inland waterways is expected to increase even further in this decade. The major types of freight being carried are sand, gravel, stones among other materials, fuel oil, hard coal and iron ores.

On the Rhein, German, Dutch, French, Belgian and Swiss barges convey iron ore, grain, petroleum and timber from Holland, where they have been transshipped from oceangoing ships and carry coal and coke, brown-coal briquettes, steel, fertilisers and chemicals downstream. Duisburg–Ruhrort, Europe's largest inland port, is situated at the confluence with the Ruhr. It is of paramount importance for the whole Ruhr and in 1973 more goods were loaded and unloaded here than in any of West Germany's seaports except Hamburg. Other important ports further upstream are Köln and Mainz.

All major tributaries of the Rhein can take the standard European 1350-tonne barges. The Neckar is canalised as far as Plochingen, just beyond Stuttgart, the Main as far as Nürnberg, and the Mosel—completed as part of the Franco–German agreement on the return of the Saar to Germany—right into Lorraine. Barrages with locks provide the necessary depth and also serve as sources of electric power. The Saar between Saarbrücken and its confluence with the Mosel is being made navigable. The Donau because of its dependence on Alpine waters is an unreliable navigational channel but traffic below Regensburg into and from Austria and beyond is increasing. Here, as was the case with the north German rivers Elbe, Weser, and Ems, a great deal will depend on the completion, scheduled for 1985, of the long-projected canal connection with the Rhein system between Nürnberg and Regensburg.

All of Germany's canals date only from the end of the last century and did not, as in Britain, precede the building of the railways. Leaving aside the 99 km-long

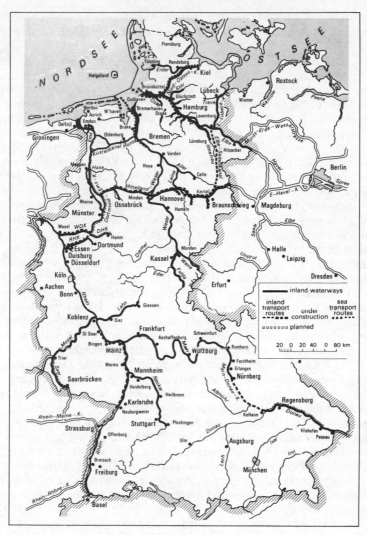

Map 6   Inland waterways (1974).

Nord–Ostsee–Kanal (Kiel Canal) in Schleswig–Holstein, completed in 1895 and allowing the passage of seagoing vessels of up to 9.5 m draught between the two seas, West Germany's most important canals are the *Rhein–Herne–Kanal* and the *Wesel–Datteln–Kanal* through the Ruhr district, the *Dortmund–Ems–Kanal* (West Germany's longest at 265 km), which continues these further north and provides the link between the Rhein system and the German Nordsee, and the *Mittelland–Kanal*, branching off the *Dortmund–Ems–Kanal* and providing connections with East Germany and Berlin and the Weser sea ports through locks. An entirely new canal, the *Elbe–Seitenkanal*, will link the Elbe with the Mittelland–Kanal on West German territory (the former link is now in the DDR) and will include Europe's largest ship-hoisting plant near Lüneburg, bridging a 38 m difference in water level. It is scheduled for completion in 1976.

Sea Ports

The coastline of the Bundesrepublik is only approximately 600 km long (total length of borders 4244 km) and is confined to Northern Germany. It borders on the eastern side of the Nordsee and the west of the Ostsee. Germany's main sea ports, in decreasing order of importance in terms of total tonnage of freight handled, are Hamburg (49 million tonnes in 1973), Wilhelmshaven (27 million), Bremen (16 million), Emden (15 million) and Lübeck (6 million). Both Hamburg and Bremen are old Hanseatic towns, which (unlike Lübeck on the Ostsee) did not decline with the collapse of the League. Their common problem in the 1970s is that they are too remote from both the main Atlantic shipping routes and Western Europe generally. The Dutch port of Rotterdam on the Rhein estuary provides a much closer and cheaper link with the Ruhr industrial centre and south and south-west Germany.

Hamburg is also a river port a great deal of whose trade was with eastern Germany and eastern Europe before the war. It has suffered from the termination or diversion of much of its former traffic. However, Hamburg is, after Rotterdam and Antwerp, still the third port of continental Europe. It lies some 100 km up the river Elbe. Although the Elbe channel is now 12 m deep it is too shallow for the largest cargo ships and its depth is currently being increased to 13.5 m. Cuxhaven used to be the outport of Hamburg but now specialises as a fishing port. In line with all major German ports, receipt of goods—in Hamburg's case mostly bulk products like grain and raw materials—exceeds shipments. An increasing volume of traffic both in Hamburg and in Bremen is handled in containers for which both ports are expanding facilities.

Hamburg is West Germany's largest city (1.77 million inhabitants). It is still her most important wholesale and export trading centre and a very lively, cosmopolitan place. It is West Germany's largest shipbuilding centre, although the industry has been in difficulties for some time. It has considerable industry devoted to the processing of important commodities, like oil-refining, rubber, asbestos and tobacco-processing. Mechanical and electrical engineering industries also flourish.

Bremen's main imports are more specialised commodities, like wool, cotton, wood and wine. Bremerhaven is its main outport (10 million tonnes freight was handled in 1973), with which it forms the smallest Land of the Bundesrepublik. Bremerhaven is still Germany's ocean passenger port but with its decline the facilities are being used to unload bulk iron ore carriers, for example. As goods imported through Bremen were in the main always carried by rail, the port suffered less than Hamburg from the ending of traffic with the east and was able to rebuild and achieve its former volume of traffic more quickly. Its own industry includes shipbuilding and raw-material processing.

Wilhelmshaven, until 1945 Germany's chief naval base, now handles mainly crude oil and is the terminal for the pipeline to the Ruhr. It is being developed as West Germany's main deep-sea port and can accommodate vessels of 250 000 deadweight tonnes. Emden is linked by the Dortmund–Ems–Kanal to the Ruhr. It handles mainly bulk commodities, especially ore.

Lübeck, on the Ostsee, chiefly trades with Scandinavia and its traffic has increased rapidly. Kiel, always associated with the German navy and with shipbuilding, is principally a fishing port.

In 1950 the newly established Bundesrepublik had a fleet of 2078 merchant and fishing vessels of altogether 826 000 gross registered tonnes. In December 1973 West Germany had 3767 oceangoing craft of altogether 8.3 million g.r.t. and most of her ships were less than ten years old. Among these ships there were only four large passenger vessels but 173 tankers. New ships put into service are chiefly tankers, ore freighters and container ships. In 1973 the Bundesrepublik took eleventh place in the merchant fleets of the world. She had just over one-quarter of the gross registered tonnage of the United Kingdom (excluding vessels below 1000 g.r.t.).

Air

The total number of passengers carried in 1973, 25.8 million, was slightly lower than in 1972, thus interrupting a pronounced upward trend. This was, however, only a temporary drop, as a result of prolonged industrial action by Germany's air traffic controllers. Some 17.7 million passengers used scheduled services, the rest charter flights. While domestic air freight fell, mainly because of a reduction in traffic to and from West Berlin, the overall amount of freight carried increased by 8.6 per cent, totalling 413 000 tonnes in 1973. In addition, 88 000 tonnes of mail were transported.

West Germany's national airline, Lufthansa, was refounded in 1953. It rapidly expanded its route network and now ranks as one of Europe's major air-carriers in terms of passengers (eight million in 1973) and freight (287 000 tonnes) carried. The airline's fleet of eighty-one aircraft (in 1973, almost exclusively Boeing) completed 124 000 flights and covered 453 million flight km. In addition, there were over thirty other companies operating passenger and freight air services.

West Germany (excluding West Berlin) has ten airports that are regularly serviced by Lufthansa and other international airlines: Hamburg, Hannover, Bremen, Düsseldorf, Köln/Bonn, Saarbrücken, Frankfurt, Stuttgart, Nürnberg and München. The largest and only really major international airport is Frankfurt. It handled 202 000 aircraft movements in 1973, 11.4 million passengers and 445 000 tonnes of freight. Düsseldorf, München, and Hamburg rank next in importance.

Telecommunications and postal services

The *Bundespost* claims to be the largest enterprise among service industries in Europe. It employs 487 000 people (1973) and deals every day with 30 million letters, one million parcels and 3.2 million newspapers. It carries out the usual postal and telecommunications services, although charges are generally much higher than in Britain. It also instals and maintains television and radio transmission and receiving equipment for the second and third TV programmes of the central and regional radio and television corporations, collects TV and radio licence fees at the door and runs an extensive bus service, often in conjunction with the Bundesbahn (430 million passengers carried in 1973). The German postman also delivers newspapers and collects their monthly subscription.

Early in 1974 there were 17.9 million telephones installed (Britain 19.1 million). Their rate is increasing by some 900 000 every year, one of the fastest growth rates in the world. Almost all inland and 95 per cent of all international calls made are by STD. Telecommunications is the only sector that has consistently made a profit, subsidising especially the parcels, money, letter and newspaper delivery services. Overall, the Bundespost made a loss of about DM 2000m in 1974 in spite of increased charges. In addition, there is mounting criticism of the quality of service given. Social needs forbid drastic increases in charges for loss-making services, so the deficit will grow further. The dilemma is the same as for the Bundesbahn. Salaries and wages amount to 56 per cent of total expenditure and the possibilities of rationalisation are limited. Hitherto the Bundespost has not received any regular subsidies, unlike the Bundesbahn, but on the contrary had a statutory obligation to pay 6.6 per cent of its net receipts to the Federation in lieu of tax. It is unlikely that the proposed reorganisation of the Bundespost into a semi-independent corporation with fairly independent management will alter the situation substantially.

4 Economy and Economic Policy

Industrialisation and Industrial Development

The basic industrial pattern of present-day West Germany is to a considerable extent the product of the nineteenth-century economy, in spite of the ravaging effects of two world wars, the division of Germany into two independent political units and the loss of territory both to east and west, which formed part of Germany in the second half of the nineteenth century.

Germany's industrialisation on a large scale began in the 1830s and a true industrial revolution occurred in the 1850s and 1860s. In 1830 Germany was still predominantly an agricultural country but in the following thirty years or so she achieved what Britain had completed in about a hundred years. One can give several reasons for Germany's delayed industrial development. Adverse geographical and geological conditions played a part: her most important mineral resources were located on the periphery of the country and her principal sea-coast was in the Ostsee, away from the main trading routes of the world. Communications by road and water were poor and the construction of a railway network was necessary before industry could get under way. A system of canals was not begun until towards the turn of the century.

Germany had the crucial asset of vast natural resources of coal, lignite, and iron ore. Their output increased at an astonishing rate, stimulated in turn by newly developed industries. In 1846 Prussia mined 3.2 million tonnes of coal in a year and in the 1860s she was ahead of her continental rivals and independent of imports. In 1871 and after the annexation of Alsace and Lorraine German annual output of coal and lignite amounted to 37.9 million tonnes, and by 1913 Germany's total output had almost caught up with Britain's and reached 279 million. The industry was then dominated by a few companies which were often owned by big steel firms.

'The German Empire was built more truly on coal and iron than on blood and iron' wrote Keynes. In 1860 all German states between them produced 529 000 tonnes of pig iron, less than one-sixth of the output of the United Kingdom. In 1910 Germany manufactured 14.8 million tonnes against Britain's 10.2 million, and in addition 13.1 million tonnes of steel, as compared to Britain's 7.6 million. In Germany the primary iron and steel industry moved to the coalfields, especially to the Ruhr and the Saar basin, and the two industries together laid the foundation of economic wealth. Also, new processes of smelting and steelmaking enabled Germany to use the phosphoric iron ores of Lorraine and Luxembourg, and coke from the Ruhr coalfield was sent there.

In former times the metal industry in Germany consisted of town craftsmen (Solingen is an outstanding example) who were organised in guilds, and of small family establishments in the Siegerland and Silesia concerned with smelting the ore and processing the iron and steel. In the 1840s some larger concerns were founded and soon flourished—iron and steel works in Ruhrort and Oberhausen in the Ruhr district and Borsig in Berlin. The growth of the metal industry was stimulated by the railways, not merely because transport was made easy but also because the railways used the products of the industry, among them rails and locomotives. Numerous secondary iron and steel firms for ironworking and engineering were started, especially after 1871, and a powerful metallurgical industry of great variety developed, whose products helped to modernise other industries.

Textile production was formerly a cottage industry carried out by peasant craftsmen (as in the case of flax and wool in Silesia and elsewhere) or in small factories (as with cotton and silk in Prussia's Rhenish provinces around Krefeld and Elberfeld). Between 1845 and 1870 textile production was still the most important industry in Germany. Modern manufacturing methods began to be introduced on a larger scale and by 1870 mass production in factories was normal. The wool industry, in particular, remained important. In spite of heavy reliance on wool and yarn imports, exports of raw or manufactured wool were considerable before the First World War, being the fourth largest group after iron and steel goods, machinery, coal and coke.

A modern shipbuilding and marine-engineering industry was created virtually from scratch and concentrated at Hamburg, Bremen and Stettin. In 1870 Germany had scarcely any steam tonnage, and most of that was not built of iron or steel. By 1900 Germany's mercantile steam tonnage was almost all of iron and steel and had reached 1.35 million tonnes, and by 1910 2.4 million tonnes. Just before the First World War Germany was able to produce almost 400 000 tonnes of merchant shipping a year, in addition to the ships built for the expanding German navy, and her merchant fleet greatly assisted her export trade.

In general, Germany's machine industry became one of the chief export industries of the Empire and its high reputation has lasted to the present day. It produced machinery of all kinds and types, including armaments. In 1912 Krupp alone employed 68 300 workers. The entire work force in the industry had risen from 51 000 in 1861 to 1 120 000 in 1907. One of the notable features of the industry as early as 1900 was the lack of very small producers, and the predominance of businesses of fifty or more employees.

Two new industries that grew vigorously during the Empire were virtually non-existent before 1850: the chemical and electrical industries. Their development was greatly stimulated by German scientific research. Education in general was of a high standard in Germany compared to other European countries and scientific and technological education and learning in particular had been deliberately encouraged, not least by the early foundation of technological institutions that soon achieved university rank (Berlin 1799, Karlsruhe 1807, Hannover 1831). Germany had become pre-eminent in the world of natural sciences, as names like Liebig and Fischer, Helmholtz, Hertz, Röntgen, Planck and Ehrlich testify. Other research produced, for example, the dynamo (Siemens) and the petrol engine (Daimler).

Germany's rich natural deposits (potassium salts, iron pyrites as a source for sulphur, and coal) provided the foundation for her chemical industry. Tar extracted from the coke in gasworks and ironworks was the basic raw material. The dyestuffs industry gave birth to many subsidiaries, like pharmaceuticals, insecticides and eventually plastics. Before 1914 Germany had a virtual monopoly in this field.

The electrical industry has been described as the 'greatest single industrial achievement of modern Germany' (J. H. Clapham). Spurred on by American inventions like the telephone, the German electrical industry grew from a few thousand employees in the early 1880s to 107 000 in 1907. The first large firm, the *Allgemeine Elektrizitätsgesellschaft* (AEG) of Berlin, was founded in 1883. Apart from the general production of electrical appliances Germany took the lead in special applications to industry, like electrification of tramways and railways and electrical furnaces for steelworks. An extensive radio industry also developed.

The role of the banks and the creation of cartels

An essential feature of the industrialisation of Germany was the role of the German banks. They were, and still are, actively involved in industrial expansion by providing direct loans to industrial and commercial enterprises, or by taking over the issue of firms' stocks or bonds to the public. The large banks are therefore often substantial shareholders of these enterprises, and inevitably exercise considerable influence. Although originally some of the large firms like Krupp or Thyssen or those in the chemical industry were independent of the banks, the banks had a hand in most industrial development.

As early as 1850 a trend towards the formation of large enterprises can be detected. Concerns developed that controlled their own supplies of coal and iron ore, produced iron and steel, and operated engineering works. The firm of Krupp is an outstanding example. After 1870 this growth of individual firms or the merger of several smaller enterprises into one larger concern continued. In addition, several firms of the same branch would often associate to share the market and to establish fixed prices, or form a cartel (restrictive trading agreement). This form of association, which naturally was particularly popular in periods of depression, was perfectly legal in Germany and the German government furthermore introduced tariffs against foreign imports. At the outbreak of the First World War hardly any trade was without its cartel, so that after 1933 the National Socialists had no great difficulty in achieving control of industry. The Nazis also introduced public control not only of waterworks, gasworks and power stations (usually by the municipality), which already existed, but also of mines, ironworks and banks.

In 1800 the population living in the territory that later was to constitute the Empire amounted to little more than at the beginning of the Thirty Years' War. By 1900 it was about three times that number and reached 67.9 million in 1915, the percentage increase being highest between 1895 and 1915. Germany now had to import food in spite of improved agricultural techniques and increased productivity of the land, and ceased to be self-sufficient. There was a great movement of the population away from the rural areas into the towns and industrial centres, a trend which continues. The population of Berlin increased from 400 000 in 1848 to four million in 1914, that of Bochum from 5800 in 1850 to 65 000 in 1900.

The inter-war years

By 1914 Germany was one of the leading industrial powers of the world, taking third place behind the United States and Britain, but leading Britain in heavy industry and rivalling her in coal production. By 1920 she had not only lost a major war, she had also lost, as a result of the Versailles peace settlement, 13.1 per cent of her prewar territory (including Alsace–Lorraine and part of Silesia), ten per cent of her population (including the Saar), 14.6 per cent of her arable land, 74.5 per cent of her iron ore, 68.1 per cent of her zinc ore and 26 per cent of her coal production. Reparations to her conquerors were crippling. The Ruhr, the industrial heart of Germany, was for a time occupied and paralysed by passive German resistance, and the currency completely depreciated. While the middle classes were the chief victims of the inflation some industrialists made substantial profits. No industrial reform, reorganisation or nationalisation worth mentioning took place in this post-war period, in spite of the outwardly 'socialist' revolution of 1918. During an era of false prosperity between 1923 and 24 (when a new currency was introduced) and 1930, German industry recovered, modernised itself and regained many of the leading positions it had occupied before the war, especially in the chemical, electrical and engineering fields.

After the great depression of the early 1930s and the futile efforts of the last governments of the Weimar Republic to rescue the state and its economic system, the Nazis in 1933 came to power in a state whose economy was substantially controlled by the government. This helped Hitler to gain absolute control of the economy without further nationalisation. Trade and industry, in fact, collaborated with the government in establishing a tightly planned economic system.

In pursuance of the Nazi policy of independence from imports heavy investment was directed towards increasing domestic production of certain raw materials like flax, wool, natural oil and iron ore, but only with partial success. Capital was poured into the establishment of plant to manufacture *Ersatz* (artificial) materials. Buna (synthetic rubber) was produced at enormous cost and other synthetic materials included synthetic oil, dyestuffs, artificial silk (rayon and acetate). Only later in the war was industrial production totally subjected to military requirements, so that any normal industrial activity ceased.

Post-war Economic Policy and Development

Economic recovery

On the defeat of Germany in 1945 her entire economy lay in ruins. Considerable damage had been caused by bombing and street-fighting. Communications and power supplies were disrupted, factories destroyed and over the whole country about one-fifth of all dwellings were uninhabitable. Hardly any large town or industrial concentration had escaped air-raid damage. There was no central government, and local and regional German administrations were only gradually restored. In addition, large territories in the east and west were detached from Germany and put under foreign administration. The remainder of Germany was divided into four initially isolated zones of occupation under the strict control of the Allies. Although the Potsdam Declaration of 1945 proclaimed that Germany was to be treated as an economic entity, there was little effective co-ordination between the four Allies.

This applied even to the execution of the Level of Industry Plan on which the Allied Control Council agreed in March 1946. Its aim was not only to indemnify through reparation payments the countries that had suffered during the war and to forbid the production of military equipment, including all types of ships, but to restrict German industry in general and thus emphasise her agriculture. Most branches of industry, including the steel, machinery, chemical and car industries, had severe limits imposed (the permitted production capacity of steel was approximately 25 per cent of the 1938 capacity and that of electricity approximately 50 per cent), and a plan for reparations and dismantling of complete factory installations was drawn up. The Allies also began to carry out a programme of deconcentration of economic power, especially in the chemical and coal and steel industries and the banks. Not surprisingly in 1946 the industrial production of the four zones of occupation, including Berlin, was only a quarter of what it had been in 1936 in the whole of Germany. Similarly, the wheat and rye harvest amounted to only 5.5 million tonnes when in 1936 it had been 9.2 million tonnes. The new, smaller territory now housed 66 million people, an increase of eight million. Hundreds of thousands of city-dwellers had fled from the bombing and were accommodated in primitive conditions in the country. Others lived crammed together in the town housing that had survived. The situation in those early years was aggravated by the expellees from east of the Oder–Neisse line and other non-German eastern territories who arrived in ever greater numbers. By 1950 at least 12 million had sought refuge in the occupied territories, eight million of them in the three western zones which by then formed the Bundesrepublik. In addition, there arrived in the British, French and American zones refugees from the Soviet zone of occupation, by 1952 already some 1.9 million. The total number of expellees and refugees who have settled in the Bundesrepublik exceeds 13 million. In the years immediately following the end of the war they exacerbated the housing and food shortage. Many were old and infirm, and they were concentrated in the agricultural parts of West Germany near the eastern frontier, especially in Schleswig–Holstein, Niedersachsen and Bayern. In Schleswig–Holstein, for example, 32 per cent of the population were refugees in 1951, and this was only remedied when resettlement took place from about 1950 onwards, partly government-sponsored, partly due to private initiative. Rationing in the western zone was strict—more severe than at any time during the war—and covered food, clothing, fuel and furniture. Food consumption per person per day was often below the necessary minimum.

The prospects of a constructive collaboration between the four Allies receded very quickly, and this led to a gradual revision of the policies of the three Western Powers. Reparations, for instance, were reduced and the dismantling of factories ceased altogether in 1951. Also, the American and British zones were economically fused in 1947, with a German central administration under Allied supervision in Frankfurt, and in 1948 the Western powers, after the effective end of the Four-Power administration of Germany, decided to establish a Bundesrepublik on the territory of their three zones of occupation. It was formally founded in September 1949.

An essential prerequisite to the political and economic success of the new state was the currency reform that was undertaken separately in the East and West in June 1948. In the early post-war period a universal shortage of goods existed so that proper trade had largely given way to barter and the black market, but there was an abundance of money. The currency reform was designed to reduce this and was planned and organised by the Allies, assisted by German advisers, in great secrecy. The entire huge debt of the former Reich was virtually eliminated. Overall, the rate of monetary devaluation amounted to one-fifteenth, and appeared to affect everyone equally. However, shares, land and valuable moveable property were hardly touched so that it soon became apparent that the owners of such securities, only a small section of the population, had been treated especially favourably.

On the other hand, government and parliament recognised the special plight of those who had, through bombing or expulsion, lost all their possessions. In 1952 the *Lastenausgleichsgesetz* (Equalisation of Burdens Act) was passed, which imposed a 50 per cent levy on all assets owned in 1948 (assessed at well below their real value) to be paid into a special fund over thirty years, and also a tax on certain devaluation profits. Payment to war victims or their dependants, which started only very slowly, is still in progress.

The 1948 monetary reform would have been wasted without a definite economic policy to follow it up. This was provided by the *Soziale Marktwirtschaft* (social market economy), based on the theories of the so-called Freiburg School. Professor Erhard (then in charge of economic affairs in the fused American and British zones of occupation and later Minister of Economics in the first and successive federal governments until 1963) and the ruling CDU/CSU embraced it as their basic economic policy. Hitherto all aspects of the economy—prices, wages, rents, allocation of foodstuffs and materials, etc.—had been strictly controlled, and the Allies had simply continued the previous Nazi system. Now that the management of the economy was put into German hands Erhard and his advisers decided to reconstruct the economy on neo-liberal principles to go hand in hand with the newly won democratic freedom in the political sphere. A 'free market', that is freedom from controls especially of wages and prices with only very few restrictions, was to be created to allow the freest possible operation of market forces. 'Competition is the most promising means to achieve and to secure prosperity. It alone enables people in their role of consumer to gain from economic progress. It ensures that all advantages which result from higher productivity may eventually be enjoyed' (Ludwig Erhard).

As a first step the control over several hundred commodity items was lifted on the day of the currency reform. An act of the bizonal Economic Council gave Erhard wide powers to decontrol freely, and by July 1948 90 per cent of the then existing price controls had been abolished. Erhard was fundamentally opposed to almost any state interference and planning, although the state by no means withdrew totally from the scene and certain price controls, for example in the housing sector and in agriculture, persist in the 1970s. Opponents of the doctrine, notably the SPD and the trade unions, were sceptical and hostile. They advocated the maintenance of price controls and stressed the importance of planning the growth and expansion of the devastated Germany economy. The critical voices became stronger when, although production increased spectacularly, prices also rose, unemployment exceeded 9 per cent in 1950, and a serious balance of payments deficit developed. However, these largely inevitable initial difficulties were relatively quickly overcome. As the overall success of the government policy became evident, the overwhelming majority of the German electorate heartily accepted it. The SPD opposition abandoned its former dogmatic objections, including its demands for nationalisation, and from 1959 onwards became an equally strong advocate of the market economy base of the German economy, while not totally excluding planning where it might be socially necessary. The Soziale Marktwirtschaft is still the principle on which West Germany's economic system is based.

The German achievement

By stimulating the freest possible competition the government hoped to encourage production in order to satisfy the strong demand for consumer goods. It offered private industry the chance to make profits, and it was an essential element of this policy to have these profits ploughed back into the plants. Substantial tax and depreciation concessions were granted to entrepreneurs to encourage this self-financing of investment out of undistributed profits, and the government itself pumped back surpluses (obtained through high taxation and relatively low public expenditure, due for example, to the absence of a German army) into housing, public utilities, and state-owned firms. In the early years more than 22 per cent of the gross national product was made available for investment purposes.

While the private entrepreneur occupied a privileged position and was encouraged to accumulate wealth quickly wage increases generally lagged behind. But the German workers and their unions accepted this situation arising from the employer-orientated capitalist policy. They remembered the instability of the 1920s and 1930s and desperately wanted security. Of course, they also wished to improve their material condition, and they realised that the harder they worked (overtime was tax-free!) and the sooner industrial capacity was rebuilt and expanded the more they, too, would gain in the end. The average hourly gross earnings of a male industrial worker rose between 1950 and 1973 by 530 per cent in absolute figures and by 243 per cent in real terms, taking into account an average annual increase in the cost of living of 2.7 per cent (Britain 4.7 per cent, France 5.0 per cent). From 1960 to 1970 a German industrial worker took home (in terms of purchasing power) the highest hourly gross earnings in the E.E.C., excepting Luxembourg, and in April 1973 he still came third in the enlarged Community (DM 8.06) after Denmark (DM 12.69) and Luxembourg and ahead of Britain (DM 7.23) and France (DM 6.14). While the cost of living increased by 6.8 per cent in 1973 and 7 per cent in 1974 (an alarming rate of inflation for Germany, but quite moderate compared to Britain's 7.1 per cent and 18.3 per cent, respectively) gross salaries and wages increased by 10.4 per cent and approximately 10 per cent, respectively.

The basic forty-hour week had in 1974 been agreed for all public servants, for 88 per cent of all wage earners, and for 85 per cent of all salaried employees. In the European Community, Germany holds a good middle position: in April 1973 an industrial worker in Germany was actually paid for an average of 43.0 hours per week (France 44.6, Britain 43.0, Italy 41.6). The average length of his annual holidays was 27.1 working days in 1973, and many branches of industry and government pay additional holiday bonuses, frequently equivalent to a full extra month's wage. Until the 1973–4 recession the employment situation was equally satisfactory. Once the post-war economic difficulties had been overcome—the annual average of unemployment in 1950 was 10.3 per cent, in 1958

3.7 per cent—it remained (between 1960 and 1971) below the 1 per cent mark, except in the recession period 1967–8, when it temporarily reached 2.1 per cent. It has risen since then and for the first time became a serious problem in 1974 (2.6 per cent annual average). The number of wholly unemployed was 946 000 or 4.2 per cent in December 1974, the worst for sixteen years. 703 000 workers were on short time and there were only 194 000 unfilled vacancies. Unemployment will, in fact, be West Germany's most serious economic problem in 1975. The government hopes that with mild reflation unemployment will drop to around 500 000 by the end of the year but this also depends on the number of foreign workers returning to their homes.

Strikes were virtually unknown during the 1950s and 1960s and they are still rare today. Management and unions have worked remarkably amicably together, notwithstanding tough wage negotiations. The concept of *Mitbestimmung* (co-determination) in the iron, coal and steel industry and the active role of the *Betriebsrat* (works council) in all other firms has led to a better understanding on both sides of industry.

Until the beginning of this decade relatively few Germans were conscious of the rising gap between the accumulation of private wealth by the relatively small and numerically declining group of self-employed persons and the steadily growing percentage of employed people and pensioners, the vast majority of the population. Between 1950 and 1967 the wealth of this small employer group (20 per cent of the working population) increased by more than twice the amount of that of the second group. Several explanations can be offered for public acceptance of this type of incomes policy.

(1) the steady rise in real incomes and the resulting widespread prosperity;

(2) the overall relative stability of the Deutsche Mark;

(3) the lack of class-consciousness among the West Germans;

(4) the German tax system, which results in a slightly lower percentage of total tax receipts originating from direct taxes on households and encourages, as part of deliberate government strategy, all income groups to save by granting exemptions in virtually all areas of investment, from shares to life-insurance policies, and grants special tax-free bonuses; and

(5) further deliberate government measures to spread and increase ownership, for example, the issue of small shares at favourable prices to low-income groups, as happened with the denationalisation of the *Volkswagenwerk* and several other firms.

It seems, however, possible that, as this inequality becomes more obvious and the post-war generation comes to the fore, the unions and part of the electorate will become more critical of these injustices and more militant, and the government may be obliged to intervene more actively and discriminatingly in the economic process.

Instruments of economic and monetary policy

Hitherto, the main efforts of successive governments have been directed on the one hand towards establishing and preserving fair competition, and on the other towards economic growth and stability of the currency. Trade, capital movement, and the foreign exchange market were all liberalised. After a considerable delay the law that should have been one of the main pillars of the neo-liberal system was passed in 1957: the Act against Restrictive Practices. Although amended in 1973 it is, by common consent, weak. While making cartels and monopolies illegal it grants so many exceptions that industry has not found it too difficult to circumvent its restrictions. In any case, there are now about 200 legal cartels in West Germany. The *Bundeskartellamt* (Federal Cartel Office), which is *de facto*, if not *de jure*, subject to government instructions, and where cartels have to be registered, can declare cartels to be ineffective, demand a reduction in the selling price of a product and impose fines. It is now particularly concerned about the increasing number of mergers. Decisions of the Cartel Office can be contested in the ordinary courts and the Office has rarely lost a case, but matters are frequently settled out of court. Thus in a most spectacular case a fine of DM 49m which had been imposed on the chemical fibre industry in 1972 was reduced to a payment of DM 12m to the federal government. German companies are also subject to the scrutiny of the European Commission, which has taken a strict line over monopolies and restrictive practices that affect trade within the E.E.C.

Even under the German Freie Marktwirtschaft with its supposedly free play of supply and demand, direct state intervention in certain sectors of the economy is by no means rare, either for social reasons or as a direct result of pressures by individual industrial lobbies. Large direct or indirect (through tax concessions) subsidies and loans are regularly made available to certain branches of industry (coalmining, shipbuilding), commerce, communications (rail and post), housing and agriculture.

Germans on the whole do not believe in prices and incomes controls. In order to achieve the twin government objectives of price stability and steady economic growth, coupled with full employment, the government chiefly uses fiscal, monetary and tariff measures, and the Bundesbank, West Germany's central bank, plays a crucial role. Its task is more difficult because since 1958 the Deutsche Mark is freely convertible and has become one of the 'hard' currencies. Industry, foremost the investment goods industry, is especially export intensive: 21.5 per cent of the total turnover of industry went into exports in 1973. Inevitably economic and financial conditions outside the country have a considerable impact on the German economy, and inflation is easily imported. The fixing of the exchange rate is particularly important here. German governments have been reluctant to revalue the Deutsche Mark (this happened in 1961, 1969, 1971 and twice in 1973 when the joint European float against the U.S. dollar was also introduced) and repeatedly government and Bundesbank have not seen eye to eye on this issue. The Bundesbank attempts to influence the economy by monetary measures, such as the fixing of interest rates and of rediscount quotas for banks, interventions in the money market or imposing minimum reserve requirements. The federal government has the power to introduce exchange controls, for example quantitative controls on capital transactions, which are important in the event of excessive money inflows from foreign countries. Above all, however, the government can influence the economy on a short and medium-term basis by its fiscal and budgetary policies, although often measures necessary to maintain stability have been sacrificed for short-term political advantages, especially at election times.

Before 1966–7 almost any means of positive economic forecasting and planning was frowned on, as being likely to be seen as a first step towards a socialist, planned economy. In 1967, however, under the shock of the recession, when the gross national product increased by only 0.8 per cent instead of the customary 6–10 per cent, and unemployment shot up to over 600 000, the Act Promoting Stability and Growth of the Economy came into force. For the first time this Act recognizes that a highly industrialised economy cannot be left to its own processes but requires, in order to benefit all sections of the population, the guiding influence of the government. In order to achieve the objectives of the policy (now formally incorporated into an Act of Parliament)—stable prices, full employment, external equilibrium, and economic growth—medium-term financial planning and co-ordination between the Bund and the Länder is made obligatory and the Bundesregierung is required to present an annual economic report to parliament. To enable the government to fight an acute crisis the Act introduces new, and strengthens existing, fiscal measures, like deficit spending, building up of reserves in boom conditions and variations in the rate of income tax. The then Finance Minister did not hesitate to use these new policy measures immediately.

Since 1964 a five-man academic Council of Experts has prepared forecasts on the prospects of the German economy and has recommended suitable measures, but in the absence of any compulsory incomes policy (which has hitherto been unthinkable under the prevailing philosophy) the government is reduced to issuing advisory wage guidelines, based on its own expectations of the growth rate of the economy.

The reasons for Germany's performance

Without any doubt the recovery of the German economy after 1949 has been remarkable, especially during the first decade, even if it is realised that all the attributes of a very high level of economic development were still present in the country. The gross national product, the total output of the national economy, went up from a very low DM 98 000m in 1950 to approximately DM 926 000m (at current prices) in 1973. Between 1962 and 1972 the real growth of the G.N.P. amounted to 53.1 per cent, which is less than in France (67.9 per cent) or the Netherlands (64.9 per cent) but considerably more than in Britain. It can be said that West Germany's post-war growth was very steady but not especially rapid. West Germany's gross domestic product *per capita* at market prices reached DM14 950 in 1973 compared with DM 2090 in 1950. In 1972 the index stood at 140 (1963 = 100), compared with 152 for France, 148 for the Netherlands, and 121 for Britain. The contribution of industry, including power, mining, manufacturing and building, towards the G.N.P. amounted to 51.7 per cent in 1973 (1950: 49.6 per cent), and that of agriculture and forestry to 2.9 per cent. Service industries, including credit and insurance institutions, provided 15.7 per cent (10.2 per cent) and general government and private households 12.1 per cent (9.6 per cent).

The index of industrial production (including food and beverages) stood at 489 in 1973 (1950 = 100); the average annual increase between 1958 and 1973 was six per cent (Britain 3.4 per cent). A substantial part of Germany's industrial production—something like 25 per cent of its total G.N.P.—is exported, and the constantly rising annual trade surplus is the most obvious expression of West Germany's successful economic performance, especially since it was achieved against repeated revaluations of the Deutsche Mark. These could only be offset by higher productivity; in fact, since 1960 productivity (the gross domestic product per employed person) only once grew by less than 3 per cent (in 1962 prices). The relatively low rate of inflation and stable industrial relations also played a part. The Bundesrepublik has had an export surplus ever since 1952. It amounted to a mere DM 700 000 then, but climbed to DM 50 800m in 1974, an all-time record in spite of the higher cost of oil imports. In 1951, with a share of 4.5 per cent, West Germany took fifth place among the exporting nations of the world. In 1973 she had attained second position (12.2 per cent of total world exports) after the U.S.A. (12.8 per cent) and before Japan (6.7 per cent), France (6.5 per cent) and Britain (5.6 per cent). West Germany's balance of payments surplus in current transactions has been a constant embarrassment both to herself and to her trading partners. Note, however, that allowing for the deficit on invisibles (services and transfer payments, especially by foreign workers) the 1973 current account surplus was only DM 12 400m, with a trade surplus of DM 33 000m.

Together with the gross national product the nominal income, that is the income in current prices, has also risen but so have consumer prices, by 83 per cent between 1950 and 1973. This rate of inflation was, nevertheless, lower than that of virtually all other industrialised countries, from Britain (185 per cent and France (210 per cent) to Japan (225 per cent) excepting only the U.S.A. (82 per cent). On balance the real income of the Germans has risen considerably.

A further point relating to the economic growth of the Bundesrepublik is that consistently only a relatively low percentage of the gross domestic product has been appropriated to private consumption (only 53.9 per cent in 1971, compared with Britain's 62 per cent). Investment, on the other hand, accounted for a relatively high proportion (26.7 per cent, Britain 17.9 per cent), but relatively little of this, at least compared with Britain and the United States, goes abroad.

The German economy has not grown at a steady rate but so far can be seen in six clearly distinguishable cycles, which were usually determined by forces outside Germany: 1950–1954 (the Korean boom), 1955–1958 (increase in foreign demand), 1959–1963 (impact of the E.E.C.), 1963–1967, 1967–1971 and 1971–1974. These cycles (except the latest one) are characterised by an increase in demand for industrial products from abroad and a subsequent increase in productivity, since wage increases usually lagged 12 to 18 months behind. This allowed profits to rise and permitted substantial investment. When the impact of delayed wage increases made itself felt price increases usually followed, but there was by now also an increase in home mass consumption. Further wage demands exceeded productivity gains, with fewer profits as a result and so the scaling down of investment continued, while prices rose further and demand began to slacken. Until recently there has never been a real recession, in the sense of an actual decline in the gross national product from the previous year, simply variations in the intensity of the rate of growth.

Although the fast initial recovery and subsequent performance of the West German economy, at least until 1970, are remarkable it is hardly correct to speak of a 'miracle'. There are, in fact, sound financial, economic and social reasons for this growth.

Bombing and the dismantling of factories caused tremendous damage to Germany's industrial potential, yet it enabled reconstruction to bring about a thorough modernisation of industrial installations and techniques. Germany was helped by the favourable international climate, as the Korean War brought a continuous expansion of world trade, and also by American money through the Marshall Plan. From the middle of 1948 onwards, under this scheme, essential foodstuffs, raw materials, and machinery were made available, which did not have to be paid for immediately. Indirectly the Marshall Plan also provided investment, since the German recipients had to pay for these imports in German currency into special funds. These were then used by the government over many years to make investment grants to industry, from power stations to iron and steel plants, coal mines and housing. Of course, other countries profited from the same source, Britain with a total of $7340m even more than Germany with $4400m. But for Germany this aid came at a crucial point in her reconstruction where it could be used to achieve the best long-term effects.

In the early 1950s West Germany was not yet rearmed and had no costly military commitments, save some contributions to Allied occupation costs. She was thus in a position to take full advantage of the worldwide demand, especially in capital goods like machinery and equipment, unleashed by the war in Korea. Even when she later built up her own army, initial defence expenditure remained lower than, for example, in Britain and the U.S.A. Later it rose steeply, for instance by 141 per cent between 1957 and 1963.

Refugees and expellees had initially been a serious liability, but at the time of buoyant expansion they proved a valuable source of labour both because of their numbers and their skills; so did the many hundreds of thousands of unemployed in the 1950s. Shortage of labour became a problem in the 1960s and led to the large-scale importation of foreign labour without being fully able to satisfy the demand at boom periods.

Finally one must not forget what is, perhaps, the most important reason for West German prosperity: the capability and determination of the Germans to work hard, coupled with their ability to organise. The efforts and devotion to his job of almost every German in the early period of the Republic were without doubt remarkable. Even today, when most Germans appear to have acquired a quite different outlook, one finds very little opposition to rationalisation and modernisation.

The economic system of the Bundesrepublik was intended to have a 'social' component as well—hence Soziale Marktwirtschaft. In this respect it was much less successful, and the omissions of successive governments have by now become very clear. Not without reason the SPD/FDP social–liberal coalition entered its first term of office in 1969 with an ambitious programme of social reforms to redress some of the existing social injustice. Only a few of these reforms were actually realised.

In the early years of the Bundesrepublik certain sections of the population and the economy received preferential treatment in terms of special regulations, payments or loans. Refugees, expellees and other war victims were among these. Rents remained controlled until the housing shortage had, at least statistically, been eliminated. In order to reduce the shortage of dwellings, housing construction was assisted by public loans and grants. Similarly, agriculture and certain 'lame duck' branches of industry, like coalmining or shipbuilding, were subsidised in a rather indiscriminate fashion. The state's share in social security expenditure increased to over 50 per cent in 1965, but has declined since then. As explained previously, the government also endeavoured to increase the spread of wealth by means of tax allowances and bonuses.

On the negative side, whole sections of the population, in particular old-age pensioners, have gained relatively little from the overall prosperity. A positive, comprehensive structural policy hardly existed. The government's regional policy was deficient; urban, regional and environmental planning has hardly begun, public transport is characterised by alarmingly growing deficits to be met from the public purse in the absence of government-established priorities and the educational system is totally antiquated and starved of funds.

Germany has now at last been caught up in the general trend of inflation. Until recently, a 5 or 6 per cent rate of inflation, which is regarded as quite normal in other countries, was in inflation-conscious Germany totally unacceptable and any political party that wants to win an election must make the restoration of the stability of the Deutsche Mark its first priority. Much of the German problem since 1971 has come from abroad but exceptionally high wage settlements in 1971 and 1972 have probably also contributed. The federal government and the Bundesbank in 1973 clamped down on the booming domestic demand by floating and revaluing the currency and using various measures of monetary and fiscal policy, including a withdrawal of tax concessions, special 'stabilisation supplements' on income and corporation tax, and even charges on investments, increases in the tax on spirits, tobacco and petrol and, for a time, foreign-exchange controls (a new departure, vigorously opposed by 'pure' free market economists), to curb the inflation. Internal demand promptly fell and companies were forced to sell more overseas. It remains to be seen whether the 1974–5 economic downturn is of a more serious nature than previous troughs. The minimal growth of the G.N.P. in 1974 (approx. 0.4 per cent), the general weakness of the home market and the staggering rise in unemployment finally persuaded the federal government towards the end of 1974 to reflate the economy slightly, thereby risking the hard-won price stability. It announced a public investment programme and provided private industry with a financial stimulus to invest in capital equipment, in the hope that this would create new jobs. The winter round of wage negotiations was also crucial. Wage awards were modest (around 6 per cent) so that there is a good chance that inflation can be held down and eventually industry will be able to increase its profits to stimulate investment.

Germany and the European Community

The *Montanunion*, the European Coal and Steel Community established by the Treaty of Paris in 1951, ended the discriminatory controls over Germany's coal and iron and steel industries imposed by the Ruhrstatut in 1949 and replaced them with a voluntary agreement by six European states to create as equals a common market for coal, iron ore, steel and scrap. The Coal and Steel Community was an important step in Germany's eventual swift achievement of complete equality with her neighbours, politically as well as economically, but it also represented a widespread desire inside Germany to overcome the old national frontiers and move towards greater European unity. Liberalisation of foreign trade relations and willingness to collaborate in the establishment of international agreements on the exchange of capital and goods was in line with the prevalent German neo-liberal philosophy, and the majority in the Bundestag was prepared to sacrifice certain aspects of German sovereignty to a supranational High Authority. Certain provisions under the Treaty, like those establishing a genuine free market and those forbidding cartels on a supranational level, were welcomed. In German eyes the Montanunion was moderately successful, even in the late 1950s when a huge surplus of coal built up and steel slumps occurred.

However, it became obvious that one sector could not be managed in isolation from the rest of the economy. The *Europäische Wirtschaftsgemeinschaft* (E.W.G., European Economic Community) of 1958 set out to create gradually a common market for all goods, services and capital movements. This not merely involved the creation of a common tariff against outside countries. Under the guidance of an independent, supranational Commission it also meant the gradual harmonisation of many aspects of economic, fiscal, and social policy of the member states and thus impinged very strongly on domestic policy aims and their execution. Germany, which is the most populous and the most highly in-dustrialised member state of even the enlarged Community, has subscribed to the idea of the *Gemeinsamer Markt* (Common Market) wholeheartedly and until recently generally subordinated her national interests to those of the Community and her partner countries, especially France. One would find scarcely one politi-cian, economist, or indeed citizen in West Germany who would doubt the benefits brought by the Community during the first decade or so of its existence. They would genuinely welcome further monetary, economic and political in-tegration but would, like the German federal government, be wary of any scheme that imposes the highest financial burden on Germany. The gross national product at market prices of the Community increased between 1960 and 1970 by 5.3 per cent annually (at constant prices), that of EFTA by 3.6 per cent and that of the United Kingdom alone by only 2.8 per cent (Germany alone 4.8 per cent). It has also been shown that there was a marked improvement in the pace of growth of productivity in the manufacturing industry of all E.E.C. countries during the second half of the decade 1960–70, when the Common Market had become fully effective, while that of Britain was considerably inferior. Every member country's percentage share of intra-Community trade in the total of foreign trade has increased since the Community was created in 1958. Germany, an export-intensive country whose exports have more than trebled in value over the period, illustrates particularly well how the existence of the Common Market acted as a stimulus to trade with the other countries inside the Community, for between 1958 and 1970 the E.E.C. percentage share of German imports rose from 26 per cent to 46.8, of German exports from 27 per cent to 40.1 per cent whereas the share of both exports and imports with EFTA countries dropped. West Germany always desired the inclusion of the United Kingdom and other countries in the Community, both for economic and political reasons. Among the nine member states of the enlarged Community the Bundesrepublik retains its leading position in industrial production (37 per cent of the Community total in early 1972) and exports (30 per cent in 1971). It provided one-third of the total E.E.C. gross national product in 1973 and held half of its reserves (May 1974).

Banking and Finance

The Bundesbank

The Bundesbank, West Germany's central bank, has its seat not at Bonn but at Frankfurt, the commercial capital. The Bundesbank has the sole right to issue banknotes, and by the 1957 Federal Bank Act it is charged with 'safeguarding the stability of the currency, by means of regulating the money circulation and the credit supply to the economy' [article 3]. To this end the Act empowers it to determine the level of the bank rate and other interest rates and the minimum reserve requirements of the commercial banks. The federal government, on the other hand, under the 1967 Stabilitätsgesetz, may restrict borrowing by the public authorities and determine the terms and the maximum amounts of these loans. The government also fixes the exchange rate that the Bundesbank is then obliged to defend. Thus, necessarily, the Bundesbank closely co-operates with the government and especially with the Ministers of Economics and Finance, whom it advises and whose general economic policy it is expected to support.

Yet the freedom of action of the Bank is considerably greater than that of central banks in other countries. It is not subject to parliamentary control nor to government instructions or supervision and can be characterised as an independent part of the executive which is entrusted by law with autonomous powers to run German monetary and credit policy. An open disagreement between the President of the Bundesbank and the Minister of Finance or the Minister of Economics on some aspect of monetary policy is thus not at all excluded. It occurred in 1971 over the government's decision to float the Deutsche Mark which the Bundesbank opposed, in line with the very strict anti-inflationary policy that it has consistently advocated. A divergence of view on the introduction of foreign currency controls led in the summer of 1972 to the resignation of Professor Schiller, who then combined the offices of Minister of Economics and Minister of Finance. He had voted against the Bundesbank's proposals at a cabinet meeting, when all his colleagues supported the proposals of its President, who was present at the time.

The Bundesbank's president is nominated by the Minister of Finance and appointed by the Bundespräsident for eight years. Once installed he cannot be removed before his term of office expires. The presidents of the Bundesbank have usually been men of independence of mind but have tended to accept the guidance of the *Zentralbankrat* (Central Bank Council), composed of the eight members of the directorate of the Bundesbank (also nominated by the government) and the presidents of the 11 central banks of the Länder, the main regional offices of the Bundesbank.

Other financial institutions

The three leading German banks in the private sector, the Deutsche Bank (Europe's fourth biggest bank), the Dresdner Bank, and the Commerzbank also have their headquarters in Frankfurt. Like most German banks they are completely universal institutions and combine the business of the British joint stock bank, merchant bank and stockbroker. In 1973 their volume of business was about 11 per cent of all German banking groups. Their balance sheet totals have risen year by year. The totals for 1973 will give an indication of their relative size: Deutsche Bank DM 46 300m, Dresdner Bank DM 39 100m, Commerzbank DM 28 400m.

One interesting aspect of their operation is their direct involvement in German industry. They not only handle the issue of shares and loans to the public (often in syndicates) and act by proxy for small shareholders, but have substantial shareholdings themselves. Thus the Deutsche Bank, for example, holds over 25 per cent of the shares in the Daimler Benz company. Since this not only applies to the big three but to a number of other commercial and savings banks, the larger banks are in a position to exercise a considerable influence on industry in general and on the management of individual firms in particular.

The big three and several of the other banks also have an expanding foreign business. They are often linked in organised groups with foreign credit institutions and they handle the floating of foreign loans on the German market. The German capital market, which is virtually free from government control, except for regulations relating to the purchase of German bonds by foreigners, is among the leading European markets in terms of its annual net volume of issues. In 1973 DM 25 000m worth of domestic bonds and DM 3500m of new shares were sold. Banks were the largest issuers of bonds.

From among the remaining 307 commercial banks special mention must be made of the largest regional institute, the Bayerische Hypotheken- und Wechselbank of München (balance sheet total in 1973 DM 25 600), which controls 18 per cent of the German beer market, and the dynamic Bank für Gemeinwirtschaft, another all-purpose bank (DM 17 700m in 1973), only twenty years old and completely owned by the German Trade Union Federation. The forty-two public and private *Hypothekenbanken* (mortgage banks) issue debentures and raise long-term loans to finance their lending. Their business accounted for 12 per cent of all banking groups in 1973.

Private savings in the Bundesrepublik reached an all-time high in 1974 (DM 86 000m), in spite of inflation and the bitter German experience of two major inflations and currency reforms in the course of the last fifty years. In order to encourage private accumulation of wealth—one of the chief aims of West Germany's economic policy—federal legislation provides for special tax-free bonuses for various types of longer-term private investment, including savings deposits, funds placed with building and loan associations, life insurance policies and property acquisition. In 1973 private households saved an annual average of 13.5 per cent of their disposable income, and the 1974 savings ratio is likely to be a record, probably because of the relatively low rate of inflation in West Germany. Predominantly the banks and life insurance companies profited from these private savings deposits. On the other hand, the nineteen independent *Bausparkassen* (building and loan associations), the equivalent of the British building societies, are experiencing a decline in new business, signalling the end of the boom in savings for house purchase. Private ownership of fixed-interest securities and shares and of investment certificates is modest in West Germany (approximately only 22 per cent of all longer-term investments in 1973 and even less, approximately 10 per cent, in 1974).

Fifty-seven per cent of all savings deposits with banking institutions were in 1973 held by the *Sparkassen* (savings banks), municipal institutions under public law. They have over 16 500 branch offices in all parts of the Bundesrepublik. Together with the *Landesbanken/Girozentralen* (their central giro institutions), which rate among the large commercial banks in West Germany, and the *Deutsche Girozentrale* (the central clearing bank of the Landesbanken/Girozentralen) their volume of business amounted in 1973 to 39 per cent of the business of all banking groups. These savings banks transact all the normal business of a banking institution but are, unlike the private banks, subject to certain restrictions in regard to the investment of their funds. There also exist several credit co-operatives, among them especially the *Volksbanken* and *Raiffeisen-Kreditgenossenschaften*. They, too, have central institutions with functions parallel to those of the savings banks, and the individual banks and branches (almost 19 000) transact much the same business as other banks.

The independence of the Bundesbank and existing bank legislation, including a special bank supervisory body, did not prevent a crisis in a number of German banks in 1974, as a result of losses through bad loans and in foreign currency dealings. It is planned to tighten up bank supervision and to establish a greater joint liability of all banks for the protection of creditors. A so-called joint liquidity bank has been established in which the Bundesbank participates.

The leading German *Börse* is in Frankfurt, although the German stock exchange cannot compare with that of London. An interesting difference is that banks are usually the contracting parties and are represented by their own staff so that stockbrokers in the British sense do not exist in West Germany.

Industrial Relations

Trade unions

All *Gewerkschaften* (trade unions) were banned by the Nazis in 1933 but were reestablished by the Allied powers after the end of the Second World War. At that time a decision that has proved of inestimable value to German industry was made: it was decided to replace the religious and political divisions of the pre-war period with sixteen new industrial unions. In practice, therefore, the German employer has to deal with a Gewerkschaft that represents many of his workers without creating a 'closed shop' whereby all of his workers are obliged to belong to one Gewerkschaft. Inter-union conflicts are substantially reduced. For example, the *I.G. Metall* represents 2 300 000 workers and covers the entire iron and steel industry, the car manufacturers and the shipbuilding and engineering industries.

The Grundgesetz guarantees [article 9 (3)] the right to form associations to safeguard working and economic conditions and makes illegal any measure directed to prevent or hinder this right. Every worker therefore has a right to belong to a Gewerkschaft and by interpretation to refuse to belong, though the Bundesverfassungsgericht has never ruled on this. In practice, slightly fewer workers join Gewerkschaften than in Britain: only 39 per cent were members of unions in 1973 (Britain, just over 40 per cent). Union dues are much higher than in Britain. The law requires that the benefits negotiated by union representatives shall be conferred not only on union members but also on all other employees. There is no legal obligation on any Gewerkschaft to register and the most important West German Gewerkschaften are unregistered and therefore completely independent. By law a valid collective agreement can only be concluded by a Gewerkschaft that is independent of party-political or denominational control.

Most unions are members of the *Deutscher Gewerkschaftsbund* (DGB, Federation of German Trade Unions), the equivalent of the British T.U.C. The *Christliche Gewerkschaftsbund* (Christian Trade Union Association) is an insignificant rival association. Organisations representing white-collar workers only are the *Deutsche Angestelltengewerkschaft* (DAG, German Salaried Employee's Union) and the *Deutscher Beamtenbund* (DBB, German Civil Service Federation). Comparative membership of these organisations at the end of 1973 was: DGB 7.18 million, DAG 463 000, DBB 718 000.

Employers associations can voluntarily choose to become members of the *Bundesvereinigung der Arbeitgeberverbände* (Confederation of German Employers' Associations) to which belong employers associations from all branches of the economy, industry and commerce as well as those of artisans, banks, insurance companies, agriculture and traffic. Throughout the Bundesrepublik there were forty-four associations with between them 369 individual membership associations in 1973. The Bundesvereinigung has, like the D.G.B., no direct bargaining function and corresponds to the Confederation of British Industry.

Collective bargaining

In West Germany a collective agreement is a written agreement between one or more employers or employers associations on the one hand, and one or more Gewerkschaften on the other, for the regulation of their rights and duties and for the establishment of legal standards governing detailed conditions of employment. It may also include provisions for the settlement of disputes (procedure agreements as they are known in England). Such an agreement is legally binding and the Gewerkschaften do not challenge the law's authority in this field, but accept without question the decisions of the *Arbeitsgerichte* (labour courts), of which there is an established hierarchy at Land and federal level. The courts resemble the British industrial tribunals and the former National Industrial Relations Court, being composed of a legally qualified chairman sitting with two lay assessors representing both sides of industry. Most cases before the courts are settled by agreement.

Legally binding collective agreements must be entered in a federal register and displayed by the employers at the factory or office. Wage agreements are normally concluded to last a year and the two sides usually begin negotiation of a new agreement well before the termination of the old one. In West Germany the typical agreement is negotiated between an employers association and one Gewerkschaft at Land or regional level. Individual employers covered by the agreement cannot contract out of it, though the collective agreement will only set a minimum standard, which can be varied at plant level in favour of the worker. The federal government may in some circumstances make such agreements binding on employers and employees not party to the agreement where a committee representing both sides recommends that this would be in the public interest.

Plant bargaining

The major difference in ideology between the average British and West German worker is that the former tends to see himself as in perpetual conflict with his employer while the latter likes to believe that he can by becoming part of the capitalist system work with the employer to the advantage of both. The key word is *Mitbestimmung* (co-determination). It must, of course, be said that the great prosperity of German industry and of the workers means that there is necessarily less friction. If the standard of living of the German worker were as low as that of his British counterpart no doubt conflict would arise. West German unions in the 1970s have shown sympathy towards their British colleagues because wage levels here are still low by West German standards. One reason for the prosperity of the Bundesrepublik is her record of industrial peace.

The Betriebsrat

Worker participation in management takes two forms. The first is embodied in the *Betriebsrat* (works council), established by law in 1952 and now made even more important by the revised 1972 *Betriebsverfassungsgesetz* (Industrial Constitution Act). Every employer who employs at least five workers over the age of eighteen must every three years provide for the election of a Betriebsrat to represent his employees. The main plant of Volkswagen at Wolfsburg, for instance, must under the 1972 Act have a Betriebsrat consisting of at least sixty-five members. This council is independent of the employer, although members of the council must be allowed time off work with pay by their employer where it is necessary to fulfil their function and for training and education courses. A minimum number of Betriebsrat members must be totally freed from work on full pay; for example, the employer of between 1000 and 2000 workers must release at least three Betriebsrat members. The costs of the Betriebsrat must be borne by the employer, who must provide facilities like offices and secretarial assistance.

All workers over eighteen have a right to vote in the election, including foreign workers. Only employees can be elected, so that full-time Gewerkschaft officials would not be eligible. Aliens and nationals are now equally eligible for election. Both wage earners and salaried employees must be represented, in proportion to their numbers. A minority group is in any case entitled to at least one representative if it consists of five or more employees. The 1972 Act also provides that both sexes should be proportionately represented. In the past most Betriebsrat members were active trade unionists, and the first elections under the new law in April 1972 brought little change in that respect (78 per cent trade union members), even though foreign workers were included.

The Betriebsrat's general duty is to co-operate with the management for the welfare of the employees and the enterprise. In practice, therefore, bargaining at plant level is between the employer and the Betriebsrat rather than with the Gewerkschaft directly. The Betriebsrat has a right to be consulted by the employer on a large number of issues. For example, the employer must obtain their consent to any appointment of new staff, any dismissal, and for any transfer or reclassification of existing staff. If the employer acts without consent he can be taken to the Arbeitsgericht, which can order him to rescind the measure and fine him if he refuses to do so. A dismissal without consulting the Betriebsrat is legally invalid. Management must obtain the consent of the Betriebsrat to any change in the beginning or end of the working day or in working hours. The Betriebsrat must approve the method of assessing piece rates.

In addition, management must inform and discuss with the Betriebsrat wider issues of policy, such as mergers, major changes in production methods, proposed redundancies, and so on. What happens if there is a clash between management and the Betriebsrat about, say, the introduction of a new method of production? The 1972 Act provides that an appeal may be made by either side to the Land government for mediation, and failing agreement, the Minister may refer the matter to a conciliation board containing representatives of both sides with an impartial chairman. Management is in theory free to ignore the recommendation of the conciliation board but would have to compensate any workers dismissed as a result of doing so. In some cases, not usually policy issues, the 1972 Act provides that the decision of the conciliation board is binding on both parties. This applies, for example, in disputes about hours, timing of holidays, rules for accident prevention, piece rates and efficiency bonuses, and amounts to compulsory arbitration.

Worker participation in management

Worker participation also takes place at a different level. German workers participate in the management of companies through their own representatives on the *Vorstand* (board of management) or on the separate part-time supervisory *Aufsichtsrat* (supervisory board of directors). This happens in two types of company: the coal and steel companies and most joint stock companies (a term which covers most public companies). In the iron and steel industry since 1951 workers have equal representation with shareholders on the Aufsichtsrat, which also includes an independent member so that no side has an absolute majority. In addition the supervisory board must elect a workers' representative, the *Arbeitsdirektor* (labour director), to the Vorstand, which is charged with day-to-day administration. The Aufsichtsrat supervises company accounts, appoints and dismisses members of the Vorstand and is responsible for most policy decisions, such as mergers and reorganisation schemes. Often the Aufsichtsrat is advised by, and gives only formal approval to decisions of, the Vorstand. In other public companies since 1952 only one-third of the members of the Aufsichtsrat are employee-elected and there are no provisions for worker representation on the main board.

The SPD/FDP coalition is committed to extend Mitbestimmung to all companies with more than 2000 employees, although in early 1975 both parties were still not agreed on all details. The government's proposal is to have complete parity, that is to dispense with a neutral chairman of the Aufsichtsrat, which would have twenty members, ten elected by the employees and ten by the shareholders. Neither unions nor industrialists are totally happy with the proposed new scheme. The existing, less-complicated system has worked well for over twenty years. It gives the employees several real advantages of which perhaps the most important is information. The workers can, through their representatives, discover the real financial standing of the company and may therefore be more willing to co-operate with policy changes. Greater confidence may be placed in management when the workers know that their interests are directly represented.

Industrial disputes

Conciliation and arbitration

There are no provisions in federal law for conciliation and arbitration, which is left to the laws of the individual states. All have ministries offering conciliation services, though compulsory arbitration is not generally found. However, a law of 1946 passed by the Allies before the foundation of the Bundesrepublik is still in force, except in Rheinland–Pfalz and Südbaden. This law provides that in the event of a dispute the matter shall be referred to a conciliation board with an independent chairman and an equal number of representatives of both sides. However, the decision is not binding on the parties unless they agree to be bound. The recommendations of the board are usually put by the unions to their members who are asked to vote by secret ballot (the vote by show of hands is considered unreliable).

Most collective agreements provide for voluntary arbitration in disputes and these agreements are legally binding on the parties who are not therefore free to ignore them by, for example, taking strike action before arbitration has taken place.

Industrial action

There is no universal legal regulation of industrial disputes. There is no guarantee in the Grundgesetz of the 'right to strike' or anything similar to it. Various Länder have different restrictions on industrial action, but certain principles have been evolved by the courts and apply throughout the Bundesrepublik. A strike or lockout is illegal if it is in breach of a collective agreement or if it is resorted to while negotiations for a new agreement are proceeding, or before an agreed conciliation procedure has been exhausted. Political strikes—those aimed against the government—are illegal, as are all unofficial strikes, or, those not sanctioned by the trade union membership by means of a ballot with a 75 per cent majority. Peaceful picketing is lawful. Civil servants are generally denied the right to strike because of their special duty of loyalty to the state. Any unlawful act carries an obligation to pay damages to anyone injured by it, but there are no criminal sanctions against strikes or lockouts except in special cases like an attack on the constitution or the stoppage of essential services. Whether the strike is legal or not, the workers lose all social security benefits during the strike (in some cases their families are also affected; for example they lose the protection of health insurance based on the striking worker's contributions). Strike pay for trade union members, however, is almost equivalent to regular earnings.

In West Germany the taint of illegality is taken seriously. The unions and the workers are always reluctant to take any industrial action, let alone withdraw their labour, and the history of industry since the war shows a remarkably small number of days lost through strike action. The average figure per 1000 employed persons for the two years 1972 and 1973, for several countries, will serve as illustration: Bundesrepublik 14, Netherlands 94, Belgium 108, France 231, Britain 700, Italy 1449. It must, however, be said that the rights of the worker guaranteed by law are much greater than in England, where the right to belong to a union and to sue for unfair dismissal were only conferred in 1972. This may in some part have contributed to the German worker's greater willingness to cooperate with his employer, though the traditional German respect for authority must also have been a factor.

Trade Associations

There are a number of central trade associations. The most important is the

Bundesverband der Deutschen Industrie (Confederation of German Industry) at Köln. It represents the interests of industry but does not deal with salaries and wages. Membership, which is voluntary, is not open to individual companies as in Britain but only to associations representing sections of industry, as iron and steel or metal goods. The membership associations are estimated together to represent some 100 000 firms. The president of the Bundesverband, who is assisted by a board of twenty-five members, a large number of committees and working groups, and two chief executive managers, has become an influential spokesman for industry, especially since the first president after the war held office for twenty-two years.

Similar central associations exist, for example, for the banks, wholesale and foreign trade, retail trade, artisans and agriculture. All these central associations belong to the *Gemeinschaftsausschuss der deutschen Wirtschaft* (Joint Committee of the German Economy). This voices the opinion of all branches of the German economy on basic matters of common interest, including questions of taxation, competition or traffic.

Numerous voluntary associations have been founded to further the interests of specialised groups of employers or specific careers. Independent craftsmen of the same or related trades may combine, on a local level, to form *Innungen* (guilds), which are entitled to negotiate wage agreements and to operate their own insurance schemes.

Membership of the *Industrie- und Handelskammern* (Chambers of Industry and Commerce), of the *Handwerkskammern* (Chambers of Artisans), and of the *Landwirtschaftskammern* (Chambers of Agriculture) is compulsory by law. They have the status of public corporations and represent the interests of the appropriate group on a regional level. The Industrie- und Handelskammern to which anyone or any organisation carrying on a trade or business in the area (except artisans) has to belong are the most important. The *Deutscher Industrie- und Handelstag* is their central representation at the federal level. Handwerkskammern are established by the government, although they have the right of self-administration. They hold the register in which any independent master craftsman has to be entered (in order to obtain a licence he must produce proof of competence), regulate examinations requirements, and, like the Industrie- und Handelskammern, nominate experts and provide opinions and reports for courts of law and government departments.

Manufacturing Industry and Industrial Regions

Iron and steel

In the boom year 1973 Germany's iron and steel output amounted to 37 million tonnes of pig iron and almost 50 million tonnes of crude steel, more than was produced by any other European state and one-third of the production of the whole Community. Over 70 per cent of the iron and steel-producing capacity is concentrated in the Ruhr area and some ten per cent in the Saar region (see map 7). In both, the furnaces and mills have been established near the supply of coking coal rather than near the source of iron ore. For example, the largest blast furnace in the West is at Duisburg in the Ruhr, with an annual production of 3.5 million tonnes of pig iron. On the other hand, the plant near Salzgitter in Nieder-

Map 7   Industry and industrial regions.

sachsen with an output of 5.2 million tonnes in 1973 is in the vicinity of ore fields. Other smaller works near a source of ore are in the Sieg–Lahn district, especially at Siegen and Giessen, and in Bayern. Finally, there is Germany's only coastal plant at Bremen, which takes advantage of iron ore and coal imported by sea. It has recently been modernised by installing modern oxygen converters and is intended to produce over 3 million tonnes of steel annually.

The Ruhr

The main Ruhr plants, in the west of the district at Rheinhausen, Oberhausen, Duisburg and also in the east at Dortmund (on the Dortmund–Ems–Kanal) rely chiefly on imported ore which is brought via Rotterdam on inland waterways, and on scrap. The whole industry was badly affected by the war and took some years, following the reversal of Allied policies of dismantling and restricting output and the creation of the Montanunion to reach its pre-war output. In 1973 Ruhr production of crude steel (30 million tonnes) alone was 60 per cent of the federal total (50 million tonnes). It exceeded that of the entire United Kingdom (27 million tonnes) and amounted to one-fifth of the total production of the European Community (150 million tonnes). Competition from within the original

Common Market and from further afield (America and Japan), a general gradual erosion of the industry's competitive position as a result of spiralling wage costs, high coal prices, and several revaluations of the Deutsche Mark since 1969 have forced the industry since the mid-1960s to contract and rationalise. Four steel sales offices were formed in 1967, to which all big steel companies belong, and older Bessemer and open-furnace plants are being replaced by oxygen converters.

In 1968 the Thyssen group, through a number of mergers, became the continent's largest steel manufacturer. In spring 1973 the concentration of the industry went further when Thyssen took over its Ruhr rival Rheinstahl. The new combine had a crude-steel output of 15.7 million tonnes in 1973 and employs more than 150 000 people. It is West Germany's second largest company in turnover terms, second only to the nationalised British Steel Corporation in annual steel output, and occupies sixth place in the world steel-making league, which is led by American and Japanese firms. Cross-frontier mergers are also taking place, like the 1972 merger between the German number two steelmaker Hoesch and the Dutch Hoogovens, which resulted in Europe's third largest steel-producing concern. German steel firms are, of course, private companies, although the federal government and the Land government of Nordrhein–Westfalen assist individual firms by guaranteeing export credits. They took a hand in rescuing the giant family firm of Krupp from bankruptcy in 1967–8 and turning it into a public company, which by 1970 again began to make a profit.

The Krupp concern with some 100 000 employees provides a good example of another characteristic feature of the German iron and steel industry—the size of firms. They frequently include coal and iron ore mines (since 1968 the former are generally separated), coke ovens, iron and steel plants, and engineering works. Not surprisingly it was a particular policy of the Allied occupation powers after 1945 to split up these huge concerns into smaller units, for many of the powerful industrialists had supported Hitler and had been immensely influential in making his aggressive policies practically possible. The Vereinigte Stahlwerke, for example, formed in 1925, controlled about 90 per cent of Ruhr steel and about one-third of its coal and coke output. Allied measures divided the twelve largest coal and steel companies into twenty-eight independent companies. These efforts at fragmentation were only partially successful and after Allied control ceased and German sovereignty was restored regrouping created new giants like Thyssen and Flick. Krupp had been asked to dispose of his coal and steel holdings yet no purchaser could be found. Since then the coal mines of this concern have, like those of all other steel companies, been detached from the group and brought into a separate organisation as a rescue operation for the ailing coal industry.

The Ruhr industrial region has been described as a 'policentred metropolis' (Peter Hall). The total population in 1973, 5.56 million was 8.9 per cent of the total West German population. The predominance of coal and steel, the declining fortunes of coalmining, and new steel furnaces powered by fuels other than coal, have created special problems for this, the continent's largest (and the world's fourth largest) industrial area. Between 1962 and 1970 221 000 workers (excluding agricultural workers) or ten per cent of the total work force, left the Ruhr. As a result the economic growth rate of the district was for several years, until 1969, below that of the rest of the Bundesrepublik. The task of restructuring the area by diversification of industry was begun with some success in the 1960s, and the process of transformation is still going on. This is not only a matter of attracting new growth industries. Here government investment grants have helped to create many thousand new jobs, for instance in a new car factory at Bochum, employing more than 18 000 people, or in new chemical, electrical and aluminium works. The entire transport system needs to be reorganised and developed on a regional rather than a piecemeal local basis (a beginning has been made by the construction of a comprehensive high-speed suburban railway network), more new roads have to be constructed and waterways improved. Apart from this modernisation of the infrastructure the entire district urgently needed to be totally reorganised administratively in order to create fewer but larger and more powerful local authorities. This finally occurred in 1975 when seventeen towns, fifty-two small Gemeinden and three Landkreise were amalgamated to form nine 'super' towns and one Landkreis. A programme to improve the image of the area is also under way and urban renewal is proceeding with vigour, while new universities at Bochum, Essen, Duisburg and Dortmund are expected to provide intellectual stimulus. The effects are beginning to be felt, and just over half of the Ruhr's labour force is now employed outside the old basic industries.

The Saar

The problems of the Saar region today are not political, as after both World Wars, but economic. Like the Ruhr it depends predominantly on the coalmining and iron and steel industries, and the decline of the first and the varying fortunes of the second, partially a result of its disadvantageous competitive position (use of imported high-grade ores), have aggravated the position of the entire region, which was always precarious owing to its isolation from the rest of the Bundesrepublik. The provision of better access by rail through electrification of the main west–east lines, by road through the construction of a west–east Autobahn, and by water through the canalisation of the Mosel has helped. In spite of greater competition the opening of the frontiers to the Saar's immediate neighbours France (Lorraine) and Luxembourg, the combined attack on the similar problems of these regions, and the planning of industrial development across the frontier has also benefited the region. The region itself has attempted, like the Ruhr, to attract new industries. Thus, in addition to the iron and steel works in Saarbrücken, Neunkirchen, Völklingen and Dillingen, and the old-established coal mines, we now find some industry producing machinery, electrical equipment, clothing and foodstuffs.

Heavy engineering and machine tools

The Bundesrepublik is the leading European producer of heavy machinery. The industry is located where raw materials and labour are most easily available and communications are easy. Thus, once again the Ruhr is the centre of this important branch of German industry. The Ruhr heavy-engineering industry produces bridges, cranes, locomotives, rolling mills, boilers, agricultural machines, machine tools and other heavy machinery. On a smaller scale the Saar has at

Saarbrücken and Zweibrücken a similar concentration of heavy engineering plant. It is common to both regions that their relative importance (in comparison to other branches of industry, especially car-making, chemical and consumer goods) is declining.

Secondary centres of heavy-engineering industry, usually mixed with medium and light machinery, exist at München (locomotives, wagons, aircraft engines, machine construction), Nürnberg (cranes, diesel engines), Kassel (railway engines, rolling stock), Hannover (heavy vehicles, machinery) and Hamburg and Bremen (subsidiary industries of shipbuilding). Agricultural machinery is often produced in rural areas and textile machines in Württemberg (Esslingen, Ebingen) and the Lower Rheinland (around Krefeld and Mönchen-Gladbach) (see map 7).

In 1973 the machinery industry exported 39 per cent of the total value of production (the machine-tool industry, the world's leading exporter in this field, over 50 per cent). In the same year these exports were the second largest single group among investment goods exported and amounted to almost 20 per cent of all industrial exports.

Vehicles

The German motor industry deserves special mention, not only because of its history (which is particularly associated with the names of Daimler and Benz who independently built in 1885–6 the first motor car), but also because of its importance in West Germany's economy. It occupied fourth place among manufacturing industry in 1973 and employed 632 000 people with several millions indirectly depending on it. In 1973 Germany was the world's third largest vehicle producer (3.6 million units) after the U.S.A. (9.7 million) and Japan (4.4 million) and followed by France (2.9 million) and Britain (1.7 million). The German vehicle industry is particularly export-intensive—in 1973 59 per cent of all units produced were sold abroad (Britain 35 per cent), just over half in Europe and 36 per cent in the U.S.A. For this reason it is especially dependent on the economic situation in other industrialised countries, and sales abroad inevitably dropped in 1974. At the same time, the oil crisis and the uncertain state of the German economy caused a pronounced downward trend in the home market, where German makes have a share of about 75 per cent. Car sales and production in 1974 were some 17 per cent down compared to the previous year, and many car workers had repeatedly to be put onto short-time working. It thus appears that the phenomenal boom in the vehicle industry (whose index of production reached 197 in 1973 (1962 = 100) and was only exceeded by the chemical (302), mineral oil (240) and electrical (231) industries), has given way to an, at least temporary, decline.

The industry, with the exception of Ford's at Köln and Saarlouis and a new Opel plant at Bochum in the Ruhr, is located outside the old centres of heavy industry, largely in southern Germany (see map 7). The main plant of the Volkswagen AG is at Wolfsburg, a completely new town near Braunschweig, which was established together with the factory when the National Socialist government decreed that the first *Volkswagen* (people's car) should be built there in the then centre of Germany and in the immediate neighbourhood of the Mittelland–Kanal. Cars and components are also produced at Braunschweig (engines), Kassel (components), Hannover (commercial vehicles), Emden (export) and Salzgitter (new models). The firm has around 200 000 employees and up to 1971 and again in 1974 it sold more cars inside Germany than any of its competitors. In 1973 70 per cent of its production was exported, again more than that of its rivals. In that year total production amounted to 1.5 million vehicles, more than any other vehicle manufacturer in Europe except Fiat. In terms of turnover Volkswagenwerk was Germany's largest enterprise in 1973.

The success of the company is based on the almost legendary 'beetle', of which more units have been sold than of any other model in the world, even the Ford Model T. Only recently did profits decline and the firm made a loss of some DM 500m in 1974. This promptly brought the company, in which the federal government and the Land government of Niedersachsen have a 40 per cent holding—the rest of the shares being held by thousands of small shareholders—into difficulties. It had not sufficiently diversified its production or drawn up long-term development plans nor had it attained sufficiently high sales figures for the remaining models of its range. Although a whole series of new models was launched in 1973 and 1974 and they have recaptured a substantial share of the German market VW still has problems with foreign sales, partly because its cars cost too much to produce. Substantial rationalisation measures are being undertaken in 1975 to restore the company's profitability.

A few years ago Volkswagen acquired the firms of Audi and N.S.U. They produce passenger cars at Ingolstadt (Bayern) and near Heilbronn, north of Stuttgart. Audi cars had a 9.6 per cent share of the new car registrations in Germany in 1973. The former N.S.U. owns the rights of the revolutionary Wankel engine. VW also owns the Porsche sports car company at Stuttgart.

The Stuttgart region is a centre of German car production. In addition to the firms mentioned, several plants for the manufacture of Mercedes passenger cars are concentrated here. Although in 1973 Daimler–Benz produced a comparatively small number of passenger cars (only 331 000) of all types and supplied only eight per cent of new car registrations inside Germany, Germany's reputation in car manufacturing is to a considerable extent based on this firm's quality of design and output. The company, in which since late 1974 Kuwait has a 14 per cent stake, certainly produces Germany's most prestigious range of passenger cars, about half of which are exported, and in terms of turnover occupies fifth place among all German companies. West Germany's second largest car manufacturer is Opel, a subsidiary of General Motors. It turned out 840 000 cars in 1973, less than, for example, Renault or British Leyland, but commanded 21 per cent of the German market. Its main production units are situated in the Rhein–Main region, especially at Rüsselsheim. As the second American manufacturer Ford had in 1973 a smaller (12 per cent) share of new registrations in Germany and produced 160 000 vehicles less than Opel. The BMW (Bayerische Motoren Werke), centred on München, have achieved with their fast saloon cars a steadily increasing share of the German market.

Most of the big companies, including Ford, Daimler–Benz and Volkswagen, also produce commercial vehicles, sometimes in special plants at different locations, as does Daimler–Benz in the Heidelberg–Mannheim region. Other commercial vehicles, including tractors, are manufactured by specialised firms (for example MAN–Büssing) or subsidiaries of engineering companies (like Klöckner).

Shipbuilding

The shipbuilding industry of the Bundesrepublik produced 1.9 million gross registered tonnes in 1973, only 6.3 per cent of total world production, but its order books were full for several more years. In 1973 it exported 70 per cent of the gross tonnage launched and is in strong competition with Japan, Sweden and Britain, although it has long surpassed the latter. In common with the international industry it underwent a crisis in the early 1960s out of which it emerged with greatly modernised engineering techniques and shipbuilding facilities, and fewer firms through mergers. The Howaldtswerke–Deutsche Werft AG at Hamburg and Kiel, Europe's largest shipbuilding firm, which is 50 per cent owned by the nationalised Salzgitter company, is the outcome of such a merger. Other large shipyards are at Hamburg, Bremen, Emden, Flensburg, Rendsburg and Lübeck. The shipbuilding industry, which now produces mainly large vessels such as tankers and container ships often on fixed-price contracts with a long construction period, is particularly affected by currency fluctuations, rising world steel prices and wage increases. It has repeatedly needed the assistance of cheap government bridging loans.

Aircraft

The German aircraft industry, which once led the world, totally ceased production at the end of the war, when it was either destroyed or dismantled. Even after the lifting of Allied restrictions and in spite of encouragement by the federal government it has never reached its former status. With some 40 000 employees in factories mainly in the Bremen–Hamburg and München–Augsburg areas the aerospace industry in the Bundesrepublik counts today only as a minor investment goods industry. With the exception of the development and manufacture of a medium-size passenger plane it is chiefly engaged in joint European projects (the European Airbus, the European fighter plane) or with participation in American contracts.

Medium and light engineering, precision engineering

The Bundesrepublik prides herself on a very extensive and varied industry in this sector with numerous specialisations. The industry generally is a growing one, and in some branches, for instance in the precision and optical goods industries, export plays an important part. The industry is dispersed throughout the Bundesrepublik between many industrial regions and towns, often mixed with other branches of industry. Some places specialise in one single group of product, as for example Solingen (cutlery), Remscheid (hand tools), Triberg/Furtwangen/Villingen (clocks, precision engineering, optical instruments), Oberkochen (optical instruments and cameras), Trossingen (musical instruments), Schweinfurt (roller and ball-bearings).

The Stuttgart and Frankfurt regions

The two regions where light engineering industries dominate are Schwaben, especially along the Neckar valley and centred at Stuttgart, and the Rhein–Main region (see map 7). The whole of Baden—Württemberg is West Germany's fastest expanding area (a population increase of 19 per cent between 1960 and 1973), and—another indication of industrial growth—in 1973 almost ten per cent of its population was foreign. In Stuttgart, this figure was as high as one-quarter of all gainfully employed persons—the highest percentage in the entire Bundesrepublik. In addition to the vehicle-building and textile-machinery industry there is an important electrical engineering and textile industry and production of vehicle components. Also manufactured here are railway equipment, precision instruments, musical instruments and a host of other engineering products.

Similarly, the Rhein—Main region specialises in engineering and vehicle building, which complement the extensive chemical industry. Whereas Frankfurt had for many centuries been a town of political, commercial and financial importance Stuttgart, rather inconveniently situated in a hollow surrounded by hills, only achieved significance in the nineteenth century. It is still essentially an industrial, commercial, and administrative regional centre, albeit a flourishing one. Frankfurt, on the other hand, is today the undisputed commercial and banking centre of the continent, famous also for its twice-yearly consumer goods fair.

Other industrial regions have developed around München (machine construction, light and precision engineering, vehicle and locomotive building), Nürnberg/Fürth (typewriters, toys, precision instruments, and also cranes, diesel engines, electrical equipment, vehicles and chemicals), Hannover/Braunschweig (agricultural engineering, machinery for canning, and vehicles and electrical equipment), Berlin (machines, consumer goods, electrical equipment) and Hamburg and Bremen. Hannover has the added attraction of being Germany's leading exhibition centre, with a hall area approximately four times that of Olympia or Earls Court, where the annual international industrials goods fair is held.

Electrical engineering and electronics

After engineering this is the second most important sector of the iron and metal processing industry in the Bundesrepublik. In 1973 the industry employed 1.06 million people and exported 23 per cent of its total production (excluding office machinery and data-processing equipment, where the export rate was 52 per cent. Eleven per cent of all industrial exports in that year came from this source, the fourth largest group after engineering, vehicle construction, and chemicals. The largest electrical-equipment companies are Siemens, with a payroll of over 300 000 in 1973, the largest private employer in the Bundesrepublik, and the third largest enterprise by turnover in the same year (DM 15 500m, exceeded only by Volkswagenwerk's 17 000m and BASF's 16 000m), AEG Telefunken, with whom it collaborates closely in the power engineering field, and Bosch. While the old-established plants are located in major industrial centres many new factories have been built in more rural areas in search of labour. West Germany's fairly young but vigorously expanding electronics industry is concentrated near Stuttgart, Konstanz and Mainz. The country is now Europe's largest computer user.

Chemicals

The German chemical industry is expanding at a breathtaking pace. The index of industrial net production in 1973 stood at 302 (1962 = 100) and sales in that year had reached DM 64 600m, 15 per cent up on the previous year and more than eight times as much as in 1950. In 1974 the industry was scarcely affected by the downturn of Germany's economy. It is the largest industry of its kind in western Europe. Thirty-four per cent of the turnover of this most dynamic of all German industries was exported, and in addition a considerable number of German chemical works have been built abroad.

After the war the giant IG Farben concern was broken up by the Allies and three main successor groups were created: Badische Anilin und Soda Fabriken (BASF), centred on Ludwigshafen, stretching along the Rhein there for several kilometres, and with new plant at Antwerp in Belgium and in South Carolina (U.S.A.), Farbwerke Hoechst near Frankfurt and numerous other locations, including Ireland, and Farbenfabriken Bayer at Leverkusen, near Köln, and a new complex on the German Nordsee coast. All three firms are now giants in their own right and in 1973, in terms of turnover, individually ranked among West Germany's top six and among the top twelve European companies. In recent years they have not only grown through mergers and rationalisation measures within the chemical industry inside Germany, but also as a result of investing in new plant in Germany, in European countries inside and outside the original Common Market, and overseas, especially in America, and through acquiring control of existing firms outside Germany. Bayer alone is reported to own over 120 foreign companies. Most of the remaining German chemical firms, with a few exceptions like Schering of Berlin, are tied in one way or another to the big three, which produce everything from fibres and plastics to paints, pharmaceuticals, cosmetics and fertilisers. BASF supplies some 90 per cent of Germany's potash.

Formerly the industry was predominantly coal-based and located near the Ruhr. Today oil is the industry's essential raw material. It is pumped to the vast chemical complexes by pipeline from Nordsee and Mediterranean ports and has permitted the installation of new plant in south and south-west Germany, for example in the Saar and near Basel. Natural gas is a new base for the industry, especially at Marl, north of the Ruhr.

Other industries

The textile and clothing industry is dispersed throughout the Bundesrepublik. It is not, as in Britain, concentrated near the coalfields, and individual regions do not specialise in particular branches as they used to before the war, with the exception of the Krefeld area in Nordrhein–Westfalen, where most of the silk industry is located. Baden–Württemberg houses about one-quarter of West Germany's textile industry: Württemberg, especially the Schwäbischer Jura, produces knitted textiles (at Stuttgart, Reutlingen and Ebingen) and hosiery and women's outer clothing (Stuttgart), and in the southern Schwarzwald cotton and silk are manufactured. Textiles and clothing are also manufactured at Augsburg (woollen textiles), Wuppertal (woollens and specialised textile goods like ribbons and tapes, corsetry, linings, upholstery fabrics), Bocholt (cotton spinning), Mönchen–Gladbach (cotton spinning and weaving) and Bielefeld (linen and clothing).

The Bundesrepublik is a big producer of ready-to-wear clothes, and this branch has increased its turnover since 1960 by almost 80 per cent. Berlin alone has over 300 manufacturers, which produce especially women's clothes, and the former capital together with München and Düsseldorf is a centre of 'high fashion' with international fairs. The production index for the entire textile industry stood at 142 in 1973 (1962 = 100). However, for the clothing industry it stood at only 126, and the leather and especially the footwear industries have performed even less well.

Another industry for which Germany has a good reputation and a successful export record is glass, glass products and fine ceramics. Glass is produced at Kaufbeuren south of Augsburg by German refugees from Czechoslovakia, in the Bayerischer Wald, Fichtelgebirge and Frankenwald, at Neunkirchen in the Saar, and at Gelsenkirchen. Pottery is also made near the Bavarian–Czech frontier, especially at Weiden and Selb, and at München, in the Saar and near Neuwied.

The food, beverage and tobacco industry has grown by an average of five per cent per annum since 1960. The brewery industry stands out: Germany brews 41 per cent of all the beer consumed in the Common Market and is the second largest producer of beer in the world after the United States (94 million hl in 1973), yet it exports very little. Many mergers took place in the early 1970s and this trend is expected to continue.

Handicrafts and the retail trade

In common with other highly industrialised countries the number of independent craftsmen is steadily diminishing. While in 1963 there were 686 000 firms, in 1973 there were only 544 000 employing a total of 4.3 million persons and contributing 11 per cent to the G.N.P. With certain exceptions, notably in the food sector (butchers, bakers), their dependence on industry is constantly increasing. They supply manufacturers with their specialised products or carry out the servicing and repair of industrially manufactured goods. Nevertheless, in spite of industrial manufacturing, automation and new forms of selling, the independent artisan appears to have survived in greater numbers and in more sectors in Germany than in Britain. They still owned 16 per cent of all businesses, employed 15 per cent of all employees in the Bundesrepublik and trained 34 per cent of all apprentices in 1973. The fall in the number of independent artisans has been accelerated because the master craftsman finds it difficult to keep his trained staff and to attract young school-leavers as apprentices. These prefer to go into industry or commerce where conditions and pay are more attractive.

The development of the German retail trade clearly points towards an increase in the multibranch or chain-type businesses (their share of the total turnover increased from 10 per cent in 1962 to 17 per cent in 1973) and further expansion of the big stores (now a 12 per cent share), with a corresponding decline of the small businesses, which, nevertheless, still account for just under two-thirds of the total turnover and whose future, in spite of self-service stores, multimarkets, etc., appears to be assured in Germany. Germans definitely like to shop in specialised shops, whether for food, electrical goods, or clothes, and they like to receive more individual attention, though they are also price-conscious and may turn more to hypermarkets as prices continue to rise. Competition is somewhat restricted, since the opening hours for all types of shops are regulated by law and allow little flexibility even to the small family-operated business. No shop is permitted to remain open in the evening or on Saturday afternoons (except the first Saturday in the month). Exceptions apply only to shops in airports, stations and holiday resorts, and to certain special kinds of retailers, like chemists, patisseries, florists or hairdressers. In spite of a proliferation of mail-order firms and an extension of their business, their turnover accounted for no more than 5 per cent of the retail trade total in 1973.

5 Education, Arts and Sciences

Education in the Federal System

In the Bundesrepublik all aspects of education, from kindergarten to university, and the arts and sciences in general are in the main the responsibility of the Länder. This is without doubt their most important area of legislative competence. In recent years, however, there has been a distinct shift towards greater federal involvement such that, as the result of several constitutional amendments, the Federation now not only provides finance for certain sectors of education and research but also has functions of planning and co-ordination. It can, for example, legislate (with the consent of the Länder) on the production and use of nuclear energy, the promotion of scientific research, the regulation of student grants, and the legal status and salary scales of Länder employees, including school and university teachers [articles 74, 74(a), 75]. It has the power to make general rules of principle regarding institutions of higher education, the Press and the film world [article 75]. Articles 91(a) and 91(b) enable the federal government to collaborate with the Länder in the planning and financing of the extension of existing and the construction of new institutions of higher education (universities as well as art, technical and teacher training colleges), in general educational planning, and in the support of research institutions and projects on a supraregional level.

Thus the federal government has become an indispensable partner of the Länder governments. Since December 1972 these federal responsibilities have been shared by two ministries. The first is *Forschung und Technologie* (Research and Technology) which co-ordinates federal policies and activities in research (excluding, however, all university-based research) and technological development, and guides and sponsors, for example, research in atomic energy, data-processing and space. The minister is also the Minister of Posts and Telecommunications; the second is the *Bundesministerium für Bildung und Wissenschaft* (Federal Ministry of Education and Arts and Sciences), within whose competence fall all aspects of education.

The co-ordinating body for the eleven *Kultusminister* (Minister of Education and Cultural Affairs) of the Länder is the *Ständige Konferenz der Kultusminister der Länder* (Standing Conference of the Ministers of Education and Cultural Affairs). The Kultusministerkonferenz deals with cultural and educational matters of supraregional importance and attempts to arrive at a common Länder view in such matters as the beginning of the school year, teacher training, student discipline and university and school reform. Unanimity is required for any positive recommendation, which then has to be approved and implemented by the governments and parliaments of the individual Länder whose interests are diverse and whose desire to retain cultural and educational independence is paramount. The Kultusministerkonferenz is not noted for its initiative, nor for its positive planning and policy-making rôle. In fact, it is by its very nature an eminently conservative body, so that—although most of the basic features of the German educational system are fairly uniform throughout the Bundesrepublik—effective co-ordination is still absent.

Nothing illustrates this more clearly than Germany's poor record in university reform. Until recently, prospective students had almost unimpeded access to university, provided they passed the *Reifeprüfung* or *Abitur*, the grammar school leaving examination. In consequence university student numbers swelled almost uncontrollably from 108 000 in the winter of 1950–1 to 206 000 in 1960–1 and reached 417 000 in the winter of 1972–3 (662 000 in all institutions of higher education). All Länder had to spend vast sums of money to extend existing and build new universities. The poorer Länder soon found it difficult to shoulder this ever-increasing burden, yet it took them until 1964 to agree to set up a special joint fund to finance certain new universities and medical academies. This belated arrangement soon proved to be insufficient, so that federal help was sought and given.

A *Wissenschaftsrat* (Council for Arts and Sciences), with a carefully balanced membership drawn from the Länder, the Federation, the universities, and industry and commerce, had existed since 1957 and was the first body in which representatives of the federal and regional governments collaborated in a major sector of the educational system producing a great many thoroughly researched volumes of recommendations. Its main weakness was, and still is, that it is only empowered to issue recommendations, which remain to be implemented by each individual Land. Most of the Länder attempted, through their own laws, a piecemeal modernisation of the institutions of higher education within their jurisdiction, which inevitably resulted in widespread confusion throughout German higher education.

It was at this stage that the Federation, with the reluctant agreement of the Länder, was granted its new powers of initiation, co-ordination, and planning. However, some of the Länder, probably more from party-political motives than for reasons of their cherished educational independence, appear to be reluctant to co-operate with the Federation, so that West Germany in 1975 still lacks an effective national higher education policy. In 1970 the federal government, after intensive consultation with all interested parties, proposed a *Hochschulrahmengesetz* (General Law for Institutions of Higher Education), the object of which was to re-establish a uniform legislative and administrative framework for all such institutions. It was finally passed by the Bundestag in December 1974 yet because of opposition in the Bundesrat may never become law. The most successful co-operation between Federation and Länder has been over medium-term building programmes and the allocation of funds for specific building projects. The Federation now contributes 50 per cent of all costs of the expansion of all types of institutions of higher education; a total of DM 9608m was spent between 1970 and 1973.

Educational planning

The most important co-ordinating and planning instrument at government level in the Bundesrepublik is the *Bund–Länder–Kommission für Bildungsplanung* (Federation–States Committee for Educational Planning), set up in 1970 and designed as an umbrella for educational policy-making in all sectors. It is charged with the preparation of a long-term development plan for the entire educational system, the drafting of a joint educational budget for federal and Länder governments, and with the encouragement of educational research. The *Bund–Länder–Kommission*, where the Länder governments together have the same number of votes as the Bund, takes into account the recommendation of two advisory bodies, the Wissenschaftsrat, for the higher education sector, and the *Deutscher Bildungsrat* (German Education Council), for the remainder of the educational system, but it also considers the decisions and recommendations of the conferences of the relevant Länder ministers, and of the appropriate government departments in Bonn. Its work is hampered by deep-seated and party-political differences of view between the Federation and some Länder on the one hand, and the rest of the Länder on the other.

The *Bildungsgesamtplan* (Comprehensive Education Development Plan), the major result to date of the Bund–Länder–Kommission, was completed and agreed in 1973. It is the first comprehensive goal-based long-term development and reform programme for all sectors of West German education up to 1985. The underlying aim of this planning exercise was to reintroduce a uniform educational policy throughout the Bundesrepublik and to establish a framework for its future development. The objectives emphasised are structural reorganisation, curriculum reform, and quantitative expansion, in the interest of the twin principles of *Chancengleichheit* (equality of opportunity) and *Leistungsfähigkeit* (educability).

The plan provides a clear picture of what West German pre-primary, primary, secondary, higher and further education are likely to look like in 1985. In the absence of reliable statistical information and in view of many additional uncertainties—not least those brought about by the oil crisis—many of the forecasts and targets must be tentative; some, as the predicted number of full-time students in higher education, have already been proved wrong. The figures of the accompanying educational budget, which estimates the costs that are likely to be incurred if the targets of the plan are to be fulfilled, are particularly vulnerable in this respect. They nevertheless allow us to see the importance attributed by West Germany's educational planners and their governments to the education programme in relation to other main areas of public spending, and they indicate future priorities within the education programme. According to the budget total public expenditure for education and research will rise from DM 29 200m in 1970 to DM 67 000m (at constant 1970 prices) by 1980 and DM 90 500m by 1985, or from a share of 16.9 per cent of public expenditure (4.8 per cent of G.N.P.) in 1970 to 22.6 per cent (7.6 per cent of G.N.P.) by 1985. Throughout most of the period tertiary education (excluding student grants and housing) has the highest growth rate but by 1985 the annual rates of growth in the upper secondary and tertiary levels will be about the same.

Administration and Finance of Education

The entire West German educational system is under the close supervision of the state (Grundgesetz [article 7 (1)]) and most of the schools and all institutions of higher education are state establishments. Although the Grundgesetz guarantees the right to establish private schools, with important restrictions on private preparatory and primary schools [article 7, (4)–(6)], only a very small percentage of all children attend these. Since virtually all full-time schooling is on a half-day basis only, parents are expected to play a greater part in the education of their children than in Britain. Their status is recognised by the Grundgesetz, which states explicitly that 'care and upbringing of children are the natural right of the parents and a duty primarily incumbent on them' [article 6 (2)].

Religious instruction is available in all primary and secondary schools but parents and older children have the right to decide whether a child should attend these classes or not. The majority of the primary and virtually all of the secondary schools are now non-denominational but Christian in outlook. However, in some of the Länder most primary and some secondary schools are denominational state schools and in others Protestant, Roman Catholic, and non-denominational state primary schools may exist side by side. Only in a few Länder are teacher training colleges for the training of primary and certain secondary school teachers still organised on a denominational basis. There has been a heated debate for many years about the question of denominational schools and colleges.

Most of the old-established universities and a few of the more recent foundations have faculties of Protestant and/or of Catholic theology, which train future clergymen as well as secondary school teachers. Separate Protestant or Roman Catholic theological colleges, a few of which have had full university status for centuries, still exist in some Länder, especially in Nordrhein—Westfalen and Bayern; they will gradually merge with universities.

Primary, secondary and most tertiary education is free. Public expenditure on education is shared between local authorities, the Länder, and the Federation. West Germany, part of a country whose culture, learning, and educational system once aroused admiration the world over, spent in 1955 a mere 2.4 per cent of her G.N.P. on education and science (including government-sponsored research), less than most other developed countries. Although this percentage began to grow in the early years of the 1960s, West Germany still fares badly in comparison with other nations. In 1965 only 3.7 per cent of the G.N.P. went to this sector, in 1973 4.9 per cent (approx. DM 45 000m, an increase of 70 per cent over 1970). Both federal and Länder governments are committed to further substantial increases in the next decade and the current rate of growth in this sector is among the highest of any head of government expenditure. Through its growing involvement in education the central government's share of the total recurrent and capital expenditure rose from 5.2 per cent to 9.2 per cent between 1963 and 1973. Its contribution was most substantial in higher education and research (excluding university hospitals), where, according to the 1973 budgets, approximately DM 1900m (16 per cent) out of a projected total of DM 11 700m originated in the federal budget, and lowest in primary and secondary education, where it contributed a mere DM 82m. Here, on the other hand, the local authorities provided DM 8700m (33 per cent) of the total of DM 26 400m. Local authorities frequently administer primary and many secondary schools, but nowadays the regional governments finance a substantial proportion of the educational expenditure in the school sector. A common arrangement is that a local authority bears the cost of erecting and maintaining school buildings (although even here frequently aided by government grants), while the regional government pays for the teaching staff. In 1971 DM 2400m were spent on theatres, libraries, museums and cultural activities in general, of which over 50 per cent come from the local authorities.

The *Bundesausbildungsförderunggesetz* (Federal Educational Grants Act) of 1971 (amended in 1974) co-ordinates all student grants throughout the Bundesrepublik. The federal government contributes 65 per cent and the Länder governments between them the remaining 35 per cent of the money required. Grants are awarded on the basis of a fairly stringent means test to cover the fees and living expenses of students in full-time or part-time education beyond compulsory school age and to students who as part of their course are required to undergo a period of practical training. A small percentage of a student grant is given as a loan. There is separate legislation dealing with grants to graduate students. Further grants are available under a separate act to assist individual students during periods of vocational training, retraining or further training, and while attending training courses. The reform of West Germany's grants legislation was long overdue and although grants still lag behind British provision recent improvements are dramatic.

Every one of the eleven Kultusminister is in his Land responsible for primary, secondary and tertiary education as well as for museums and the performing arts, though galleries and theatres are often municipal institutions. Under this regionally centralised system his powers of control are considerably greater than those of the British Secretary of State for Education and Science. The regional government trains, appoints, and promotes teachers (who are all civil servants), and determines curricula, syllabuses and teaching methods. All examinations, including the Abitur are state examinations and are set and marked by schoolteachers under the close supervision of the civil servants in the appropriate ministry of education. Lay Boards of Governors of schools are unknown. The freedom of an individual school, its teachers and headteacher, is limited. An individual headteacher, too, has fewer powers and less discretion than his British counterpart.

Hitherto, the role of parents in the school system was only peripheral and, at most, advisory. Changes are, however, contemplated in several Länder, which would give both pupils and parents greater rights in the running of their schools; some proposals even envisage the election of headmasters of secondary schools by a committee on which teachers as well as pupils and parents would be represented.

Nine years' full-time schooling is compulsory throughout West Germany followed by three years of obligatory part-time (day release) education in connection with vocational training (see figure 3). A child enters school at the age of six and leaves at fifteen. Plans exist to raise the school-leaving age to sixteen and at least one Land has done so. Proposals have also been made to bring forward the age of entering primary school to five. Secondary education begins at about ten years and takes place in three types of institution: the upper primary school (leaving age usually fifteen), the intermediate school (leaving age sixteen) and the grammar school (leaving age nineteen). For those who have left full-time education before the age of eighteen part-time vocational education is compulsory. There is also the possibility of full-time vocational, specialised technical or advanced technical education. Teacher training colleges, universities and other university-type institutions stipulate the Abitur as the entrance requirement. It takes from three to six or seven years to obtain a first degree.

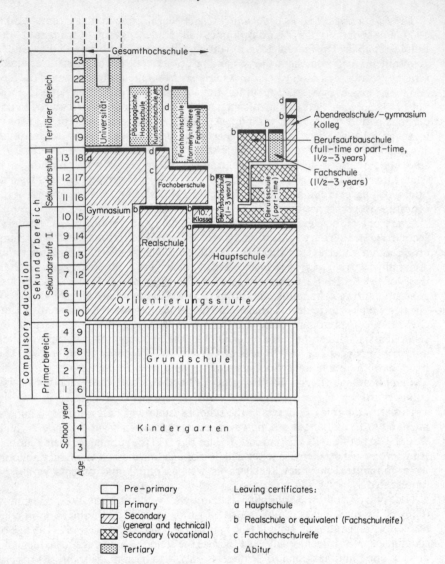

Figure 3   Educational facilities in the Bundesrepublik.

Pre-primary and Primary Education

Most pre-primary education takes place in *Kindergärten* for children between the ages of three and six. However, in 1972 only about 15 per cent of all children in this age group were able to obtain a place, considerably fewer than in some other West European countries, and the provision of new places has only just kept pace with the increase in population. At present the Kindergärten fall outside the official state system and some 80 per cent are maintained by welfare organisations, including the churches, and the rest by local authorities. Plans exist but have hardly been put into practice to develop this sector.

The *Grundschule* (primary school) is a four-year school (six years in the city states of Hamburg, Bremen and West Berlin) common to all children and 35 per cent of all pupils are in this type of school. Because of its universal nature the Grundschule was regarded as the most successful, democratic and egalitarian base of the German school system, which consequently needed little reform. Only in the 1960s was this assumption questioned and the paramount importance of early learning in a child's development taken seriously. Reforms, especially of outmoded syllabuses, are very gradually being introduced. One of the most drastic new departures so far, based on an agreement between the ministers of education in 1968, was the introduction of 'new maths' in all Grundschulen throughout the Bundesrepublik as from the beginning of the school year 1972–3. Other proposals aim at replacing general, usually vaguely local history- and geography-based instruction by more subject-orientated syllabuses, with a greater emphasis on the ability and interest of individual pupils. Foreign-language tuition has been introduced in third and fourth forms in some Länder as an experiment.

Curriculum revision in West Germany is a slow and protracted process. This applies to all types of schools and is not merely a result of the difficulty of coordinating the efforts of eleven different education ministries. Unlike British practice, curricula are determined by the ministries, on the advice of curricula committees composed of small groups of practising schoolteachers. These are frequently unacquainted with modern research in educational psychology and the social sciences. Existing curricula tend to be amended rather than rethought and the existing division into types of schools goes unquestioned. Curriculum research, like educational research in general, is still in its infancy in the Bundesrepublik.

Children attending the Grundschule receive instruction for 16 to 26 periods (of 45 to 50 minutes) a week during their first two years at school, and between twenty-four and thirty periods in their third and fourth years, less than in many other countries. They do not stay at school outside these teaching periods and they do not have meals at school. School hours are (as in secondary schools) distributed over six (sometimes five) days of the week; they tend to be erratic and are by no means the same every day. This is caused by a shortage of both classrooms and teachers. Classes of over forty pupils are not rare; in Bayern in 1971 18 per cent of all Grundschule classes fell in this category.

Special Schools

Provision of *Sonderschulen*, special schools for the mentally or physically handicapped at primary and secondary level, has been rapidly expanded, yet is still far from adequate, especially in rural areas. In 1972 365 000 children of school age attended these schools, far below the 5 to 10 per cent thought to need this type of education. Another 66 000 children went to 2280 *Schulkindergärten*, pre-primary classes for children of school age who are physically or mentally retarded. These are the only nursery classes attached to state schools. It is still common, nevertheless, to defer school attendance in the case of children who are not ready for school at the appropriate age.

Secondary Education

One type of secondary institution, the *Hauptschule* (upper primary school), is attended by well over 50 per cent of all pupils of the ten to fifteen age group. The percentage is particularly high in predominantly rural areas. Progression from the primary stage is automatic and Grundschule and Hauptschule, often bracketed together as *Volksschule*, are usually in the same building and form one administrative unit.

After completion of primary education, parents decide, usually after consultation with the teacher, whether or not to apply to have their child enrolled in either the six-form *Realschule* (intermediate school) or the nine-form *Gymnasium* (grammar school). Both of these may lead to higher education, but generally only the Gymnasium provides a route to college or university. Thus pupils and their parents have to make a choice at the age of ten between three different types of school with different objectives. Pupils are recommended by their primary-school teachers for acceptance at either a Realschule or a Gymnasium. A final decision is deferred until they have completed an observation period, which lasts from six months to two years.

This early selection and specialisation has been criticised in Germany, not least because it tends to perpetuate class divisions within the educational system. In Baden–Württemberg (a Land with a mixture of urban and rural areas) in 1971 14.6 per cent of pupils in their fourth, fifth, and sixth year at school attended the Gymnasium, 11.9 per cent the Realschule and the remaining 73.5 per cent the Hauptschule. But a 1968 sample survey revealed that, broken down according to the father's monthly income, only 9.4 per cent of those earning less than DM 1000 per month went to the Gymnasium (as compared to 14.3 per cent to the Realschule and 76.1 per cent to the Hauptschule), whereas 66.8 per cent of the children of the high DM 2000 plus income group did so. However, this issue appears to have caused less public controversy in Germany than in Britain and few drastic measures of reorganisation have hitherto been implemented. Perhaps the reason for this is the less rigid class system in West German society, coupled with expansion of facilities for secondary education outside the Hauptschule. Statistics show that the percentage of all thirteen-year olds attending a Realschule throughout the Bundesrepublik increased from 11.3 in 1960 to 16.6 in 1967, in the case of Gymnasien from 15 to 18.7, with an appropriate fall in those remaining at the Hauptschule. Yet in 1971 still only 12 per cent of all school leavers had obtained the qualifications for university entrance (less than Germany's Western neighbours), while 21 per cent had completed six years of secondary education and the remaining 67 per cent had simply reached compulsory school-leaving age.

Attempts are being made to introduce during the first two years of secondary education a so-called 'orientation level' which would be common to all pupils and would enable each individual to make a better choice in his type of school according to his inclination and ability. Transfers from one type of school to another are becoming more common. It is possible in some Länder to be transferred from a Hauptschule to a Realschule or a Gymnasium even after the sixth year at school, and to this purpose *Aufbauzüge* (extension or promotion courses) may be provided for transfer pupils. Transfers from Realschule to Gymnasium are especially encouraged in a suitable case. In the other direction, the not uncommon move back from Gymnasium to the other types of secondary school, which may occur in any year, usually means that the pupil has not been able to respond to the demands of the more academically orientated school. Many children leave the Gymnasium, which is designed to be a nine-year school, or the Realschule altogether after completion of the compulsory period of schooling (more than 24 000 in 1972). It is the social prestige attached to the German Gymnasium that leads many parents to send their children to this type of school rather than to the 'inferior' Hauptschule or even Realschule, to which they might be better suited. Although *Gesamtschulen* (comprehensive schools) are favoured by the SPD/FDP coalition in Bonn as the best means of achieving greater flexibility, up to 1972 only about 150 experimental comprehensive schools existed in the entire Bundesrepublik.

The Hauptschule is still seen as providing an essentially practical education. It is the most widespread type of secondary school, attended in 1970 by some 2.4 million pupils aged from ten to fifteen. Taken together with the Grundschule, with which it is combined, there were in 1972 19 600 Volksschulen with 210 000 full-time and 50 000 part-time teachers and 6.5 million pupils. In 1972 there were still, on average, 31.2 pupils per class (Realschule: 32.2, Gymnasium: 29.9). The Hauptschule suffers from its image, which associates it with the education of those children who did not achieve entry to the more demanding types of secondary school. Some Länder endeavour to escape from the narrow aim of training the pupils for life as skilled craftsmen or unskilled workers and seek to provide an education that prepares them better for the problems they will face in modern society. In 1969 the Kultusministerkonferenz passed a recommendation that stressed the need to introduce new subjects and methods. They suggested *Arbeitslehre*, to introduce the pupils to aspects of their future economic and working environment, and recommended the compulsory study of a foreign language, usually English. For the advanced forms they also proposed instruction in mathematics, physics and chemistry in small groups. One important change has been the virtual elimination of the once standard one-class village school, where children between six and fourteen years of age were taught together in one class just as 'family grouping' has become fashionable in England. Now at least the upper levels of these schools are combined in larger centrally situated units, and the total number of primary and upper primary schools has been reduced quite substantially in the past decade.

Given the threefold division of secondary education in the German educational system the Realschule leads a somewhat uncomfortable existence between the other two major types. It, too, has expanded and in 1972 some 133 000 pupils obtained its leaving certificate—either after simply completing the tenth form or after a special examination. The Realschulen are meant to prepare their pupils for 'tasks with high demands on independence, responsibility, and leadership in predominantly practical jobs'. Compared to the Hauptschule the course of study is longer and a greater variety of subjects is studied at greater depth, for example at least one foreign language, biology or chemistry. There are approximately thirty to thirty-five hours of instruction a week.

While Hauptschulen and Realschulen are the principal types of full-time schools within—to use recent German terminology—*Sekundarstufe I* (secondary level I), or between the fifth and tenth year of schooling, the Gymnasium embraces both secondary level I and secondary level II (between the eleventh and thirteenth years of schooling). Gymnasien are secondary schools leading to higher education. Their leaving certificate, based on the Abitur examination, qualifies its holder for university entrance. The education offered is of a more theoretical and academic kind than in the other types of secondary school. German, mathematics, biology, geography, a first foreign language (usually English or Latin), music, art and physical education are compulsory subjects from the beginning, a second foreign language, social studies, physics and chemistry follow after two or three years, and a third foreign language may be added later. Not all subjects are carried through to the final year of the Gymnasium and some may be dropped after the sixth or seventh year. It is here, in the last two or three forms during secondary level II, that an element of choice is introduced and the three kinds of Gymnasium truly come into their own. They are the *Neusprachliches Gymnasium* (modern language type), where the emphasis is on teaching of modern languages (mainly English and French) in addition to Latin, the *Mathematisch–naturwissenschaftliches Gymnasium* (mathematics and science type), where the emphasis is on teaching of mathematics, physics and natural sciences, as well as two foreign languages, and the *Altsprachliches Gymnasium* (classical type), where the emphasis is on the teaching of classical languages with English and/or French. One school may contain two branches but in all three disciplines German and mathematics are compulsory in the last two years, as are usually physical education, art or music and one science subject chosen by the pupil, as well as two other subjects, depending on the kind of school.

Many of the features outlined above were only introduced during the 1960s yet already further experiments with revised syllabuses are undertaken in several Länder, and a drastic restructuring of the curricula of all types of secondary school is subject to discussion and experiment. The Bildungsrat's Plan for the Structure of the Educational System of February 1970 provided the decisive stimulus. The federal government, which is only to a limited extent able to influence educational planning directly, published its own Educational Report 70, whose ideas largely coincide with those expounded in the Bildungsrat's Plan, and the Bund–Länder–Kommission has translated these and other recommendations into a more concrete, politically acceptable and financially viable form in the Bildungsgesamtplan.

Meanwhile the Kultusministerkonferenz agreed in July 1972 on a reorganisation of the secondary level II of the Gymnasien. This seeks to achieve even greater flexibility. It abandons the traditional concept of dividing pupils into forms according to their school year and replaces it by courses that allow greater differentiation according to ability and inclination. This system would do away with the traditional German practice that a pupil who has not attained the required grades for the whole year's work has to repeat that year. This happens so often that the average school-leaving age for students going on to higher education is twenty, not nineteen as it should be. The education ministers' resolution allows much greater freedom of choice and encourages greater specialisation. If implemented the scheme would constitute a drastic break with the tradition of the German grammar school and the German secondary level II would come to resemble the English sixth form. Furthermore, it is also proposed to introduce a system of assessment by points in the last two years at school and these points would count for more than half of the final Abitur marks.

A total of 122,500 pupils obtained their Abitur qualification in 1972. This gives access to all branches of higher education or, in certain cases, only to certain sectors of higher education, for instance to faculties of economics or teacher training colleges.

An *Abendgymnasium* is a part-time school, designed for young people or adults (minimum entrance age nineteen), who left school at the end of compulsory schooling and completed a vocational training course or were at least three years in employment. These evening courses last for at least three years, and students must continue their employment during their studies except for the last eighteen months when they may receive a grant. In 1972 12 400 students were registered at forty-eight such institutions. A *Kolleg* provides mature students with a similar route to the full Abitur qualification but by means of full-time, often residential, study.

Vocational Education

Part-time schooling is compulsory in West Germany for anyone below eighteen years of age not in full-time education. Thus any young person who has left a school offering a full-time general education and who does not attend a full-time vocational school or college is required whatever his job, to attend a *Berufsschule* on a day-release basis (see figure 3). This dual system, which has a long tradition in Germany, is in the process of being modernised. After having been neglected for many years the whole field of vocational education and training, which affects almost 80 per cent of the appropriate age group, is receiving special attention from the Bildungsrat, the federal government and Parliament, and from the Bund–Länder–Kommission für Bildungsplanung, which singled it out as a priority area for reform. The federal government is particularly anxious to increase the number of training places and to improve the quality of training.

Well over 50 per cent of all school leavers without the necessary qualifications to proceed to higher education become apprentices or trainees. By international standards this is a very high proportion. These young men and women follow one of several hundred recognised vocational training courses covering, for example, clerical jobs (the largest group), farming and bakery, as well as retail selling and eleven different occupations in the textile industry. Since 1969 Bonn has the legislative competence in the field of vocational training, and the 1969 Vocational Training Act stipulates, among other things, that the syllabus and examinations of such courses must be approved by the government.

In 1972 there were 1.3 million apprentices and trainees (60 per cent men) in the fifteen to twenty age group—63 per cent of all employees in that age group. In absolute figures and as a percentage of the total population this figure is declining, a sign that a larger number of young people are staying on longer at school. Practical training takes place on the job and lasts from one to three-and-a-half years, depending on the trade. Instructors are mostly part-time and often have little training themselves. Since many small firms can no longer meet the demands of modern apprentice training and frequently use apprentices as cheap labour the need to establish outside central workshops and supplementary training has been recognised. Implementation of training regulations, supervision and examinations are the responsibility of the chambers of industry and trade, crafts and agriculture, who between them are responsible for over 90 per cent of apprentices and trainees. In spite of the shortcomings of the system the rate of failure at the final examinations compares favourably with the percentage of failures in school and university examinations.

The 1969 Act provides for the setting up of vocational education committees at federal and Land level, composed of representatives of employers, employees and government-nominated vocational education experts. Furthermore, a Federal Institute for Vocational Educational Research has been established as a public corporation.

Berufsschulen are the other half of Germany's dual system of vocational education, and are under the authority of the Länder. As part-time schools they were attended by some 1.6 million young people in 1972 on a day-release basis. This theoretical part of vocational instruction clearly plays only a secondary role to on-the-job practical training. Only eight hours of instruction a week are prescribed and, because of a shortage of teachers, buildings and equipment, students often receive less. Instruction is both in general subjects, like German, social and economic studies, and religion (together 40 per cent of the time available) and in specialised subjects related to the trade the pupil is learning. It is intended to enable pupils learning the same or a related trade to be taught together in specialised classes on, for instance, technical drawing. However, this is not possible at every school, particularly in rural areas, and specialised classes are held in certain centres, which are attended by apprentices from the entire district. Furthermore, there are Berufsschulen catering exclusively for apprentices in one particular trade, say mining, agriculture, commerce or home economics.

German authorities are alive to the need for an all-round improvement in vocational education. This sector is to be put on the same level as general secondary education and curricula are to be reviewed with the aim of putting more stress on the systematic teaching of fundamental theory and on the broad understanding of individual occupations. The main obstacle to effective reform is the difficulty of co-ordinating the overlapping powers of the federal government, the chambers of industry and trade, agriculture, etc. and the Länder governments. Federation and Länder agree, however, on the desirability of gradually introducing a one-year, full-time general vocational education course that would count towards the qualification for any trade.

Apart from the dual system, vocational training can also be acquired in *Berufsfachschulen* (full-time vocational schools), which vary considerably from one Land to the other in conditions of entry, courses, duration of studies (one to three years) and certificates awarded. Their pupils receive a general education up to the standard of the Realschule leaving certificate and are exempt from attending classes at Berufsschulen. The certificate awarded also partially or wholly exempts the pupil from industrial vocational training. Indeed, the Berufsfachschule may prepare for occupations for which there are no recognised training regulations and courses. Altogether in 1972 there were 239 000 pupils at these schools, which ranged from the commercial (the most important) and industrial/technical to the home economics, nursing, fine arts and language variety.

There are two further types of vocational school in the secondary sector, where attendance is voluntary. The *Berufsaufbauschule* (voluntary extension school) accepts pupils who have completed the Berufsschule, or have had at least six months' successful attendance there. This type of vocational school, which must be attended for one-and-a-half years full-time or three years part-time, provides through its leaving certificate, called *Fachschulreife*, a route to specialised, more advanced technical education in the tertiary sector, as does the *Fachoberschule*, which admits pupils with the leaving certificates of the Realschule or its equivalent. In 1970 they had between them 143 000 pupils. Eventually they are likely to be integrated in a reformed secondary level II.

Vocational education in the tertiary sector

Once again the variety of institutions offering distinct courses leading to separate certificates is bewildering (see figure 3). *Fachschulen*, specialised colleges for, for example, agricultural occupations, professions in industry, careers in commerce, transport, catering, administration or social welfare, or professions in the arts, stipulate, as a rule, completed vocational training and/or professional experience as entrance requirements. These Fachschulen are a well-developed branch of tertiary education, not usually leading to higher education but providing better qualifications in the various occupational sectors. In many ways, they take the place of the British professional institutions, which are unknown in Germany.

Höhere Fachschulen, another type of technical college, are distinguished from the Fachschulen by a longer period of study (three to four years as a rule), slightly higher entrance requirements (Realschule leaving certificate and practical training, or equivalent), and a leaving certificate that gives admission to certain branches of non-university higher education. In fact, most Höhere Fachschulen are being converted into *Fachhochschulen* (advanced technical colleges), thus becoming more advanced professional colleges.

Advanced Technical Education

Institutions of advanced education in the tertiary sector fall into three broad groups: advanced professional colleges together with institutions of higher education for the fine arts, music and sport, colleges of education and universities and institutions of university rank (see figure 3). However, with the foundation and development of *Gesamthochschulen* (comprehensive universities) growing apace the dividing lines between these groups are becoming more and more blurred.

The Fachhochschulen are the most recent recruits to higher education and the Länder governments favour the expansion of these institutions as an alternative to the traditional university. Their upgrading from the secondary sector followed an agreement between the Länder in 1968 and received a decisive stimulus from attempts to harmonise engineering education throughout the European Economic Community. Entrance requirements were stiffened and the nature of these colleges is changing too: the academic content of their courses has been considerably increased, research is being encouraged, and they have been allowed a limited measure of internal self-government. They are rapidly developing into something like the former English colleges of advanced technology.

Students who have successfully completed the three-year (six-semester) course will obtain an academic qualification awarded by the state and may call themselves *graduiert*. This diploma is distinct from, and academically inferior to, the *Diplom* (first degree) awarded by a German university or technical university. Holders of the diploma will, however, be granted exemption for a year or more should they wish to proceed to study for a university degree. Fachhochschulen exist in various fields, the most common being engineering and commerce. In 1972–3 112 000 students were registered at 147 colleges of this type.

Kunst-, Musik- and Sporthochschulen (colleges for fine arts, drama, music and physical education) are also moving closer to universities, although in fine arts and music candidates without Abitur but with proven artistic and musical ability are accepted. In spite of high unemployment among former art students the number of students at these colleges is increasing (14 100 in 1972–3), if not quite as rapidly as in the other institutions of higher education.

Colleges of Education and Teacher Training

Pädagogische Hochschulen (colleges of education) are probably more immediately affected by the reorganisation of German higher education than the other institutions in this sector. Only a few years ago almost all these used to be divorced from the universities. Now their heads are members of the German Vice Chancellors' Conference and links with universities are common, sometimes on the basis of informal collaboration, frequently in much closer association. Students might complete their academic training as a Realschule teacher in a Pädagogische Hochschule and subsequently transfer to a university in the same Land to study further to qualify as a teacher in a Gymnasium (as in Baden–Württemberg), or the entire college might be integrated as a faculty of a university (as in Bayern) so that all types of schoolteachers may be said to be university-trained.

In general, however, the training of teachers for Grundschulen and Hauptschulen is separate from that of teachers for Realschulen and Gymnasien. While the training of the latter is usually reserved for the universities, with the occasional exception of teachers in Realschulen, the Pädagogischen Hochschulen specialise in the training of the former. Students must study for six semesters (three years), and their courses include theory of education, psychology and sociology, as well as the subjects taught in the Volksschule. Depending on the regulations of the Land one subject may be chosen for intensive study and specialisation is possible according to whether a person wishes to teach in the Grundschule or the Hauptschule.

In the winter of 1972–3 the independent Pädagogischen Hochschulen had 72 000 students, well over half of them female. Most of these were planning to become teachers in Volksschulen, a small number to teach in Realschulen. In addition, some Pädagogische Hochschulen have special institutes attached, which, after completion of the basic course and some practical training at a school for handicapped children, prepare students in a further four semesters as teachers in Sonderschulen. Such teachers are also trained at at least two old-established universities. Indeed, in 1971–2 altogether some 89 000 university students were studying for qualifications to teach in Volksschulen, Realschulen and Sonderschulen.

After the first *Staatsexamen* (state examination) a second phase of practical training as probationary teacher follows, which is supplemented by theoretical instruction, and lasts for at least two and at most four years. In some Länder students attend theoretical courses at *Studienseminare*, special institutes which are not part of the universities or colleges and are directly controlled by the minister of education. These courses last one or two years and are supplemented by teaching practice. In either case, the second phase of teacher training is terminated by the second Staatsexamen.

Most teachers in Realschulen and all teachers in Gymnasien and vocational schools are educated at universities. Here they normally study two subjects taught at their type of school, together with theory of education for at least six to eight semesters (three to four years). Their studies may include a practical introduction to teaching. They end with the first Staatsexamen, which is followed by a period of preparatory service at the special Studienseminare as described above. Teacher training is completed by the second Staatsexamen after another eighteen months or two years. Teachers in vocational education of all branches, who teach the theory of vocational subjects, also undergo practical training, before and during the course, in private or public enterprises.

Teachers of all categories are appointed Beamte, initially on probation, and later for life. Promotion is to a certain extent automatic but is otherwise based on merit. Appointments and promotions are for the Kultusminister to decide. In 1972 the governments of the Länder employed altogether almost 411 000 full-time teachers and lecturers (excluding university staff). The largest group (210 000) taught at Grund- and Hauptschulen, the next largest (76 000) at Gymnasien. In 1971, there were 21.5 pupils per teacher in Volksschulen, 17.5 in Realschulen and 13.6 in Gymnasien. In spite of a substantial expansion of teacher training the supply of teachers has not kept pace with the overall increase in the number of pupils, which is the result of the general increase in the age group, the extension of the school-leaving age and also the general trend towards more and better education, especially in the secondary sector. However, manpower forecasts suggest that some time after 1978 teacher supply and demand will be in balance, chiefly because of the dramatic drop in the birth rate. 40 per cent fewer pupils will attend primary schools in 1982 than in 1974.

One of the characteristic features of the German system of teacher training is that it is divided vertically according to the various types of schools. Apart from the inherent inequalities of this system (teachers at Volksschulen are treated as inferior to teachers at Realschulen and Gymnasien, even if they teach the same age group or the same special subject, and their promotion prospects are limited) a transfer from one type of state school to another is rare, even if the same special subject would be taught to the same age group. A post at a Gymnasium would normally be filled by a teacher who is trained for that type of school in preference to the one trained in the subject.

A thorough reform of teacher training was recommended in the 1970 Plan for the Structure of the Educational System of the Bildungsrat, and a host of other models for the reform of the structure and content of teacher training have been developed. Course requirements should be modified to allow for more academic training in fewer subjects for teachers in Grundschulen and Hauptschulen, and in the theory of education and its practical application for teachers in Gymnasien. New methods of instruction are required, also possibly a combination of practical professional training with more academic instruction into one integrated 'one-phase' programme. Above all, however, it is proposed to introduce the grade-teacher concept: teacher training courses should in future be differentiated horizontally according to educational level (primary, secondary I and II) and subjects to be taught, not according to type of school, so that all teachers would have equality of status. It is the declared aim of this structural reform to upgrade teachers in the primary and less academically orientated secondary schools by putting them on an equal level with their hitherto privileged Gymnasium counterparts. In the tightly controlled West German state system any such change can be initiated and implemented only by the Länder governments. In general the SPD-led governments favour more far-reaching reforms than the CDU-led Länder. For this reason the Kultusministerkonferenz failed to reach an agreement in 1970. In 1972 the socialist-led Länder took a surprise decision to begin a reorganisation on their own—yet another split seemed to be threatening in the West German educational system.

Universities

In the winter of 1972–3 West Germany's forty-eight universities and institutions of university rank had 417 000 undergraduate and postgraduate students, including 27 000 foreigners; 27 per cent were female, and there were 83 000 students in their first semester. Over 50 per cent were arts based, but there is no shortage of science and technology students. The increase in student numbers during the past twenty years has been spectacular—student numbers more than trebled between 1950–1 and 1970–1 and are still rising. Almost 90 per cent of all Gymnasium leavers want to go to university and are only prevented from doing so by the increasingly common imposition of a *numerus clausus,* a restriction on admission, which is totally alien to the German tradition and violates the constitutionally guaranteed right of all Germans 'to choose their trade or profession, their place of work and their place of training' [article 12]. However, in the summer of 1972 the Bundesverfassungsgericht ruled that under the circumstances—available laboratory places for chemists, dental and medical students for example, were oversubscribed two or three times—a *numerus clausus* was permissible as a temporary measure. In the summer of 1974 only 21 700 places were available for 65 000 applicants for the fifteen subjects with restricted access. In spite of a planned additional provision of 38 500 new student places annually between 1975 and 1978 at all institutions of higher education, the *numerus clausus* will have to be extended to other subjects and the number of unsuccessful candidates will grow.

Although there appear to be many more university students in Germany than in Britain (autumn 1972: 241 000) comparisons are misleading not only because of the different structure of the tertiary sector but also because German students take much longer to complete their studies (four to six years) and because the failure rate is considerably higher than in Britain. While German universities are subject to considerable state control in awarding undergraduate degrees they have the right to award their own doctorates (4200 in the summer of 1972) and a further research qualification, the *Habilitation,* which used to be essential for university teachers and is still important for promotion.

Several of West Germany's universities are medieval foundations, but none is as old as Oxford and Cambridge. The university of Heidelberg (founded in 1386) is the oldest and there is a continuous history of university foundations throughout the centuries. After the Second World War, the Freie Universität in West Berlin and the University of Saarbrücken began their existence followed by the first 'new' universities of Konstanz, Bochum and Regensburg. More recently there has been a whole series of new foundations, which are usually started on a small scale with one or two faculties. It is planned to enlarge some existing Pädagogische Hochschulen into universities.

The *Technische Hochschulen* (technical universities) are a group apart. They originated in the nineteenth century as colleges for applied science and technological subjects and were granted full university status, with the right to award doctorates, towards the end of the century. In the late 1950s and 1960s many of these were expanded into full Technische Universitäten by adding faculties of arts, social science and sometimes medicine.

Universities were always founded by the state, never through local civic initiative or by private individuals. They remain state institutions and are totally dependent on the state for finance (the university budget is part of the annual budget of the Land), their administration (all staff are government employees), their academic appointments (all permanent teaching staff are Beamte and only the minister of education, on the recommendation of the university senate, can make an appointment to a chair), even their academic work (inevitably syllabuses are influenced by the fact that most examinations are state-controlled). While university independence was always rather restricted in comparison with the autonomy enjoyed by British universities, recent university legislation has extended state control even further. The so-called *Akademische Freiheit* (academic freedom), a university lecturer's freedom to choose his lecturing and research topics, and a student's freedom to choose which lectures to attend, has been considerably eroded, by, for example, the imposition of revised staff structures and the introduction of a maximum period study.

Formerly all German universities had a common organisational pattern. The comparatively few full professors enjoyed an exceptionally powerful position as heads of their departments, and each faculty was virtually independent. The *Rektor* (head of a university), elected for a short term of office from among the professoriate, was usually unable to speak or act on behalf of his own university. Since 1968 new university laws have come into force in all Länder and almost every university has had new charters and statutes approved by the Länder governments. In the absence of a federal university law establishing a uniform administrative framework for all institutions of higher education, the new detailed legislative provisions vary substantially from one Land to the next, thus destroying the once uniform internal structure of the German university, which dates back to the early nineteenth century. They frequently lead to a reduction in the autonomy of the individual institution and a corresponding increase in the influence of the government. They have in common the creation of new elaborate and democratic decision-making bodies at all levels, where professors are joined by non-professorial staff, students, and even technical and service staff. The old faculties have been replaced by smaller schools of study, the autocratic powers of a professor and head of department have been considerably reduced, and the accent is now on participation teamwork and collaboration. However, confrontation between groups within the universities occurs all too frequently, especially when professors, nonprofessorial staff, and students each have one-third of the votes in committees. The new system is not working well. Everyone has wasted time, effort and resources to force through superficial and merely technical improvements rather than concentrating on revising syllabuses, co-ordinating and planning research activities and thinking about the place and function of institutions of higher education in modern West German society.

Comprehensive universities and university reform

One of the more promising developments in West German higher education is the widespread acceptance of the idea of *Gesamthochschulen* (comprehensive universities) although again the discussion seems too often to be bogged down on questions of organisation. The basic idea is to unite virtually all institutions of higher education in one area—Universitäten, Pädagogische Hochschulen, Fachhochschulen—into one large superuniversity either on a co-operative or closely integrated basis. These comprehensive institutions would combine the tasks of research, teaching and learning, which hitherto have been the responsibility of different types of institutions. They would offer courses and award qualifications at different but co-ordinated levels and the student would be able to transfer from one course to another within one and the same institution and would not need to make an early irrevocable selection of his course. The gap between the more vocational courses at the colleges and the more theoretical curricula at the old universities would be narrowed, and the inequality and class structure of German higher education could be more easily overcome.

In any case the old-established German universities, not so long ago one of the most élitist and middle-class dominated structures in the entire Bundesrepublik, are on the way to becoming mass institutions, preoccupied with turning out as many teachers, engineers and doctors as can be processed in the shortest possible time. Students, who used to enjoy a great deal of freedom, who could choose their own courses, who were able to change university as they liked, and who often wasted a whole semester in finding their way around the university and their own department are now generally advised by staff on aspects of their studies and more often than not follow a suggested (though rarely compulsory) course programme. Also, the influx of tens of thousands of students who previously would not have thought of going to university and are now supported by grants (47 per cent of all full-time students in higher education received a grant, although only one in three students does not get any support from home at all) has led to a readjustment of the formerly excessively high and rigorous standards. On the other hand, lack of motivation and lack of interest in the subject of study is also notable among students.

Students, who earlier had justifiably demanded greater investment to overcome the intolerable overcrowding, played an important part in bringing about university reform in West Germany. From 1965 they insisted on a far-reaching reorganisation of the universities in order to make them more democratic, and since 1967 violent disorder has again and again erupted in almost every university and has brought many faculties and whole universities to a temporary standstill.

Student unions exist but they organise relatively few social functions. Students in many universities elect an *A.St.A.* (*Allgemeiner Studentenausschuss*, General Student Council) which is invariably dominated by very vocal and active political, usually left-wing groups. The political involvement of the vast majority of German students is negligible, notwithstanding an apparent abundance of political activity. Since 1968 the *Verband Deutscher Studentenschaften* (German National Union of Students), the central organisation to which most student unions are affiliated, has been dominated by left-wing radical students and for a time concerned itself solely with the organisation of militant action against the university establishment and capitalist society. Apart from compulsory contributions from its student members the Union used to receive a handsome subsidy from the federal government. This has now stopped.

A reform of the university staff structure is under way almost everywhere. Most universities are now headed by a *Universitätspräsident* (Vice Chancellor) who is more powerful than the former Rektor. In order to improve the dismal staff–student ratio in German universities, where teaching still takes place mainly through lectures attended by hundreds of students and tuition in small groups is rare, an entirely new career grade, collectively known as *Mittelbau* (middle level), equivalent to the British lecturer grade, has been introduced. Staff in this category, who have a variety of titles and now far exceed the professoriate in numbers, have a fairly independent position in the university and department. On the other hand, the *Assistenten* (junior lecturers) who used to be dependent on their professor for their employment and future career, still have to rely on the continued support of a professor for advancement. But here, too, things are changing and in a few of the Länder some Assistenten have been converted into *Assistenzprofessoren*, comparable to the American assistant professors, with limited tenure, usually for six years.

Research

Expenditure on research and development in the Bundesrepublik increased from DM 9600m in 1967 to approximately DM 20 000m in 1972. This increase of over 100 per cent is only slightly lower than the rise in the total higher-education sector and represents a growth in the share of the G.N.P. from 1.9 to 2.4 per cent. This trend runs parallel to that in other European countries. Approximately DM 9800m or 49 per cent were spent by industry in 1971. Compared with the research and development expenditure in 1969 the share of the Federation, Länder and Gemeinden has increased fairly rapidly from 47 per cent (Britain 51 per cent) to 51 per cent (or 4 per cent of total public expenditure in 1972). This merely confirms the growing support given by the state to research and development inside and outside the universities. Thus the federal government, apart from supporting research in general, has initiated a number of priority research programmes, in, for example, atomic energy and space research.

Although the universities spent 18 per cent of total research funds in 1969, most research was undertaken outside the universities, chiefly in industry (59 per cent of expenditure in 1969). The most research-intensive branches of industry are the chemical, precision mechanics and optics, steel construction, electrical engineering, mechanical engineering and car industries. Between them they spent almost 90 per cent of funds. Certain small and medium-size firms in the same field (for instance, sheet metal and printing) co-operated after the war to form research associations. Later, individual industrial research associations, the majority with their own research institutes, combined to form the *Arbeitsgemeinschaft Industrieller Forschungsvereinigungen* (Confederation of Industrial Research Associations), which now has over seventy members. It finances specific applied research projects in the field of natural science and technology. The *Fraunhofer–Gesellschaft zur Förderung der Angewandten Forschung* (Fraunhofer Society for the Support of Applied Research) and the *Batelle Institut* both specialise in research under contract from public authorities or companies. The former was founded in 1949 by representatives of industry, science and the governments, and is financed chiefly by the Federation and the Länder. It also obtains income from research contracts placed with one of its seventeen research institutes and maintains two documentation centres, having close contacts with other public and private research organisations. The latter is a totally private international institution, one of four research centres of that name.

Both the Federal and the Länder governments maintain research establishments. There are more than thirty federal research institutes, some closely associated with the appropriate ministry. *Grossforschungseinrichtungen* (large science research establishments), which were set up jointly or severally by the Federation and the Länder and receive their main income from government grants, are legally independent, frequently in the form of a limited company. They deal with research projects that require costly facilities and staff beyond the resources of universities or industry. Some eighty research stations are each financed by the Land where they are located and another thirty-three establishments, including the *Institut für Zeitgeschichte* (Institute of Contemporary History) and the *Deutsches Museum* (German Museum for Science and Technology) as well as the *Institut für Meeresforschung* (Oceanographic Institute) are maintained jointly by the Länder.

The *Max–Planck–Gesellschaft zur Föderung der Wissenschaften* (Max Planck Society for the Advancement of Arts and Sciences) has over fifty research institutes, which carry out research in science and humanities and is the largest and most eminent research organisation of the Bundesrepublik. It employs over 4000 people and in 1973 had a budget of approximately DM 580m, 90 per cent of which came from the Federation and the Länder, each contributing a half.

West Germany's five Academies of Science in Göttingen (the oldest, founded in 1751), München, Heidelberg, Mainz and Düsseldorf have no research laboratories or institutes but carry out long-term research projects, like the editing of important manuscripts or the compilation of dictionaries. They are supported by the Länder governments.

The *Deutsche Forschungsgemeinschaft* (German Research Association), again financed on an equal basis by Bund and Länder, is the central organisation for the support of the arts and sciences in the Bundesrepublik. It is an autonomous organisation with only institutional membership, that is by universities, academies of science and the Max–Planck–Gesellschaft. It finances research projects, encourages co-operation between research workers and supports the research of young scholars. The Association's grants in 1973 amounted to DM 512m.

Furthermore, a dozen or so *stiftungen* (foundations) grant research fellowships—like the Alexander–von–Humboldt–Stiftung to foreign scholars—or make grants to universities or research institutes within the Bundesrepublik or abroad, like the Volkswagenstiftung.

Further Education

Further education in Germany is commonly divided into further vocational training or retraining, and adult education of a general nature, covering everything from further political education to courses in languages or science subjects and preparation for leisure activities. Generally speaking, further education does not yet occupy an important place in the German educational system. It is characterised by a lack of co-ordination and is organised by a large number of private and social organisations as well as by the federal and Länder governments and the Gemeinden but never by universities. Teachers in further education have no special training or qualifications.

Only a few Länder have so far passed legislation concerned with one or more aspects of further education. This may deal specifically with *Volkshochschulen* (adult education centres) or regulate the conditions under which private institutions of adult education in general can be supported financially by the Land government. At present Länder activity is concentrated on in-service training for teachers on a fairly modest scale and on sponsoring radio and television courses, like the Bavarian *Telekolleg* or courses in data-processing.

Local authorities either run Volkshochschulen themselves (632 of the total of 1127 in 1973) or afford considerable financial support to the independent associations and foundations organising them. A German Volkshochschule provides, with often only part-time administrative staff, a loose institutional framework for a comprehensive range of educational facilities. It offers lectures, courses, organised tours and visits in both general and vocationally orientated education.

Since 1969 the federal government has extensive organisational and financial responsibilities for vocational training and further training. The Bundeswehr also gives its long-serving soldiers the opportunity of general adult education at its own schools, leading, for example, to the leaving certificate of the Realschule, the Fachhochschulreife and even the Abitur. Two new universities run by the armed forces for its personnel opened in the autumn of 1973.

Private sponsors of further education include the churches, political parties, trade unions, individual companies, employers associations and chambers of commerce. Commercial firms offer an increasing number of correspondence courses which so far do not need to be approved by the Länder governments. However, they have established a centre that tests and grades the courses on the market, in order to protect the general public from abuse.

The Mass Media

The Press

In the absence of specific federal legislation article 5 of the Grundgesetz and the Press Acts of the Länder provide the legal basis for the German Press. The Grundgesetz states that 'everyone has the right freely to express and to publish his opinion by speech, writing, and pictures and freely to inform himself from generally accessible sources'. It expressly guarantees the freedom of the Press, and states further that 'there shall be no censorship'. The individual Press Acts of the Länder, whilst differing in detail, generally acknowledge the 'public function' of the Press, giving it special protection under the penal code and encouraging a critical attitude. The administration is required to provide the media with information about matters of special public concern, and German papers are uninhibited when reporting on judicial proceedings. Obviously the freedom of the Press is limited by the provisions of the general law, especially the penal and civil codes, the legal provisions for the protection of youth (certain publications, but not newspapers and political periodicals, may be declared to constitute a danger to young people and can be put on an 'index' and eventually be banned from public sale for a limited period), and the laws of defamation. Creating 'the danger of a serious disadvantage to the external security of the Bundesrepublik by passing on, and publishing state secrets' is an offence. The Bundesverfassungsgericht may ban a publication that abuses the freedom of expression of opinion 'in order to attack the free democratic basic order' [article 18]. The Press's own rather weak *Deutscher Presserat* (German Press Council) has ten publishers' representatives and ten journalists. Its chief aims are to protect the freedom of the Press and to criticise defects and abuses in the Press sector, to resist the creation of monopolies and to represent the Press *vis-à-vis* the government, parliament and the public.

The concentration of ownership is progressing at an alarming rate. Instead of the 610 independent daily papers at the end of 1965 there were only 404 in the fourth quarter of 1973. Many of these daily papers (evening papers are comparatively rare in West Germany) are merely local editions of a regional newspaper with identical non-local material, or they are papers in independent ownership but with central editorial offices for all but local news and comment. Such an association may consist of over fifty *Heimatzeitungen* (local papers). In 1974 there remained only about 120 independent editorial organisations.

The Axel Springer publishing firm, the largest in Europe, is an outstanding example of such concentration, which is by no means restricted to the daily papers and equally affects periodicals. Springer publishes, among others, West Germany's largest popular national daily paper, the vigorously expanding Bild-Zeitung (average circulation of almost 4m in the last quarter of 1974), its Sunday counterpart, Bild am Sonntag (2.3m) the second largest Sunday paper, Welt am Sonntag (322 000), one of the three quality national dailies (Die Welt, 215 000), two daily papers in Berlin, the largest evening paper (Hamburger Abendblatt, 290 000) and the largest radio and television programme weekly (Hör Zu, 3.7m). In the second quarter of 1971 Springer's publications accounted for 32 per cent of the circulation of all dailies, including Sunday papers; in Berlin this percentage amounted to 91 per cent. A similar concentration has taken place in the illustrated and women's weekly or monthly magazines and periodical field, where all major publications now originate from only three publishing groups.

Financial considerations above all force this concentration on the publishing industry of the Bundesrepublik. Costs of production, newsprint and postage are soaring and in spite of a steady increase in circulation and a well-developed subscriber system sales cover only 30 per cent of the production costs of the daily papers and advertising revenue the remaining 70 per cent. But here the competition of television, which broadcasts twenty minutes of commercials every weekday, makes itself felt; before its introduction dailies accounted for almost 60 per cent of all supraregional advertising expenditure, but now their share has dropped to a mere 35 per cent.

In the Bundesrepublik virtually all morning papers are financially independent of a political party and not obliged to follow any particular party line. All parties themselves issue a variety of information services for the press and their own party members. Both CDU and SPD own publishing groups which publish a number of daily and weekly papers with over one million copies each. However, they follow a fairly independent, if generally Christian or Social Democratic line, respectively. Two official party organs are owned by political parties: the weekly Unsere Zeit by the DKP, and the weekly Bayernkurier (118 000) by the CSU. This does not, of course, mean that other independent papers are not politically orientated. There is the nationalist right-wing weekly. Deutsche National-Zeitung, the Catholic conservative weekly, Rheinischer Merkur (circulation of both well below 100 000), the conservative Die Welt, the liberal–conservative Frankfurter Allgemeine Zeitung and West Germany's most prominent weekly Die Zeit (342 000), which is also liberal in its politics.

Although in the last quarter of 1973 there were 458 daily and weekly newspapers, Germans are less avid newspaper readers than the British, to judge by the average number of copies sold: 21.5 million in the last quarter of 1973, equivalent to 34 per cent of the population. (In Britain the national dailies and weeklies alone had a circulation of 37m in the first half of 1974.) On the other hand, 80 per cent of the German population claim to read a newspaper.

The Süddeutsche Zeitung (289 000) of München, the Frankfurter Allgemeine Zeitung (276 000) and Die Welt of Hamburg are the only daily papers with a nationwide circulation. By international standards, they are first-class papers with very full coverage of home and foreign news and especially good *Feuilletons* (arts pages), but they retain a notable regional flavour, especially the Süddeutsche Zeitung. The only really national paper, the poor quality but immensely popular Bild Zeitung, has nine different regional editions. Regional quality newspapers are particularly strong in the Bundesrepublik and their circulation is high, usually exceeding 150 000.

While Sunday papers are rare there are some seventeen quality weekly journals. The best known, apart from Die Zeit, is the nonconformist leftist liberal Der Spiegel (approx. 881 000), an outspoken and informative journal in the style of the American Time Magazine. Only four big general illustrated periodicals (each with a circulation around 1.5 million) are left (Bunte Illustrierte, Stern, Neue Revue and Quick) but there are five illustrated radio and television programme periodicals and numerous other periodicals with high circulation, appealing to a more restricted readership.

The most important source of information for all German papers and periodical publications is the Deutsche Presseagentur (dpa, German Press Agency), jointly owned by publishers and the broadcasting corporations. Foreign news agencies, like Associated Press, also serve the German press and broadcasting organisations, and many national and regional papers have their own foreign correspondents.

Broadcasting

The freedom of broadcasting is guaranteed by article 5 (1) of the Grundgesetz, which deals with the right to free expression in general and refers explicitly to the freedom of reporting by broadcasting and films. Broadcasting by television and radio is regulated by separate Acts of the Länder, by treaties between several of these Länder, and by a 1960 Federal Act. The latter established the only two federal stations, the Deutsche Welle and the Deutschlandfunk, which chiefly provide broadcasts to foreign countries. All other radio and television corporations are organised on a regional basis, or are based on agreements between these regional stations or between the regional governments.

On the regional level, there are nine separate broadcasting corporations: the Norddeutscher Rundfunk (NDR, Hamburg), Radio Bremen (RB), the Westdeutscher Rundfunk (WDR, Köln), Saarländische Rundfunk (SR, Saarbrücken), Hessischer Rundfunk (HR, Frankfurt), Südwestfunk (SWF, Baden-Baden), Süddeutscher Rundfunk (SDR, Stuttgart), Bayerischer Rundfunk (BR, München) and the Sender Freies Berlin (SFB). These are the backbone of West Germany's radio and television network and were originally set up by the occupation powers in their respective zones. Undoubtedly they reflect and strengthen the cultural variety of different regions but reorganisation is long overdue. Companies vary enormously in size as measured by the number of receiving licences; while in January 1974 there were 4.77 million television and 5.10 million radio licences in the area covered by the WDR, the largest company, Radio Bremen had only 237 000 licensed viewers and 259 000 listeners. In the whole of the Bundesrepublik, including West Berlin, there were 19.3 million radio and 17.4 million television licences in January 1974. There were slightly more TV receivers in Germany than in Britain, although less per thousand of population (1971: West Germany 272, Britain 293). More than 20 per cent of all television sets were able to receive colour transmission.

The services of these nine stations are financed from licence fees, amounting in 1973 to a total of DM 1243m from television and DM 582m from radio licences, and from advertising revenue (DM 130m). The Bundespost, which is in part responsible for transmitters and other technical equipment and collects the monthly licence fee, charges the radio and TV companies for its services (DM 427m in 1973). In addition, 30 per cent of the TV licence fees (DM 373m) go to the second television channel, which is operated by a separate national company, so that the regional stations in 1973 had a net income of DM 1155m, which they regarded as too low. They were granted an increase in the licence fees from January 1974. In addition the small and poorer corporations in Berlin, Bremen and Saarbrücken receive financial assistance each year from the richer ones under a financial equalisation scheme.

Each regional company operates a first and second radio programme (except that the NDR and WDR have a combined first channel) and many an additional third channel. First programmes are usually transmitted on medium, short and VHF wavelengths, second and third programmes on VHF only. There are altogether twenty different radio programmes in the Bundesrepublik. Since stations and transmitters of different corporations are located relatively close to each other a listener in any part of West Germany may choose between some half-dozen different radio programmes, even on VHF. As in Britain, the character of radio broadcasting is changing and new techniques are being tried. An example is the institution of a special continuous 'service' programme of music and information for the motorist. On the other hand, radio, apart from popular music programmes, appears not yet to have regained a position comparable to that in Britain, and local broadcasting stations do not exist.

To facilitate collaboration between the corporations the *Arbeitsgemeinschaft der öffentlich–rechtlichen Rundfunkanstalten Deutschlands* (ARD, Association of the Public Broadcasting Corporations of Germany) was founded in 1950. Its real importance dates from 1953, when it was charged with the organisation of West Germany's first television programme *Deutsches Fernsehen* (German Television). It plans the programme and coordinates the contributions of the individual member corporations, which each supply a predetermined share of the joint programme. This arrangement means that each corporation has a fully developed studio complex where all types of programmes can be produced. The individual corporations retain full responsibility for their contribution.

A regular television service began in West Germany in December 1952 (four days later than in the DDR). The joint Deutsches Fernsehen combining the previous separate programmes started in November 1954 and transmissions in colour date from August 1967. Hours of broadcasting are not regulated by the governments and are shorter than in Britain. In 1973 37 per cent of the joint programme time of the first channel was devoted to news and current affairs in which there is a special interest, and only approximately 17 per cent to entertainment. Old films are popular. Live TV transmissions of important parliamentary debates are frequent. All stations transmit their own regional programmes before the main evening broadcasts between 18.00 and 20.00 hours each weekday, except Saturday. These are interspersed by a total of twenty minutes of advertising. This limit was set by the Ministerpräsidenten of the Länder and also applies to the second channel, which similarly broadcasts commercials during the early evening. Sponsored programmes are not permitted on German television, but do exist on radio.

A few corporations, or groups of corporations, produce third programmes on a regional basis, which particularly stress educational, cultural and regional aspects. A good example is the Bavarian Telekolleg, now transmitted by most third programmes. This might be called a rudimentary 'school of the air'. It leads, after examinations held and approved by the government, to the Fachschulreife and later to the Fachhochschulreife, which gives access to Fachhochschulen. Nothing comparable to the British Open University is planned as yet.

A second nationwide television service was inaugurated in April 1964, after the constitutional dispute between the federal government and the Länder had been decided in favour of the Länder. Although all transmitters of the second channel are installed and maintained by the Bundespost, the making of programmes and the running of a service fall outside the legislative competence of the Federation. The Länder governments decided against charging the existing regional stations with producing a second joint programme and instead founded, by means of an interstate treaty, the *Zweites Deutsches Fernsehen* (ZDF, Second German Television), whose headquarters are in Mainz.

Unlike the ARD the ZDF is a centrally organised corporation, without the problems of co-ordination that at times hamper the operation of its rival. The avowed aim was to offer viewers in West Germany the possibility of choosing at any time between two programmes of comparable quality but different content. A programme pattern is agreed between the two systems and representatives from both channels meet every month to discuss programme details.

Governments and parliaments of the Länder set up and regulate the structure of the broadcasting corporations but governments do not directly interfere in programme-making and administration. In fact, all German television and radio broadcasts are provided by independent public corporations. These are controlled by a *Rundfunkrat* or *Fernsehrat* (broadcasting council), which is designed to represent the public interest. Its members are drawn from the parliaments, sometimes also from the governments, and from the churches, trade unions, universities, youth organisations and local authorities. In a few cases party-political pressures can easily be brought to bear, and on more than one occasion these have influenced the appointment of chief executives. The broadcasting council usually elects the *Intendant* (chief executive officer), who is responsible for the day-to-day running of the corporation and also for its programme. It approves the budgets, and generally supervises the working of the corporation and makes sure that it adheres to the general principles laid down in the various individual broadcasting acts. The Rundfunkrat may also choose the *Verwaltungsrat* (executive council), a much smaller body, which has a more direct say in the running of a corporation.

There are also a number of foreign stations on German soil, broadcasting to American or British troops stationed in Germany and to Eastern Europe; these stations are very popular with the West Germans.

Films

German film-making has not really recovered from the upheavals of the Nazi period. The film-making and distributing industry, hampered by the loss of Berlin as an outstanding film-producing centre, has had a varied post-war history. On the one hand, the studios in München are now among the largest in Europe and other new studios, many of which are also used for television, have been created in Hamburg, Wiesbaden and Göttingen. On the other, the number of feature films of any kind produced in the Bundesrepublik declined steadily until a few years ago. The number of films of all kinds produced in 1968 was 441 but this number had sunk to 261 in 1972. In 1971 only a quarter of the 388 feature films that had their première in that year were made in Germany, considerably fewer than those from the United States. More than half were sex films.

Inevitably, television has been a powerful competitor, and the closure of cinemas, with the exception of city centre picture houses, continues unchecked. In December 1966, there were 4786 cinemas, but by December 1972 their number had dropped to 3171. While in 1966 the average German went to the cinema 4.3 times a year in 1972 this number was only 2.4.

West Germany has an international reputation for making short films. She was unable, however, to resume her great inter-war tradition of feature film production after 1945 and only very few outstanding feature films have been produced, though at the end of the 1960s there was some sign of a renaissance. There is substantial government financial help available under the Federal Film Support Act of 1967; also tax reliefs for producers, distributors, and cinema owners are granted as additional indirect subsidies for German or non-German films that have been awarded a certificate of merit on the basis of artistic merit.

Only eleven of the eighty-five feature films produced in Germany in 1972 obtained this distinction.

The *Freiwillige Selbstkontrolle* (Voluntary Self-control) is a non-statutory authority created by the film industry itself. Its committees consist of an equal number of representatives of the industry and the public (governments, churches, youth organisations). They judge a film on moral and constitutional grounds. This amounts effectively to a pre-censorship, for a negative decision may influence a distributor against taking a film because it might involve him in legal action on a local level later, although officially the Board has no legal licensing powers. The often controversial decisions of this body made the churches decide to withdraw their members in 1971.

Libraries

The provision of public lending and reference libraries is poor by British standards, especially outside big towns, and an inter-library loan system between the public libraries scarcely exists. There are only 513 public libraries (excluding branch libraries) in the entire Bundesrepublik (1971), and their combined budget amounts to less than half of the public funds allocated to theatres. Only forty-eight libraries have a budget of more than one million DM. All public libraries are maintained by local authorities, while the Länder governments finance the research libraries in universities and also the regional central libraries from the annual state budget. These research libraries are generally financially better off than the public libraries because they have profited from the rapid expansion of higher education. Yet here, too, the annual allocation varies considerably from one library to another, and between Länder. The largest West German library is the *Bayerische Staatsbibliothek* (Bavarian State Library) in München, with 3.5 million volumes. It had a budget of DM 14.3m in 1972. The only 'copyright' library is the *Deutsche Bibliothek* (German Library) in Frankfurt, founded in 1949. It has become the country's bibliographic centre and publishes the *Deutsche Bibliographie* of books printed in both German states and in Austria and Switzerland.

Germans have always claimed to be a nation of readers, and the obligatory bookcase full of books that is to be found in every German home, rich or poor, the flourishing book societies and the 3500 bookshops seem to bear this out. In 1971 German publishers issued over 43 000 separate titles, including over 36 000 new books; this exceeds considerably the 35 000 titles published in Britain in that year, even though the English-speaking market is much wider than the German one. The list is headed by literature (over 8000 titles), followed by economics, law and public administration.

Theatre, Opera and Music

During the 1972–3 season, performances were given in 200 publicly owned theatres, opera houses, and concert and multipurpose halls in towns in the Bundesrepublik. Thirty theatres and opera houses were owned and administered by the Länder as *Staatstheater* (state theatres), and over 100 were *Stadttheater* (municipal theatres). Commercial theatres accommodating touring companies are rare, though the number of the latter is on the increase, and there are a mere eighty-one private professional theatres, comparatively few amateur dramatic societies exist. The majority of companies in Germany operate on a non-profit-making basis and are heavily subsidised by the state and local authorities.

In 1972–3 subsidies from this source totalled DM 717m, over DM 37 per inhabitant of the Bundesrepublik, and many times as much as the Arts Council and local authorities in Britain spend on the performing arts. On average only 20 per cent of expenditure was covered by the sale of tickets, although most theatres and opera houses claim that on average between 60 and 90 per cent of their available seats are occupied. The percentage is especially high for opera. Thus it is not surprising that the *Bayerische Staatsoper* (Bavarian State Opera), ranking among the best opera houses in the world, received in 1973–4 a subsidy of DM 26m (total budget DM 42m), that the city state of Hamburg paid in the same year a total subsidy of almost DM 49.6m to seven theatres and one opera house in the city, and that the municipal theatre of Münster, a town of barely 200 000 inhabitants, was subsidised to an extent of DM 10.2m (total budget DM 13.2m).

Every German town of above medium size of any repute is the proud possessor of a theatre, where drama and frequently also opera and operetta are performed for about nine months of the year. Many of these theatres have their own permanent orchestra or there is a municipal orchestra, which in addition to giving concerts also performs in the theatre. West Germany boasts the staggering number of almost eighty professional orchestras, largely maintained out of public funds including such famous orchestras as the Berliner Philharmoniker, the Stuttgarter Kammerorchester, and the symphony orchestras of the broadcasting stations, some of which enjoy an international reputation.

Many of the theatres and opera houses of today trace their origin to the court theatres of the former German principalities. The responsibility for maintaining them was taken over by the Länder and the municipalities after the revolution of 1918. This tradition and modern civic pride combine to accept almost without questioning, the support largely out of taxpayers' money of such an astonishing variety of theatrical and musical activities. One hundred theatres and opera houses were rebuilt or newly built after the war. Although only 8–10 per cent of the population, mainly from the middle class, attend performances, the German trade unions regularly book entire opera performances for their members, at drastically reduced prices, and schoolchildren and students can get very cheap tickets. Most tickets are sold as season tickets at a 25 per cent reduction.

German theatres and opera houses attempt to preserve the traditional repertory system with a permanent company. The large number of German opera companies, each with a wide repertory, provide an ideal training ground for young players, producers and conductors. Young singers flock to Germany from all over the world.

Germany's theatres aim to offer a carefully balanced international selection of classical and modern plays. In 1971–2 the most frequently performed author was Brecht, closely followed by Shakespeare. The leading theatres, which often own an additional small experimental theatre, are able to offer a more adventurous repertory than the small municipal theatres whose *Intendant* (administrative and artistic director), although in theory enjoying complete artistic freedom, has to rely on the continued support of an often conservative public and town council. But either will produce at least seven or eight plays a year, and several will be retained simultaneously. An international opera house, like those at München, Hamburg and Berlin, has forty to sixty operas in its current repertory.

Mention must be made of the many drama and musical festivals that are held in West Germany every year. They include open-air festivals, like the series of plays performed in the ruins of the Hersfeld monastery, or those in purpose-built theatres and opera houses, like the Wagner festival at Bayreuth, the passion play at Oberammergau or the opera festival in München.

Museums and Galleries

The major institutions are not concentrated in one or two centres, as in Britain, but dispersed throughout the Bundesrepublik. The former Prussian museums and galleries in Berlin are now located mainly in the Eastern half of the city. Many German princes built up their own collections and later governments continued this tradition so that, for example, München now boasts in the *Alte Pinakothek* one of the finest picture collections in the world.

6 Social Structure

Population

The resident population of the Bundesrepublik (including West Berlin) was 62 101 000 (December 1973), compared to 56.2 million in 1961, 50.2 million in 1950, 47.0 million in 1947 and 20.4 million in 1871 (annual average in the same area). The population density was 250 per sq km, one of the highest in the world, higher than Britain (229 per sq km) but not as high as England and Wales alone (325 per sq km). The most populous Länder were Nordrhein–Westfalen (17.2 million), followed by Bayern (10.9 million), and the least populous the *Stadtstaaten* (city states) Bremen (729 000) and Hamburg (1.8 million). As a region the Ruhr had the highest population density (1220 per sq km); indeed, 9 per cent of the entire population of the Bundesrepublik lived in this conurbation.

As in all western societies, the number of older citizens in relation to other groups is growing. In 1961, 16.8 per cent of the total population were sixty and older, by 1972 this percentage had grown to 19.7. This is chiefly the result of the war and the falling birth rate (see figure 4).

On the basis of the most recent trends in the birth rate, West Germany's population is likely to fall slightly in the next few years. Whereas the general mortality rate has remained virtually stable—it was 11.7 per 1000 of the population in 1963 and 11.8 in 1973—the number of live births has fallen from 18.3 to 10.3 per 1000, the lowest in Europe. The decline has been especially drastic since 1967 when the birth rate was still 17.0 per 1000. In 1971 the excess of births over deaths was a mere 0.8 per cent or 47 800—in 1973 there was a deficit of 1.5 per cent or 95 000 (180 000, without the surplus among foreigners living in Germany). The birth rate in the big cities was low generally, but surprisingly the decline in the birth rate was most marked in rural, predominantly Catholic, areas like the Saar and Rheinland–Pfalz. The average German family now produces only 1.8 children instead of the 2.18 necessary to maintain the present level of population.

Some of the reasons given for this phenomenon are a decline in the number of marriages, the material wealth of the country, a general hostility in the average German towards small children and, above all, efficient contraception. One in five of all German women of childbearing age takes the Pill, although contraception is not provided by the state, the federal government has not formulated a specific population policy, and there is no body like the Family Planning Association with a network of clinics. The fact remains that German families are getting smaller; in 1971, half of all children were only children or had only one brother or sister, whereas in 1964 60 per cent of all children came from families with three or more children. The percentage of children born to unmarried mothers (6 per cent in 1972) has risen in recent years (1970: 5.4 per cent). This means that 94 per cent of all live births were legitimate, although a high proportion of first children were conceived outside wedlock. In 1974 the Bundestag legalised abortion (with certain restrictions) but this amendment to the Penal Code was referred to the Constitutional Court for a ruling on its compatibility with the constitution.

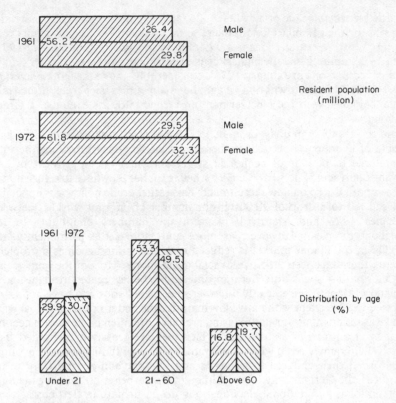

Figure 4   Population development in the Bundesrepublik.

The average age at first marriage was 25.5 years for a man and 22.9 years for a woman (1972). Since 1960 fewer Germans marry every year—in 1960 there were 9.4 marriages per 1000 inhabitants, in 1973 only 6.4 and the divorce rate is also rising (1.40 per 1000 in 1972).

Migrant workers

Immigration has had a tremendous effect on West German society since the end of the Second World War. In order to satisfy industry's insatiable demand for additional labour, refugees and expellees were succeeded from the early 1960s onwards by a wave of non-German immigrants. Some of these come from E.E.C. countries, especially Italy (17 per cent or 423 000 in December 1973), but many more come from Turkey (24 per cent or 599 000), Yugoslavia (20 per cent or 513 000), Greece (10 per cent or 243 000), Spain (seven per cent or 183 000) and a number of other countries. In December 1973 almost 12 per cent of all employed persons were *Gastarbeiter* (guest workers), a total of 2.52 million. These figures hide a constant migration in both directions across the borders of the Bundesrepublik, but at least twice as many Gastarbeiter returned to their homes as took up permanent residence in West Germany. At first only unmarried workers or the breadwinner of a family came but gradually more and more sent for their families to join them, so that the number of immigrants resident in West Germany was 3.97 million early in September 1973. Baden–Württemberg had the highest density of foreign workers (16.5 per cent of all employed persons in January 1973), considerably above the federal average of 10.8 per cent. Small towns and villages have sometimes been transformed into foreign 'colonies' with the old German inn turned into, for example, a Greek restaurant.

Foreign labour is initially brought to Germany on a short-term basis as a measure of economic policy. It is therefore relatively easy to reduce the total labour force in periods of economic strain and high unemployment by not renewing contracts of non-E.E.C. Gastarbeiter so that they have to return home, and to impose a stop on new recruitment. This rather crude policy was applied in 1974 and led to a drop of 30 000 in the number of migrant workers between December 1973 and March 1974, with the numbers continuing to fall throughout the year. However, as more and more settle permanently, the flexibility in the labour market is reduced and integration becomes a problem. Hitherto, there has been little overt racial disharmony. Most of the immigrants are white, initially speak little German, and tend to be segregated from the native population. Also, they frequently do lower-paid menial jobs and have not as yet competed to any extent with native Germans for the better positions. Most want to make as much money as possible and are therefore often content with accommodation of an inferior standard for which they are grossly overcharged. The real social difficulties begin when immigrants seek better family accommodation, want to send their children to nurseries and schools, and generally try to integrate with the German way of life. Although Gastarbeiter do not have the right to vote in local and national elections they do participate in Betriebsrat elections at plant level and are encouraged to put up their own candidates. As far as pay, social security benefits, and other rights are concerned foreign workers are equal to their German colleagues.

Personal Income and Expenditure

West Germany's active population of 26.7 million, which included soldiers and some 240 000 unemployed, constituted 42.9 per cent of the total resident population in 1973; 65 per cent of economically active persons were male, 35 per cent female. Some 9.5 per cent were self-employed, 5.5 per cent unpaid family workers, 7.7 per cent Beamte, 32.0 per cent salaried employees and 45.3 per cent wage earners; 48 per cent were employed in production, 49 per cent in services and by the government and only seven per cent in agriculture. The average monthly earnings of all employed persons amounted in 1973 to DM 1572, an increase in real terms of 253 per cent since 1950. In November 1949 an industrial worker had to work for twenty-three minutes to buy a 1 kg loaf of bread, in October 1973 for only thirteen minutes.

These figures only represent the average. Thus the average gross monthly wage of a male wage earner in industry amounted to DM 1660 in January 1974, that of a female worker to DM 1095, but the average gross monthly earnings of a male or female salaried employee in industry or trade were DM 2141 and DM 1344, respectively. These figures make clear that equal pay for women is far from being achieved. However, the percentage increase in pay during the period January 1973 to January 1974 was higher for women than for men, so the imbalance is being redressed. Average earnings vary from Land to Land (Hamburg, the wealthiest region of the entire E.E.C., leads the table and Bayern comes last, although the gap is narrowing) but also from one branch of industry to another. In 1950 miners had the highest hourly income, followed by printing and iron and steel workers. In 1973, workers in the oil industry came top (hourly rate DM 10.29), those in the printing industry second (DM 9.34), and those in the car industry third (DM 9.21) with the leather (DM 6.02) and shoe industries (DM 6.40) at the bottom of the list.

During the 1960s and early 1970s, the distribution of incomes has become fairer, insofar as the earnings of a greater number of workers fall in the middle income group and fewer in the low income group, but this is only true for men. In 1973 only 27 per cent of all employed persons earned less than DM 9600 per annum, compared to 49 per cent in 1968, 2 per cent between DM 9600 to 16 000 (39 per cent), 34 per cent between DM 16 000 to 25 000 (ten per cent), 18 per cent over 25 000 (two per cent).

In 1973, 69.6 per cent of the West German national income originated from employment, 30.1 per cent from entrepreneurship and property (1950: 58.4 per cent and 41.6 per cent, respectively). The total gross income from salaries and wages of all dependently employed persons before tax totalled DM 423 800m, or DM 1572 per head per month. Of this total gross sum 15.0 per cent was payable as direct taxation and 11.6 per cent in social security contributions, together 26.6 per cent or DM 414 (ranging from 34 per cent for an unmarried male skilled industrial worker to 22.7 per cent for a married man in the same job with three children). The figure for 1970 was only 25.8 per cent.

A detailed breakdown of personal income and expenditure in the Bundesrepublik can be obtained from the regular monthly surveys among selected social groups that the Federal Statistical Office undertakes. The households are chosen on the basis of income, social position of the head of the household, number of children, number of members of the family earning, etc. Figure 5 shows the distribution of income and expenditure of household type II, probably the most typical of all West German households. It is defined as a four-person household of employees, with the head of the household in the middle-income group. In 1973 his monthly gross income would fall in the range DM 1300 to DM 1950.

Personal Taxation

Taxation, both direct and indirect and accruing to the Federation, the Länder and the Gemeinden, amounted in 1973 to 24.3 per cent of the gross national product of the Bundesrepublik. This figure contrasts sharply with that for Britain, where the percentage was considerably higher (29.7 per cent in 1972), but social security contributions were lower. After many years of planning and debate a major reform of German tax law came into force on January 1, 1975. The aim of this first substantial overhaul of the German taxation system since 1949 was to make it fairer and simpler—a hope that was only partially fulfilled. The whole package covers a reform of property tax, gift tax and estate duty (implemented in January 1974), of the system of grants to encourage saving, and

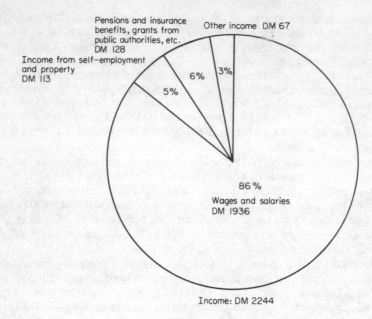

Pensions and insurance benefits, grants from public authorities, etc. DM 128

Other income DM 67

Income from self-employment and property DM 113

6%

3%

5%

86%
Wages and salaries
DM 1936

Income: DM 2244

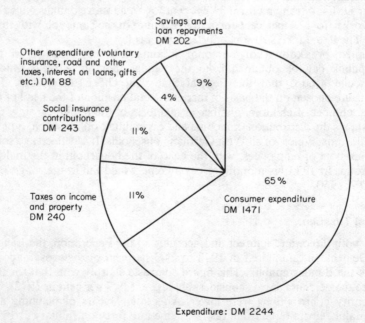

Savings and loan repayments DM 202

Other expenditure (voluntary insurance, road and other taxes, interest on loans, gifts etc.) DM 88

Social insurance contributions DM 243

9%

4%

11%

Taxes on income and property DM 240

11%

65%
Consumer expenditure
DM 1471

Expenditure: DM 2244

Figure 5   Average monthly income and expenditure of a four-person household in 1973, in the middle-income group, taken by reference to the earnings of the head of the household.

of the local trading tax. Income tax reform—which introduced new tax scales with a slightly higher maximum rate, a higher basic allowance and a substantial reorganisation of family allowances—was the cornerstone of the new legislation. All measures taken together are thought to give the taxpayer a total relief of over DM 13 000m, a strong boost to spending power at a time of economic recession. Corporation tax and motor vehicle tax are to be recast later.

The *Einkommensteuer* (income tax) represents a growing proportion of West Germany's tax revenue (39 per cent in 1973), and is levied on a sliding scale. The initial rate of tax is a flat 22 per cent up to an annual income of DM 16 000 for a single person or DM 32 000 for a married couple. For higher incomes the rate of tax rises progressively, up to the maximum of 56 per cent for any income above DM 260 000. There is no surtax. Tax allowances are granted for single people, married couples, one-parent families and old people, and tax exemption up to a fixed ceiling is given for interest payments on loans, insurance premiums and savings with Bausparkassen, etc.

Since 1968 *Umsatzsteuer* (turnover tax) is levied as *Mehrwertsteuer* (value-added tax) on goods and services at a standard rate of 11 per cent of the net price for most items, and at a reduced rate of 5.5 per cent for certain goods, like books, journals, agricultural products and certain services. Some services and transactions are exempt altogether, like exports, doctors' services, radio and television broadcasts, theatre and orchestra tickets and museum entrance charges. Other indirect taxes affecting the German consumer are the coffee and tea tax, petrol tax, beer tax, motor vehicle licence tax and also *Zölle* (Custom and excise duties). Indirect taxes constituted 55.7 per cent of the entire West German tax revenue in 1970 (UK: 50.7 per cent).

The individual German may further be affected by the *Vermögenssteuer* (property tax), which is assessed on an annual basis on agricultural land, real estate, the operating assets of a business or factory, and certain other moveable assets and securities. The rate is 0.7 per cent after certain allowances have been made. *Erbschaftssteuer* (estate duty) is less heavy than in Britain, ranging from 1 per cent to a maximum of 60 per cent, although tax is levied at a lower valuation.

Individuals as well as enterprises are subject to a levy on property under the 1952 *Lastenausgleichsgesetz* (Equalisation of Burdens Act). The tax is due quarterly and amounts to basically 50 per cent of the value of the assets affected, based on their value in 1948. Payment is spread over thirty years, from 1949. Profits arising from mortgages and loans are also taxed. This scheme aims at a substantial redistribution of wealth and has assisted the economic integration of the millions of refugees and expellees. Up to December 1973 DM 83 900m had been paid out in grants, pensions or loans.

German companies are subject to *Körperschaftssteuer* (corporation tax) at 51 per cent on retained but only 15 per cent on distributed profits, dividends being regarded as taxable income to the shareholder. All businesses in the Bundesrepublik are in addition liable to *Gewerbesteuer* (trade tax), which is levied at varying rates by local authorities and largely accrues to them. It is charged on profits and on capital, and sometimes also on the payroll.

Social Security

Most but not all employed and self-employed Germans contribute to the several social security schemes for health, old age and accident that exist in the Bundesrepublik. Like most West European countries West Germany does not possess a comprehensive and compulsory national social security system on British lines, administered by a government department and supported largely by general taxation.

The first German social-security legislation was introduced by Bismarck in the 1880s. His first Act introduced health insurance for workers with later legislation for industrial injuries and disablement benefits, and old age pensions. These three Acts were combined in the comprehensive Reich Insurance Code of 1911, which is still in force today in modified form.

The historical development of Germany's social services explains some of its present-day features. One of these is that totally separate schemes, administered under federal supervision by self-governing bodies with the legal status of public corporations, provide, for example, for old age pensions, sickness, industrial injuries and unemployment benefit. Furthermore, frequently different groups of the working population are covered by separate provisions, and different conditions apply. This is particularly so in the case of old age pensions where no less than seven separate schemes exist. Also, the outdated distinction between *Arbeiter* (manual worker or wage earner) and *Angestellter* (white collar worker or salaried employee) persists: while the former's membership of his health insurance scheme is compulsory, the latter is exempt if he earns above a certain income, but can remain a voluntary member.

The German system is predominantly insurance-based. For most schemes employees and employers, whether public or private, pay roughly equal contributions, with the exception of industrial injuries insurance to which employers alone contribute. Employers are required to pay an employee's full wage or salary from the first day of illness for up to six weeks and also during health treatment in a spa (even if the latter is paid for out of a social security fund), and civil servants in particular are covered by a generous non-contributory pension scheme. Employees in fact contributed only about 25 per cent of the total social expenditure in the Bundesrepublik in 1973 and employers (both private and public) approximately 49 per cent. Direct subsidies out of general taxation amounted to 23 per cent, less than in Britain. Taken overall, however, the public sector (Bund, Länder, and Gemeinden) provides half of all social expenditure in the Bundesrepublik. The other half originates from employees (21 per cent) and private enterprises (33 per cent).

Social security expenditure

The annual *Sozialbudget* (social budget), which is prepared by the *Bundesminister für Arbeit und Sozialordnung* (Federal Minister of Labour and Social Order) and is closely linked with the government's medium-term financial planning, gives an overall picture of all aspects of social security in the Bundesrepublik from rent subsidies and tax concessions to war pensions, family allowances and old-age pensions. It forecasts the development of these services over a five-year period. The 1974 Sozialbudget (1974 to 1978) listed a total expenditure of DM 930 300m for 1973. The total social expenditure in 1973 amounted to a very high 27.1 per cent of the gross national product. By 1978 the rate will be somewhat above 29 per cent. International comparisons undertaken annually by the Statistical Office of the European Communities which, unlike the West German statistics, do not include voluntary payments made by employers, certain specific aid measures, nor indirect benefits such as tax concessions, indicate that on this basis the Bundesrepublik, with 17.6 per cent of the gross national product, in 1971 took third place in the old Community of the Six after the Netherlands (19.9 per cent) and Italy (18.0 per cent).

Pensions

Currently some 14 million Germans are recipients of *Renten* (pensions) of one kind or another: retirement pensions, widows' pensions (60 per cent of a deceased person's entitlement), war victims, payments for orphans and for preventive and aftercare medical treatment, and benefits for an insured person's incapacity for work and invalidity. In 1972 a flexible qualifying age for retirement pensions was introduced, which become due between the ages of sixty-three and sixty-seven with the choice of retirement age left to the insured person. An individual pension is computed on the general basis of the gross average earnings of all manual workers and salaried employees over the previous three calendar years (DM 13 371 for 1973), on the personal basis of earnings while working and the length of the contribution period. The minimum contribution period before an old-age pension can be drawn is fifteen years, for other pensions five years.

Existing old-age and disability pensions are related to the movement of salaries and wages and the general economic performance of the country over the three preceding years, and regular annual adjustments are made. German pensions are thus able to keep in step with improvements in the standard of living of the working population as well as with increases in the cost of living. This revolutionary principle of 'dynamic' pensions represents the most modern form of old-age insurance in an industrial society. It applies to virtually all types of pension, including industrial injury and disablement benefits and war pensions. Since its introduction in 1957 this reform has resulted in seventeen pension increases, including that of July 1974. Since 1969 alone pensions have been increased by about 60 per cent and they have more than trebled since 1957. The 11.2 per cent increase of most old-age pensions in July 1974 resulted in additional expenditure of approximately DM 8500m in a full year.

At the beginning of 1973 a retired manual worker received an average pension of DM 383 per month, a retired salaried employee DM 631, a retired miner DM 844. This is a great deal more than a British state pension, although it must be remembered that the cost of living in West Germany is high in comparison with Britain. Without any doubt many German old-age pensioners are relatively poor in one of the wealthiest countries in the world.

In 1973 a compulsorily insured person paid 9 per cent of his or her gross monthly earnings into one of the pension funds; the employer's share was another 9 per cent. The maximum income for assessment was DM 2300; any person earning more must still pay but only 9 per cent of this ceiling, however high his income. Contributions, like those for health insurance, are retained by the employer and paid into the appropriate pension or health-insurance fund. Contributions had to be increased steadily over the years in spite of additional direct state subsidies. They are likely to rise even further in future, since the

number of pensioners is growing faster than that of the active working population. In 1973 all pension schemes together cost DM 92 900m or 37 per cent of
the social budget. While the absolute figure is expected to rise to DM 160 500m
by 1978 the percentage share will remain virtually as it was in 1973. The
Rentenversicherung der Arbeiter und Angestellte (compulsory Pension Insurance for Manual Workers and Salaried Employees) includes the two largest
schemes with almost identical regulations. There are further funds for farmers,
for miners (the oldest in the country), for skilled craftsmen and for self-employed
people. Some of the latter group, for example musicians, variety artists and
midwives, are compulsorily insured under the salaried employees' schemes.
Other so-called 'free' professions, including doctors, dentists, pharmacists and
accountants, have their own independent professional associations with
obligatory membership and occupational pension provisions. The 1972 Pension
Reform Act admitted members of these groups as well as housewives and other
hitherto privately insured people on a voluntary basis to the salaried employees'
scheme.

It is a widespread practice of medium-sized and large German firms to provide
additional pensions for their staff in order to supplement the state pension. Other
additional benefits often include surgeries, kindergartens and housing. Beamte
receive substantial benefits from the state, especially in the form of generous non-
contributory pensions and widows' pensions. At present there are some 900 000
recipients of these. In 1973 all benefits in this category amounted to DM
22 000m.

Social health insurance

An estimated 89 per cent (53.5 million) of the West German population are
members of the *Soziale Krankenversicherung* (Social Health Insurance),
although the Bundesrepublik does not have a compulsory National Health Service. All wage earners with their dependants (without extra cost) are insured,
whatever their earnings, and so are all unemployed persons, old-age pensioners
(who do not have to contribute), foreign workers, certain groups of self-
employed people and salaried employees up to a certain monthly salary, which is
in fact three-quarters of the maximum assessed income for a pension fund (in
1974 DM 1875 a month). This limit has repeatedly been raised. Those earning
more and Beamte (who obtain a variety of allowances from the state) are exempt
from compulsory insurance. However, under certain conditions voluntary
membership of the health insurance scheme is possible. In 1972 18.8 million
dependently employed persons and 8.5 million pensioners were insured on a compulsory basis and 4.9 million persons on a voluntary basis. Others (some 10 per
cent) were privately insured and only just over 1 per cent of the population had no
health insurance at all.

Contributions are paid both by employer and employee. The amount payable
depends on income and may vary from one fund to another. The average in 1973
was over 9 per cent (half each by the employer and employee) but total contributions range from approximately 8 to 13 per cent of the gross wage. As with
pension insurance there is a maximum income for the purpose of assessment of
contributions (DM 1725 in 1973); earnings beyond this figure are ignored for
assessment. Payments are made, usually via the employer, to approximately

1740 approved autonomous *Krankenkassen* (sickness funds), which operate on
a local, regional, federal, occupational or works level. Other funds, the so-called
Ersatzkassen (institutions for the refund of medical expenses) function on a
federal level, similarly to private insurance companies, and there are separate
funds for salaried staff and wage earners. They are based on voluntary
membership, which exempts contributors from compulsory health insurance.

In 1973 DM 43 400m (17 per cent) of all social expenditure listed in the social
budget and just over 4 per cent of the gross national product, were spent on the
large range of services provided by the funds of the health insurance scheme.
Cash benefits consist chiefly in sick pay in lieu of earnings after the first six weeks
of illness. Sick pay is earnings-related and amounts after six weeks to 75 per cent
of normal gross earnings, plus additional allowances for dependants. The
maximum payable is 85 per cent of gross or 100 per cent of net earnings, in
excess of any benefit in Britain. Other cash benefits are given for a parent's
absence from work due to a child's illness (up to five working days), and for death
and maternity. In the latter case a small allowance and, for working women,
fourteen weeks' benefit equivalent to her normal net earnings are granted. The
cost of all medical attention during and after pregnancy, including hospital or
maternity-home confinement, is borne by the insurance. Pre- and post-natal services, that is the education of mothers before and after birth in special centres, or
midwife and health visitor services, are much less developed than in Britain. In
general, the range of local health and social services for mothers and young
children, for children of school age, for the elderly, the mentally disordered, the
physically handicapped and the convalescent at home is more developed in Britain
than in Germany.

The health insurance funds pay the fees for medical treatment by a general
practitioner or dentist chosen by the member (most general practitioners and
dentists are recognised by the funds) or a specialist, and they pay for hospital
treatment (unlimited period), medicines (there is a small prescription charge),
spectacles and (partially) for dentures and hearing aids, and for physiotherapy.
In recent years, special attention has been devoted to preventive medicine and
rehabilitation.

The medical profession charges according to scales established by the health-
insurance funds in collaboration with the doctors. This means that not always
the best available medicines can be prescribed as they would exceed the permitted sum. It also means that 'private' patients may be charged considerably
more than subscribers to insurance funds. The system has helped to perpetuate
the class system in hospitals both as far as medical attention and facilities are
concerned. A private patient gets priority treatment from specialists who charge
very high fees, and he can generally afford to pay for a bed in the first or second
class of accommodation.

The cost of the Soziale Krankenversicherung is shooting up, above all because
of vastly increased hospital charges and the growing number of old-age pensioners in the scheme who do not contribute. The government forecasts expenditure of well over DM 80 000m by 1978 and a contribution of as much as 13 per
cent of an insured person's gross earnings.

The 3500 (1972) hospitals in the Bundesrepublik are the responsibility of the
Gemeinden, Länder, insurance funds or private organisations. For years many
have run at a deficit, since the charges they were allowed to make did not cover

costs. Many new hospitals have been built since the war and although there are few nineteenth-century hospital buildings, still a familiar sight in Britain, a shortage of beds still persists. The 1972 reform of hospital financing envisaged for the first time the substantial financial involvement of the federal government, which in future will bear approximately one-third of the capital costs of building new and modernising old hospitals (some DM 900m per year).

Industrial injuries insurance

Compared to the health insurance the 2.3 per cent share in social expenditure of the *Unfallversicherung* (industrial injuries insurance), the third major branch of the insurance sector of the West German social security system, looks almost insignificant. Nevertheless, in 1972 2.5 million new cases of industrial injuries or occupational diseases were reported. Most of the accidents occurred at work or on the way to and from work. Some 26.2 million people were insured in 1972: all those employed on the basis of a contract of employment, service or apprenticeship, and also children at kindergarten, pupils at school, students and certain categories of self-employed persons. Other self-employed persons can insure voluntarily. Beamte are exempt because they have their own accident provisions, and so are doctors and dentists. Only employers pay contributions that are based on total earnings but graded according to the safety record of an enterprise. The average levy amounts to 1.5 to 2 per cent of earnings. The industrial injuries insurance is administered by a large number of *Berufsgenossenschaften* (regional occupational self-governing industrial injuries institutions), and also by some federal, Land or Gemeinde executive authorities. All these also have important functions in accident prevention.

The Unfallversicherung compensates for losses suffered as a result of bodily injury or death. Benefits are available for medical treatment and assistance, including the provision of artificial aids, home help and home nursing, and for vocational retraining. Injury benefits (after the first six weeks of illness, corresponding to sickness benefits) or disablement pensions are paid. The latter follows on from sick pay and is based on annual earnings. Complete disability entitles an insured person to two-thirds of these. Children's allowances are also paid. In the event of the death of an insured person, the widow, widower or orphans receive a pension as well as a cash payment. Industrial injuries pensions are, like other pensions, adjusted to the movement of earnings.

Unemployment and other benefits

From the mid-1950s to 1974, when it almost reached the million mark, unemployment can hardly be said to have been a real problem in the Bundesrepublik. The *Arbeitslosenversicherung* (unemployment insurance) is a fully developed branch of West Germany's social-security system. It is based on the contributory principle, with employer and employee paying half each, approximately 2 per cent of the gross earnings of an employed person up to the maximum of DM 2800. Unemployment insurance is handled by the *Bundesanstalt für Arbeit* (Federal Labour Office), a self-governing public corporation with branches, the so-called *Arbeitsämter*, throughout the Bundesrepublik. Under a 1969 Act of Parliament the office also acts as an employment exchange. It counsels young people, including students, on the choice of career and advises older people who want promotion through further training or who want to change their profession altogether. An additional new function is to guide, promote and pay for in-service training and retraining and to assist disabled people to obtain and keep suitable work.

Unemployment benefit becomes payable to anyone who is out of work and has paid at least twenty-six monthly contributions over the previous three years. It is granted for not more than fifty weeks and is about 68 per cent of the last net income of an insured person, provided he or she has paid regular contributions over the preceding three years. If there is no claim for unemployment benefit—either because it has been exhausted or because there was no claim in the first place—unemployment assistance at a rate of 58 per cent of net earnings becomes payable. If a firm goes bankrupt and an employee has not received the pay due to him he is entitled to receive his net earnings over the last three months out of public funds.

There exists a host of other direct benefits for special social groups. One of the most widely available is the *Kindergeld* (family allowance), an allowance paid for every child up to the age of 18 (or 27 if still being educated). The new rates from January 1975 are DM 50 per month for the first child, DM 70 for the second child, and DM 120 for any further child. These increased rates, which replace several different allowances available previously, are payable to parents regardless of income.

There are also pensions and related services for people disabled or bereaved through the war, for former political prisoners, for former soldiers of the Bundeswehr (or their relatives) who were disabled or sustained injuries while in service. In 1973 2.42 million people received aid under this *Kriegsopferversorgung* (War Victims Relief Fund). Former prisoners of war are also provided for, and special legislation, the Lastenausgleichsgesetz, provides for refugees and expellees.

Sozialhilfe (social aid), comparable to British supplementary benefits and the family income supplement, are given to fill in the gaps left by the other social-security schemes to meet the cost of living or in special hardship cases, completes West Germany's social security provision. For example, a young widow with small children, a pregnant woman who is not compulsorily insured, old people whose pension is too low or who are not covered by the pension insurance have a legal entitlement to aid. Its most common form is a maintenance allowance, but aid is given for special situations, as, for example, establishing a new livelihood, vocational training, sickness, blindness or integration of a handicapped person into the community. The recipients of Sozialhilfe totalled 1.7 million in 1973 and DM 5290m was spent. The official organisations working in this field collaborate closely with voluntary organisations like the Red Cross or church welfare groups. groups.

Consumer Expenditure and Social Life

Housing

Perhaps the first thing that strikes the British visitor to West Germany is the cleanliness of its streets and public places and its well-dressed people. The average German strives to keep up appearances, even when he is relatively poor. Dirty, ragged children are rarely seen, and on Sundays the family dress in their best clothes to go out on their Sunday outing, often a visit to relatives or a stroll in the woods. Germans are also very interested in interior decoration, and the standard of furnishings available in even the smallest towns is very high. In 1973 11 per cent of the consumer expenditure of the typical four-person household went on household goods (including furniture and furnishings, household appliances, and cleaning materials)—see figure 6.

Most Germans live in flats, and in 1972 over half of all households were in buildings with more than two flats. For years the majority of new accommodation has been provided in this type of building and their numbers are increasing (60 per cent of new buildings in1973); in urban areas high blocks of ten to twenty-five storeys are a common sight. German flats are small by British standards: the majority of dwellings have only a living-room, kitchen, one or two bedrooms, and a bathroom, although the average size of all dwellings completed has increased from 70.4 sq m in 1960 to 84.8 sq. m in 1972. Well over half of the 22.6 million dwellings existing in 1973 were built after 1949, but in spite of the remarkable post-war house-building effort, following the destruction of 20 per cent of all housing stock during the war, 5.8 million dwellings were built before 1918, 3.6 million have no bathroom and 1.5 million no toilet of their own. However, all new dwellings are now so equipped and in 1971 96 per cent of all new dwellings also had full central heating.

Home ownership, although low by comparison with Britain, is growing. In 1968, only 34 per cent of all households lived in their own houses or flats, 61 per cent in rented, and five per cent in sublet accommodation. Although in 1973 29 per cent of all new dwellings completed were houses or bungalows, an increasing number of owner-occupiers (every tenth dwelling completed in 1970) are buying flats. On the one hand, more and more people in West Germany are regarding the purchase of their own home as an investment at a time of increasing inflation and particularly rapid increase in building costs, on the other, relatively few Germans are able to afford the very high cost of building their own houses, which in Germany are usually architect-designed and finished to a very high exterior and interior standard.

Of the disposable income of the typical family 16 per cent in 1973 went on rent (including the estimated rent of owner-occupiers) (see figure 6), but this percentage rose to 18 per cent for a two-person household living on pension and social security benefits. Only the rents of *Sozialwohnungen*, flats financed with the help of government grants, and those of pre-war flats in the conurbations of München, Hamburg and Berlin are still controlled, and all kinds of rents have increased considerably recently. But under a 1970 Act, rent allowances on a sliding scale are payable as of right to tenants, depending on family income, family size and rent payable. Similar allowances are available to owner-occupiers living in a flat or house and in respect of agricultural land worked as a secondary occupation. The federal government and the Länder governments contributed an approximately equal share of the over DM 1100m paid out to 1.4 million households in 1973. Since 1971 tenants also enjoy much improved legal rights. It is, for example, very difficult for a landlord to give notice if it would involve hardship for the tenant, and giving notice in order to increase the rent is specifically prohibited.

West Germany's rate of new home building is one of her most remarkable post-war achievements. Some 13.5 million new dwellings have been built since 1949, at a cost of almost DM 600 000m. This is, perhaps, the most telling feature of the 'economic miracle'. Of course, most of these new dwellings are flats, but since 1953 the figure has never fallen below 478 000 units per year. A new post-war record was set in 1973 with 714 000 completed new dwellings, notwithstanding an unprecedented rise in the price of land and in building costs, and a pronounced preference for higher-amenity housing. Statistically the housing deficit has now been eliminated: the number of households and the available housing stock are approximately equal.

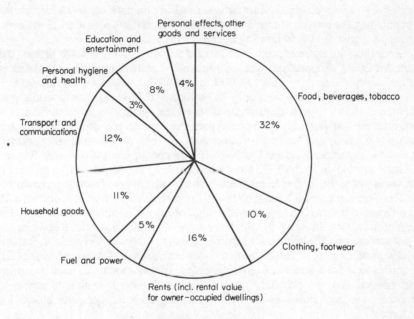

Total monthly expenditure: DM 1471

Figure 6   Average monthly consumer expenditure of a four-person household in 1973, in the middle-income group, taken by reference to the head of the household.

At present over half of all new housing is privately built. The traditional way of finance is through a *Bausparkasse* (building and loan association). Here a customer must save for several years, and a deposit of some 40 per cent of the mortgage must be accumulated before a building loan is granted. In the post-war period these Bausparkassen, which are state supervised, have been among the most successful institutions of the German credit system. In 1973 alone they made a total of almost DM 39 900m available for house-building. Other sources of finance for private house-building or purchase are mortgage banks, savings banks, insurance companies and some public organisations. The government encourages saving for home ownership by granting special tax allowances for regular savings with Bausparkassen (a total of DM 630m in 1973) and giving tax-free bonuses of up to DM 400 per annum for savings in these associations (DM 3760m). Tax concessions are also available to firms who provide money for the construction of private dwellings.

Public authorities in West Germany do not usually build or own houses but extensively subsidise house-building under federal housing construction acts. This policy was begun in 1950. During the early years of the Bundesrepublik over 70 per cent of all new dwellings were erected, whether by private individuals or private or public organisations, with the help of low-interest loans from public funds repayable over long periods. Out of the 5.8 million dwellings completed up to the end of 1960 3.2 million were such Sozialwohnungen, whose size and cost must fall within prescribed limits, whose rents are controlled, and which must be occupied by the lower-paid. In 1960 the public sector still provided 23 per cent of the capital cost of all new housing construction.

Since then the share of public funds has declined steadily (to well below 10 per cent in 1973). Accordingly the number of Sozialwohnungen completed has fallen: while there were still 152 000 in 1966 (out of a total of 605 000 new dwellings), in 1973 there were only 169 000 out of 714 000. The federal government is seeking to halt this trend. In the long term it aims to subsidise approximately one-half of all completed dwellings and to give particular assistance to certain groups of people—young couples, old people, skilled workers in economically underdeveloped regions, and owners of pre-1900 houses. The total housing allocation in the 1973 federal budget increased by 4.5 per cent over the previous year; the largest items were indirect subsidies to interest payments.

The German home is kept spotless by the meticulous German housewife. She, like German industry, has achieved a high degree of mechanisation; only 3 per cent of the above household group have as yet a dishwasher, but 38 per cent have a deep freeze and 95 per cent a washing machine and a vacuum cleaner. Relatively few families have a garden of their own but rarely feel deprived, since this is regarded as a luxury rather than a necessity. In any case most flats, whether of the council type or privately owned, have a balcony, which in summer is smothered in geraniums and petunias, making even tall concrete blocks look colourful.

Social habits

Eating and drinking are taken seriously, although the share in the monthly budget dropped from 40 per cent in 1965 to 32 per cent in 1973, a further sign of West German prosperity. Work starts early in Germany; factories begin at about seven o'clock in the morning, and offices, schools and shops are open at eight o'clock. The custom is to have a light breakfast of bread, jam and coffee, but even with a snack at mid-morning by the time midday arrives the German is ready for the biggest meal of the day. The children come home from school and the father from work if he can. German cooking is not particularly varied or exciting. Green salad, boiled potatoes, *Schweineschnitzel* (pork cutlets fried in egg and breadcrumbs), stew and cabbage, are the most popular dishes. The consumption of pork per head of population is greater than that of all the other meats together. The relative importance of veal in the German diet has declined since the early 1950s, while that of chicken has increased fivefold. Large quantities of potatoes are eaten in North Germany (although the consumption per head of population, 10 kg, is now only half of what it was in 1950–1), and noodles or dumplings are popular in South Germany. Fresh vegetables are not as common as in Britain, nor are frozen and convenience foods as popular with the German housewife.

The family evening meal is eaten between six and seven o'clock in the evening consisting often of one of many varieties of fresh brown bread (British 'cottonwool' sliced bread is rare) and cold, sliced sausage, the famous German *Wurst*, of which there are countless varieties and which bears no resemblance to the British sausage, having more flavour and a higher meat content.

Food on the whole is very expensive. Meat is a luxury not to be eaten every day, not even by the better off, and butter, coffee and tea are very expensive. Only certain fruit and vegetables tend to be cheaper and plentiful.

Germans eat very large amounts of food, an estimated average of 300 calories a day too much. Ten million Germans are overweight and as in all western societies dieting is a national hobby. Eating out in a restaurant is more common than in Britain and is relatively cheap, though again there is little variety in the menu, which has a strong regional bias. If you want something different you must go to one of the relatively few foreign restaurants, although there are now quite a number of, for example, Italian and Greek eating places. First-class international standard cuisine (and accommodation) is virtually exclusive to the big urban centres. Entertaining at home is not very common and tends to be formal.

German wines are very good and quite cheap. Wine is drunk much more frequently than in Britain (consumption per head of population in 1973 was 20 litres). Beer of the lager type, served chilled, is the most popular drink, and the beer consumption of 147 litres per head (1973) is among the highest in the world. Certain spirits, especially vodka and whisky (the latter because of lower duty is cheaper than in Scotland itself), are becoming popular. It is interesting to note that the consumption of fresh milk (94 litres per head in 1973) continues to decline. Coffee rather than tea is drunk (143 litres per head, as compared to 32 litres), especially in the afternoon, accompanied on Sundays or on special outings to a *Café* by rich cakes with whipped cream.

Germans are more formal in their social relationships than the British. Shaking hands is necessary at any meeting and titles and modes of address are still vitally important. Attitudes to one's social superiors are still respectful, although the younger generation appears to be more relaxed. Indeed, there is an even greater generation gap in West Germany than in Britain. But Germans are still notably respectful of authority and concerned with the good opinion of their neighbours. Though it is dangerous to generalise about national characteristics, the average German, hardworking and worthy citizen though he is, is inclined to be a little pompous and to lack a sense of the ridiculous. In spite of his respect for authority the average German is on the whole inconsiderate in his everyday meetings with his fellows. Queueing is unknown and people push each other out of the way on public transport and in shops, regardless of the age or sex of the person being pushed. Officials can be brusque and unhelpful—less so now than ten years ago—and neighbourliness is not regarded as a valuable quality. Apart from surface politeness families tend to isolate themselves from others, even those living in the same block of flats.

Driving a car is a particularly dangerous activity. Although in 1973 the motor vehicle density per 1000 inhabitants was only slightly higher than in Britain (286 as compared to 265) the number of fatal road accidents (16 300) was over twice as high and 488 000 people were seriously injured, compared to Britain's 346 000. There was a lessening in the number of fatal accidents (1700 less) and serious injuries in 1974, probably as a result of the temporary speed restrictions, the driving ban on Sundays, and the recommended maximum speed of 130 km h on motorways, introduced in the wake of the oil crisis. Also there is no general speed limit on German motorways, and many Germans feel personally affronted if another driver should dare to overtake. As a result aggressive driving without consideration for others is commonplace.

The Germans have a great love of nature and of their beautiful countryside. There are no enclosures here; there are few hedges and fences, and the fields and woods are accessible, no gates, no barbed wire, no notice forbidding trespassers. Acres of woodland belong to the local authority or to the state.

The prosperity of the West German economy is clearly visible. Shops are particularly attractive with beautiful displays of elegant and well-designed goods. The large department store, usually found in modern shopping precincts, is not as common as in Britain and America; and their merchandise is of the cheaper variety. 'Better' shops are almost invariably small boutiques. Since social status depends to a great extent on material possessions the average West German family spends a large proportion of its income on clothes, furniture, a car and holidays abroad (see figure 6).

More and more Germans go away on holiday. In 1973 around 30 million people undertook 36.5 million holiday journeys of five days or more; of these about half were predominantly foreign trips. The principal German holiday areas are the Alpen and the Alpenvorland in Bayern, the Bodensee and the Schwarzwald in Baden–Württemberg, the Nordsee and Ostsee coasts and the Friesischen Inseln in Schleswig–Holstein and Niedersachsen. Germany sends more tourists abroad than any other European country, the most popular destinations in 1973 being Austria (almost one-third) and Italy (just under one-quarter), followed by Spain and Yugoslavia. Charter flights showed a particular boom, and here Spain, Majorca and the Canary Islands remained the Germans' favourite destinations. Although many foreign tourists visit the Bundesrepublik they tend—to the dismay of German trade—simply to cross the country or stay for only 2.2 days on average. The number of nights spent in German hotels by foreign visitors during the summer of 1973 remained at only 7.5 per cent of the total. Although foreign tourists spent DM 5800m inside Germany in 1971, German travellers are estimated to have spent DM 17 200m abroad.

The principal vacation months in West Germany are July and August, and the long summer school vacation of six or seven weeks is staggered throughout the Bundesrepublik between late June and the middle of September. Most holiday journeys are undertaken by car (57 per cent). This places an enormous strain on West Germany's North to South communication routes, especially the Autobahnen, during the summer holiday peak periods, even more so since Scandinavian, British, Dutch, Belgian and French travellers prefer Germany's comprehensive network of fast roads to the less-developed road network of her neighbours. Rail accounts for 23 per cent of journeys, and air for 13 per cent.

The Germans are great admirers of learning and culture. Books and opera and theatregoing are not confined to the middle classes. University professors have a high social status, as do those possessing university doctorates and schoolteachers. Respect for university students has declined since some students became militant and openly disregarded social conventions. Television programmes are much more serious on the whole than in Britain. There are fewer light comedy programmes, and far more time is devoted to news and documentaries.

Another matter that Germans take seriously is their health. Serious and detailed discussion of one's headaches or the state of one's liver are frequent at social gatherings. Many Germans still undertake health cures, which involve the solemn taking of the waters in one of the 198 resorts that are permitted to add the special title *Bad* (spa) to their name. British visitors should be warned that any sign of flippancy on their part when told, for example, that someone is suffering from *Frühlingsmüdigkeit* (tiredness at the onset of spring) will be regarded as in very poor taste.

The status of women

Changes are taking place in the status of women in West German society as in Britain. Women have had the vote since 1919 and are technically free from legal disabilities (Grundgesetz, articles 3 and 117, and Equal Rights Act, 1957). However, there are few women in the Bundestag (29, but the Bundestagspräsident is a woman), in the cabinet (one), and in top jobs in the professions and even fewer in industry. And yet 35 per cent of the working population in 1972 were women, slightly less than the year before. Generally their earnings are well below those of men in the same position and with the same responsibilities; the better the job the greater the differential. It is only in certain branches of the public service, especially in teaching, that graduate women can earn as much as men. In 1973 the average hourly gross earnings of women employed in industry were DM 6.16 but those of men DM 8.76, although the annual increase over the period 1971–3 was greater for women than for men. While 38 per cent of all economically active women earned between DM 300 and DM 600 per month in 1971, only 7 per cent of men belonged to this group; on the other hand, 37 per cent of all men earned between DM 800 and 1200, but only 14 per cent of women. A 1971 survey revealed that half of all German working women had only Volksschule education and that most of the others had attended further courses of only short duration and not very high level. German women have a lower level of education than those in any other of the six original E.E.C. countries, except Italy.

It is still difficult for a mother of young children to go out to work because the schools are usually only open in the mornings and there are no school meals. German husbands of the pre-war generation do very little domestic work. The younger generation are more willing to help their wives, and marriage is becoming more of a partnership.

German couples tend to have their children at fairly widely spaced intervals; they have their second child on average five years after marriage. Half of all marriages have only one or two children and generally the Germans have a rather intolerant attitude to children. There is, however, a great public interest in their upbringing and education. Children, except for a very small minority, attend school near their home, do not go to 'better' schools and are not sent to boarding school. It is also usual for a grown-up son or daughter to continue to live with his or her parents until marriage, unless job or university take him away from his home town. Elderly parents rarely live with their married children, possibly because the average German flat is not big enough. Children are brought up to have formal manners—boys are taught to bow and girls to curtsey when introduced to someone—but otherwise German and British attitudes in this respect are fairly similar.

Sport

West Germany's most popular spectator sport is soccer. Every weekend several million watch the matches of the first *Bundesliga* (Federal League comprising eighteen teams of professional footballers) and of the teams of the two area and the many regional and district leagues. Perhaps as a result of television coverage and of the many bribery scandals in the top teams spectators have stayed away in alarming numbers in recent years, even from the big league and cup games, and many clubs are in serious financial difficulties.

Unlike rugby, which is rare in the Bundesrepublik, soccer also has a large number of active participants, and many of the 3.2 million (1973) members of football clubs, among them over 900 000 below eighteen years of age, are active players. Surprisingly, gymnastics is the second most popular German sport, followed by shooting, athletics and handball. Swimming and walking are almost universal pastimes. Although Germany's coastline is comparatively short, there are numerous lakes, and even small towns and villages have open-air swimming pools. Germans are open-air fiends, and every towndweller seems to have an urge to walk or cycle in the country at weekends, if only because he feels it is good for his health. Rambling has, in fact, a long tradition, which also explains the ample provision of *Jugendherbergen* (youth hostels) in the Bundesrepublik: in April 1973 there were 522 with over 60 000 beds. Other sports with an increasing following are skiing (many Germans now take a second holiday between Christmas and Easter), tennis, riding and golf, although the latter is rather a prestige sport. Cricket and baseball are virtually unknown.

Neither the federal nor the Länder governments are directly concerned with the organisation and promotion of sport. The Länder governments, together with local authorities, provide physical-education facilities in schools, yet physical-education instruction for school children amounts to only two or three periods a week. Gemeinden build and maintain a wide variety of recreational and sports facilities, playgrounds as well as stadia and sportshalls. The federal government provides funds to assist the work of the national associations for particular sports, especially their training schemes and international competition programmes, and towards the administrative cost of the four supreme and autonomous federal sports bodies. The most important of these are the *Deutscher Sportbund* (German Sports Federation), the national organisation of some 41 000 sportsclubs (1973) with approximately 9.9 million members (with women numbering almost one-third) and the National Olympic Committee. Governments also give capital grants for specific projects, for example for the construction of facilities for the 1972 Olympic Games in München or the 1974 Football World Cup.

Religion

Nominally at least approximately 49 per cent (1970) of all West Germans belong to one of the Protestant churches, 47 per cent are Roman Catholics, and the rest are either members of other Christian or non-Christian communities or are atheists. There are, for example, 27 000 practising Jews (1973). Only about one-quarter of the West German population go to church regularly, and the number of people leaving the Protestant or Roman Catholic churches, which in the Bundesrepublik requires a formal declaration, reached almost 140 000 and 54 000, respectively, in 1972.

Before the Second World War approximately two-thirds of the population of the German Empire was Protestant and only one-third Roman Catholic. Now Protestants and Roman Catholics are almost equal in number. This is a post-war phenomenon and is restricted to West Germany. It is a consequence of the unequal distribution of the main denominations throughout the former Reich (there were considerably more Protestants in central and eastern Germany than Roman Catholics) and the influx of millions of refugees, many of whom were Roman Catholic. Although it is still possible to state that more Roman Catholics than Protestants are to be found in the southern and western parts of the Bundesrepublik, while the reverse is true of the northern provinces, post-war population movements have meant a much greater intermingling of denominations than at any time since the Reformation. Urban areas especially are now very mixed throughout Germany, although (apart from regional differences) Protestants tend to be strongly represented in urban and Roman Catholics in rural areas; inevitably this is related to structural differences in employment and level of education.

The Evangelical Church

The *Evangelische Kirche in Deutschland* (Evangelical Church in Germany) is a federation of twenty *Landeskirchen* (regional churches), the largest being those of the Rheinland and Hannover (almost four million members each). Their boundaries very rarely coincide with the political Länder boundaries, and their origin derives from the Reformation. Until 1918 they had the status of established churches in the appropriate territories. A complete legal separation of state and Protestant churches was only effected by the Weimar constitution and the formerly established churches continued as independent Landeskirchen. Even the National Socialist oppression did not lead to more than a loose confederation of all Protestant churches after 1945. The revised constitution of 1974 envisages more links between the constituent churches, with greater powers of the central organisation and closer union, including worship and communion; yet the Landeskirchen, which are either Lutheran, Reformed or *Uniert* (the outcome of an earlier attempt in Prussia to unite these two denominations), retain a great deal of independence. The central governing body of the Evangelische Kirche is the Synod, which is composed of 120 members, both lay and clergy. One hundred of these are chosen by the synods of the constituent churches, the remaining twenty are appointed by the *Rat* (Council), the fifteen-member executive of the Evangelische Kirche. Until 1969 when the Protestant churches in the Deutsche

Demokratische Republik founded their own federation, the Evangelische Kirche was one of the very few remaining institutions spanning both parts of Germany.

The Roman Catholic Church

Within the territory of the Bundesrepublik there are five provinces of the Roman Catholic church, each under an archbishop, and a total of twenty-two dioceses. Parts of several of these are situated in the Deutsche Demokratische Republik. While still formally part of their West German dioceses they are, in fact, administered by apostolic administrators under direct authority of the Vatican. The German Catholic bishops meet in the Fulda and Freising Conferences of Bishops to discuss matters of common interest. These two powerful Conferences also represent the interests of the Catholic episcopate and church *vis-à-vis* the federal government in Bonn. The first German joint synod of Roman Catholic hierarchy and laymen met intermittently from 1971 to 1973. It was called to carry out the decisions of the Second Vatican Council and to discuss general problems of church life. Although conservative bishops, theologians and administrators opposed many suggestions, it is said to have been a moderate success.

Church and state

Article 4 of the Grundgesetz declares that the 'freedom of faith and of conscience, and the freedom of creed, religious or ideological, are inviolable'. It also safeguards the 'undisturbed practice of religion'. Article 140 incorporates *in toto* five articles of the Weimar constitution from the section entitled 'Religion and Religious Institutions'. These establish, among other things, that enjoyment of civil and civic rights and eligibility for public office are independent of religious belief, that there is no state church, that churches have in law the status of public corporations, that they may have their own ecclesiastical courts, and that they are entitled to levy taxes on the basis of civil taxation lists, in accordance with the laws of the Länder. Many additional matters covering the relationship between the church and state are regulated by treaties or concordats. Such concordats are in force between the Vatican and the Federation, as well as a number of the Länder, and there are, for example, state treaties between the evangelical churches in Hessen and Niedersachsen and the relevant Land government.

The tax provision illustrates the special and privileged position that the churches, although officially disestablished, enjoy in comparison to other associations. The church tax usually consists of a supplement of eight to ten per cent of the income tax and is collected by the tax offices of the Länder. In 1971 the income of the Evangelische Kirche from this source amounted to DM 3628m, that of the Roman Catholic Church to DM 3173. Although the West German educational system is a state system, the churches, especially the Roman Catholic church, for many years exercised powerful pressure in many parts of West Germany in favour of 'denominational' state Volksschulen. There are many other areas where direct or indirect political involvement of the churches has been considerable. Thus in many a committee, ranging from defence to television advertising, at Länder or federal level, a careful balance between Protestant and Roman Catholic members must be preserved, and quite a few high administrative and political appointments are subject to an unconstitutional shareout between Protestants and Catholics.

After the Nazi terror and the total collapse, the moral authority of the churches in the immediate post-war period was great. They had a wide appeal, as the response to the *Kirchentage*, mass assemblies of hundreds of thousands of Protestant and Roman Catholic laymen held at two-year intervals in various German towns, illustrate. Now in Germany, as elsewhere, the influence of the big churches is on the wane and they are on the defensive against accusations of a conservative outlook, of remoteness from the problems of modern society and of traditional structures.

Bibliography

The main part of this bibliography is divided into sections roughly corresponding to the chapters of the book. An introductory section lists works of a more general nature as well as the main sources of statistical material.

The bibliography contains my personal selection of books for reference and further reading, occasionally on a more specialised topic which I was unable to treat in depth in the book. Many of the publications listed are German but wherever possible the latest English translation has been given, in preference to the original German title.

General

Bracher, K. D. (Hrsg.) (1970). *Nach 25 Jahren, Eine Deutschland-Bilanz*, 2. Aufl., München.

Bundesministerium der Finanzen (Hrsg.) (1974). *Finanzbericht 1975*, Bonn.

Bundesministerium für Innerdeutsche Beziehungen (Hrsg.) (1971). *Deutschland 1971: Bericht und Materialien zur Lage der Nation*, Opladen.

— (1972). *Bericht der Bundesregierung und Materialien zur Lage der Nation 1972*, Bonn.

Claessens, D., Klönne, A., and Tschope, A. (1973). *Sozialkunde der Bundesrepublik Deutschland*, 6. Aufl., Düsseldorf/Köln.

Dahrendorf, R. (1968). *Society and Democracy in Germany*, London.

Grosser, A. (1971). *Germany in Our Time: A Political History of the Post-War Years*, London.

Hallett, G. (1973). *The Social Economy of West Germany*, London.

Leonhardt, R. W. (1967). *This Germany: The Story since the Third Reich*, Harmondsworth.

Loewenthal, R., and Schwarz, H.-P. (Hsrg.) (1974). *Die Zweite Republik, 25 Jahre Bundesrepublik Deutschland—eine Bilanz*, Stuttgart.

London Chamber of Commerce (1970). *Federal Republic of Germany: A Survey for Businessmen*, 3rd edn, London.

Model, O., and Creifels, C. (1975). *Staatsbürgertaschenbuch*, 14. Aufl., München.

Pasley, M. (ed.) (1972). *Germany: A Companion to German Studies*, London.

Payne, J. (1971). *Germany Today: Introductory Studies*, London.

Press and Information Office of the Government of the Federal Republic of Germany (1974). *Facts about Germany: The Federal Republic of Germany*, Bonn.

Presse- und Informationsamt der Bundesregierung (Hrsg.) (1975). *Bonner Almanach 1975*, Bonn (published annually).

— (1974). *Jahresbericht der Bundesregierung 1973*, Bonn (published annually).
Radcliffe, S. (1972). *Twenty-Five Years On: The Two Germanies 1970*, London.
Tilford, R. B., and Preece, R. J. C. (1969). *Federal Germany: Political and Social Order*, London.

Statistical Publications

Bundesminister für Arbeit und Sozialordnung (Hrsg.) (1974). *Statistiken für die Arbeits-und Sozialpolitik 1974*, Bonn.
Bundesministerium für Wirtschaft und Finanzen (1974). *Leistung in Zahlen '73*, Bonn, 23. Aufl. (published annually).
Central Statistical Office (1972). *Annual Abstract of Statistics*, H.M.S.O., London.
Fochler-Hauke, G. (1974). *Der Fischer Weltalmanach 1975*, 16. Aufl., Frankfurt (published annually).
Presse- und Informationsamt der Bundesregierung (Hrsg.) (1974). *Gesellschaftliche Daten 1973: Bundesrepublik Deutschland*, 2. Aufl., Bonn.
Poller, A. (1974). *Zahlenspiegel zur Politik 74*, 3. Aufl., Stuttgart.
Ruppert, F., and Stenzel, H. (1974). *Börsen- und Wirtschaftshandbuch 1974*, 111. Jg., Frankfurt (published annually).
Statistisches Bundesamt (Hrsg.) (1974). *Statistisches Jahrbuch für die Bundesrepublik Deutschland*, Stuttgart/Mainz (published annually).
— (1970). *Handbook of Statistics*, Wiesbaden (published every three years).
Statistical Office of the European Communities (1972). *Basic Statistics of the Community*, 12th edn, Luxemburg (published annually).
United Nations (1972). *Demographic Yearbook*, H.M.S.O., London (published annually).
— (1972). *Statistical Yearbook*, H.M.S.O., London.

Newspapers and Periodicals

Daily: *Süddeutsche Zeitung*, München.
       Bulletin (Presse- und Informationsamt der Bundesregierung), Bonn.

Weekly: *Die Zeit*, Hamburg.
        Der Spiegel, Hamburg.

Monthly: *German International*, Bonn.

1 Post-war History

Auswärtiges Amt (Hrsg.) (1972). *Die Auswärtige Politik der Bundesrepublik Deutschland*, Köln.
Balfour, M. (1968). *West Germany*, London.
Besson, W. (1970). *Die Aussenpolitik der Bundesrepublik: Erfahrungen und Masstäbe*, München.
Bracher, K. D. (1973). *The German Dictatorship: The Origins, Structure, and Consequence of National Socialism*, Harmondsworth.

Bullock, A. (1962). *Hitler: A Study in Tyranny*, Harmondsworth.
Childs, D. (1971). *Germany since 1918*, London.
Golay, J. F. (1965). *The Founding of the Federal Republic of Germany*, Chicago/London.
Hillgruber, A. (1974). *Deutsche Geschichte 1945–1972* (Deutsche Geschichte, Ereignisse und Probleme, Bd. 9), Frankfurt/Berlin/Wien.
Hiscocks, R. (1966). *Germany Revived: An Appraisal of the Adenauer Era*, London.
Kohn, H. (1965). *The Mind of Germany: The Education of a Nation*, London.
Laqueur, W. (1972). *Europe since Hitler*, Harmondsworth.
Mann, G. (1974). *The History of Germany since 1789*, Harmondsworth.
Meinecke, F. (1950). *The German Catastrophe*, Cambridge, Mass.
Merkl, P. H. (1974). *German Foreign Policies, West and East*, Santa Barbara/Oxford.
— (1965). *Germany, Yesterday and Today*, New York and Oxford.
— (1963). *Origin of the West German Republic*, New York and Oxford.
Morgan, R. (1972). *West European Politics since 1945: The Shaping of the European Community*, London.
Pinson, K. S. (1966). *Modern Germany: Its History and Civilisation*, 2nd edn, New York.
Taylor, A. J. P. (1948). *The Course of German History*, London.
Vogelsang, Th. (1969). *Das geteilte Deutschland* (dtv Weltgeschichte des 20 Jahrhunderts, Bd. 11), München.
Willis, F. R. (1968). *France, Germany and the New Europe, 1945–67*, 2nd edn, London, New York.

2 Government

Adenauer, K. (1965–9). *Erinnerungen*, 4 Bde, Stuttgart, vol. I published in English (1966) as *Memoirs, 1945–53*, London.
Beer, R. R. (1970). *Die Gemeinde—Grundriss der Kommunalpolitik* (Geschichte und Staat, 143), München.
Behn, H. U. (1974). *Die Bundesrepublik Deutschland: Handbuch zur staatspolitischen Landeskunde* (Geschichte und Staat, 173/174), München/Wien.
L. Bergsträsser (1965). *Geschichte der Politischen Parteien* (Deutsches Handbuch der Politik, 2), 11. Aufl., München.
Beyme, Klaus v. (1971). *Die politische Elite in der Bundesrepublik Deutschland* (Piper Sozialwissenschaft, 1), München.
Bundesministerium für Verteidigung (Hrsg.) (1974). *Weissbuch 1973/74 zur Sicherheit der Bundesrepublik Deutschland und zur Entwicklung der Bundeswehr*, Bonn.
Childs, D. (1966). *From Schumacher to Brandt: the Story of German Socialism 1956–65*, London.
Deutsch, K. W., and Nordlinger, E. A. (1968). 'The German Federal Republic', in Macridis, R. C., and Ward, R. E., *Modern Political Systems*, 2nd edn, Englewood Cliffs, N.J.
Domcke, H. (1965). *Die Rechtsordnung* (Geschichte und Staat, 112), München.
Edinger, L. J. (1968). *Politics in Germany: Attitudes and Processes*, Boston, Mass.
Ellwein, Th. (1973). *Das Regierungssystem der Bundesrepublik Deutschland, Leitfaden und Quellenbuch*, 3. Aufl., Köln.
Grundgesetz (1972). ... mit Deutschlandvertrag, Bundeswahlgesetz, Parteiengesetz, etc. (Beck Texte im dtv), 15. Aufl., München.
Haseloff, W. (1970). *Die Politischen Parteien in der Bundesrepublik Deutschland*, 2. Aufl., Frankfurt/Berlin/München.
Heidenheimer, A. J. (1965). *The Governments of Germany*, London.
— (1960). *Adenauer and The CDU*, Den Haag.

Ilsemann, C. G. v. (1971). *Die Bundeswehr in der Demokratie, Zeit der Inneren Führung*, Hamburg.
Jacob, H. (1963). *German Administration since Bismarck: Central Authority versus Local Autonomy*, New Haven, Conn.
Johnson, N. (1973). *Government in the Federal Republic of Germany: The Executive at Work*, Oxford.
Kitzinger, U. (1960). *German Electoral Politics*, Oxford.
Loewenberg, G. (1966). *Parliament in the German Political System*, Ithaca, N.Y.
Markus, W. (1972). *Die Bundeswehr: Geschichte–Aufbau–Aufgaben*, München.
Marshall, A. H. (1967). *Local Government Administration Abroad* (Report of the Maud Committee on the Management of Local Government, vol. 4), H.M.S.O., London.
Maunz, Th. (1973). *Deutsche Staatsrecht*, 19. Aufl., München.
Neumann, R. G. (1966). *The Government of the German Federal Republic*, New York/Evanston/London.
Olzog, G., and Herzig, A. (1973). *Die politischen Parteien in der Bundesrepublik Deutschland* (Geschichte und Staat, 104), 8. Aufl., München/Wien.
Pinney, E. L. (1963). *Federalism, Bureaucracy and Party Politics in Western Germany: The Role of the Bundesrat*, Chapel Hill, N. Car.
Plischke, E. (1969). *Contemporary Governments of Germany*, 2nd edn, Boston, Mass.
Preece, R. J. C. (1968). *Land Elections in the German Federal Republic*, London.
Roberts, G. K. (1972). *West German Politics* (Studies in Comparative Politics), London/Basingstoke.
Schneider, H. (1966). *Die Interessenverbände* (Geschichte und Staat, 105), 13. Aufl., München.
Sontheimer, Kurt (1972). *The Government and Politics of West Germany*, London.

Periodicals

Quarterly: Deutsche Vereinigung für Parlamentsfragen (Hrsg.), *Parlamentsfragen*, Opladen.
Deutsche Vereinigung für politische Wissenschaft (Hrsg.), *Politische Vierteljahresschrift*, Opladen.

Monthly: *Der Städtetag*, Stuttgart.

3 Economic Geography

4 Economy, Economic Policy

Agrarbericht 1975, Agrar- und ernährungspolitischer Bericht der Bundesregierung, Deutsche Bundestag, Drucksache 7/1650.
Apel, G. (1969). *Mitbestimmung, Grundlage, Wege, Ziele*, München.
Arndt, J. (1966). *West Germany: Politics of Non-Planning*, Syracuse, N.Y.
Bundesministerium für Arbeit und Sozialordnung (ed.), *Social Policy in Germany: A Survey in Monographs* (series of 50 volumes, Stuttgart, 1961ff.) *See especially*

Klein, H. *Co-determination and the Law Governing Works Councils and Staff Representation in the Public Services* (no. 23).
Reichel, H., and Ringer, F. *Freedom of Association and the Relationship between the Two Sides of Industry* (no. 18).
Reichel, H., and Wotzke, O. *Collective Bargaining and the Law Governing Collective Agreements* (no. 19).

Reichel, H., and Zschorer, H. *Conciliation and Arbitration and the Law as applied to Labour Disputes* (no. 20).

Sahmer, H. *The Labour Courts* (no. 24).

Clapham, J. H. (1936). *Economic Development of France and Germany*, 1815–1914, 4th edn, Cambridge, reprinted 1966.

Degn, Chr., Eggert, E., aand Kolb, A. (Hrsg.) (1972). *Wirtschafts–Seydlitz*, 6. Aufl., Hannover.

Denton, G., Forsyth, M., Maclennan, M. (1971). *Economic Planning and Policies in Britain, France, and Germany*, London.

Deutsche Bundesbank (1971). *Instruments of Monetary Policy in the Federal Republic of Germany*, Bonn.

— (1974). *Report for the Year 1973*, Frankfurt (published annually).

Dickinson, R. E. (1961). *Germany: A General and Regional Geography*, 2nd edn, London.

Elkins, T. H. (1968). *Germany*, 2nd edn., London.

Erhard, L. (1962). *Deutsche Wirtschaftspolitik*, Düsseldorf.

Grebing, H. (1969). *The History of the German Labour Movement*, London.

Lampert, H. (1973). *Die Wirtschafts- und Sozialordnung der Bundesrepublik Deutschland* (Geschichte und Staat, 107/108), 4. Aufl., München.

Limmer, H. (1973). *Die Deutsche Gewerkschaftsbewegung* (Geschichte und Staat, 116), 6. Aufl., München.

Manchester, W. (1969). *The Arms of Krupp*, London.

Mitbestimmungskommission (1970). *Mitbestimmung im Unternehmen*, Bericht der Sachverständigenkommission zur Auswertung der bisherigen Erfahrungen bei der Mitbestimmung, Stuttgart.

Monkhouse, F. J. (1971). *The Countries of North-western Europe* (Geographies: An Intermediate Series), 2nd edn, London.

O.E.C.D. (May, 1974). *Germany* (O.E.C.D. Economic Surveys), Paris (survey published annually).

Pounds, N. J. G. (1968). *The Economic Pattern of Modern Germany*, 2nd edn, London.

Siedlungsverband Ruhrkohlenbezirk (Hrsg.) (1970). *Bericht 1965–1969* (Schriftenreihe Siedlungsverband Ruhrkohlenbezirk, 33) Essen.

Smith, P., Atack, W. (1974). *Worker Participation and Collective Bargaining in Europe* (CIR Study 4), H.M.S.O., London.

Statistisches Landesamt Nordrhein–Westfalen (Hrsg.) (1974). *Statistische Rundschau für das Ruhrgebiet, 1974*, Düsseldorf.

Stolper, G., Häuser, K., and Borchardt, K. (1966). *The German Economy, 1870 to the Present*, London.

Vogl, F. (1973). *German Business after the Economic Miracle*, London.

Wallich, H. (1955). *Mainsprings of the German Revival*, New Haven, Conn.

Periodicals (monthly)

Deutsch Bundesbank, *Monthly Report of the Deutsch Bundesbank*, Frankfurt.

5 Education, Arts and Sciences

Bundesminister für Bildung und Wissenschaft (Hrsg.) (1972). *Forschungsbericht (IV) der Bundesregierung*, Bonn.

— (1974). *Grunddaten*, Wuppertal (published annually).

— (1970). *Report of the Federal Government on Education 1970: The Federal Government's Concept for Educational Policy* (Bildung und Wissenschaft, 2), Bonn.

— (1974) *Strukturdaten*, Bonn (published annually).

Bundesministerium für Bildung und Wissenschaft/Statistisches Bundesamt (Hrsg.) (1974). *Bildung im Zahlenspiegel*, Stuttgart/Mainz (published annually).

Bund-Länder Kommission für Bildungsplanung (1973). *Bildungsgesamtplan*, **Bd. I/II**, Stuttgart.

— (1973). Bundesanstalt für Arbeit, *Studien- und Berufswaal*, Bad Honnef (published annually).

Caty, G., Drilhon, G., Ferné, G., and Wald, S. (1972). *The Research System*, Vol. I, *Germany, France, United Kingdom*, O.E.C.D., Paris.

Dahrendorf, R. (1965). *Bildung ist Bürgerrecht*, Brahmsche-Osnabrück.

Deutscher Bildungsrat (1970). *Empfehlungen der Bildungskommission: Strukturplan für das Bildungswesen*, Bonn.

Flottau, H. (1972). *Hörfunk und Fernsehen heute* (Geschichte und Staat, 164/165), München/Wien.

Geimer, R. and H. (1974). *Science in the Federal Republic of Germany: Organisation and Promotion*, DAAD, 3rd edn, Bonn.

Hamm-Brücher, H. (1972). *Unfähig zur Reform? Kritik und Initiativen zur Bildungspolitik* (Serie Piper, 32), München.

Hess, G. (1968). *Universities in Germany, 1930–1970*, Inter Nationes, Bonn.

Hilker, F. (1963). *Die Shulen in Deutschland*, 3. Aufl., Bad Nauheim.

Inter Nationes (Hrsg.) (1970). *Die Massenmedien in der Bundesrepublik Deutschland*, Bonn.

Knoll, J. H. (1970). *The German Educational System*, Inter Nationes, Bonn.

Meyn, H. (1974). *Massenmedien in der Bundesrepublik Deutschland* (Zur Politik und Zeitgeschichte), Neuaufl., Berlin.

O.E.C.D. (1972). *Educational Policy and Planning: Germany* (Document Series), Paris.

O.E.C.D. (1972). *Germany* (Reviews of National Policies for Education), Paris.

O.E.C.D. (1972). *Training, Recruitment and Utilisation of Teachers in Primary and Secondary Education*, Paris.

Picht, G. (1965). *Die Deutsche Bildungskatastrophe*, München.

Priesemann, G. (1966). *Unsere Schulen: Ein Ratgeber für Eltern and Schüler*, Frankfurt.

Raabe, J. (Hrsg.). *Deutscher Hochschulführer 1973/4*, 48. Aufl., Bonn.

Schelsky, H. (1969). *Abschied von der Hochschulpolitik*, Bielefeld.

Scheuerl, H. (1968). Die Gliederung des Deutschen Schulwesens (Deutscher Bildungsrat, Gutachten und Studien der Bildungskommission, 2), Stuttgart.

Ständige Konferenz der Kultusminister (Hrsg.) (1974). *Handbuch für die Kultusministerkonferenz 1974*, Bonn.

UNESCO (1969). *Science Policy and Organisation of Research in the Federal Republic of Germany*, Paris.

Wetterling, H., and Oppolzer, S. (1968). *Schulführer: Handbuch für Erziehung und Unterricht* (Die Zeit Bücher), Hamburg.

Wissenschaftsrat (1970). *Empfehlungen des Wissenschaftsrates zur Struktur und zum Ausbau des Bildungswesens im Hochschulbereich nach 1970*, **3 Bde**, Tübingen.

Periodicals (monthly)

Bundesminister für Bildung und Wissenschaft (Hrsg.), *Informationen—Bildung, Wissenschaft*, Bonn.

Bundesminister für Forschung und Technologie (Hrsg.), *Mitteilungen aus dem Bundesministerium für Forschung und Technologie*, Bonn.

Inter Nationes (Hrsg.), *Education and Science in the Federal Republic of Germany*, Bonn.
— *Kulturbrief*, Bonn.
Theater heute, Velber b. Hannover (monthly, with an additional special number, *Chronik und Bilanz eines Bühnenjahres*, in the autumn).

6 Social Structure

Braun, H. (1973). *Soziale Sicherung, System und Funktion*, 2. Aufl., Stuttgart.
Bundesministerium für Arbeit und Sozialordnung (Hrsg.) (1975). *Die Einkommens- und Vermögensverteilung in der Bundesrepublik Deutschland*, 5. Aufl., Bonn.
— *Social Policy in Germany: A Survey in Monographs* (series of 50 volumes, Stuttgart, 1961ff). *See especially*

  Köllerman, H. W. *Social Policy in Germany: A Systematic and Historical Introduction* (no. 1).
  Tritz, M. *The Employment of Women in the Federal Republic* (no. 5).
  Sicha, W. and Kozlowicz, W. *Foreign Workers in the Federal Republic* (no. 6).
  Leder, H. *Unemployment Benefit and Unemployment Assistance* (no. 11).
  Rugo, H. *Wages and Salaries* (no. 21).
  Steinwender, K. *Childrens' Allowances* (no. 30).
  Jantz, K. and Zweng, J. *Basic Problems of Social Security: The Pension Insurance of Manual Workers and Salaried Employees* (no. 31).
  Schmatz, H. and Matzke, H. *The Law on Health Insurance* (no. 37).
  Linthe, H. *The Law on Industrial Accident Insurance* (no. 38).
  Doubrawa, K. *Self-Administration and the Law on the Supervision and Services of the Social Insurance Institutes* (no. 40).
  Schönleiter, W. *Pensions and Other Benefits for War Victims* (no. 42).
  Bangert, W. *Public Assistance* (no. 44).
  Nahm, P. P. *The Equalisation of Burdens Arising from War Losses* (no. 50).

Bundesminister für Arbeit und Sozialordnung (Hrsg.) (1974). *Soziale Sicherung—Ein ganzes Leben lang*, Bonn.
— (1971). *Sozialbericht 1973*, Bonn.
— (1973). *Sozialbudget 1974*, Bonn.
— (1975). *Übersicht über die soziale Sicherung*, 9. Aufl., Bonn. In English: *Survey of Social Security in the Federal Republic of Germany*, Bonn.
Deutscher Bundestag (1970). *Gesundheitsbericht der Bundesregierung*, Drucksache VI/1667.

Periodicals

Bundesminister für Arbeit und Sozialordnung, *Sozialpolitische Informationen*, Bonn (published at regular intervals).

Glossary

Abendgymnasium	part-time (evening) grammar school
Abgeordneter	deputy
Abitur	grammar-school leaving examination
Agrarbericht	Report on Agriculture
Akademische Freiheit	academic freedom
Allgemeiner Studentenausschuss (AStA)	General Student Council
Alm (pl. Almen)	high pasture
Alpen	Alps
Alpenvorland	Alpine Foreland
Ältestenrat	Council of Elders
Amtsgericht	local court
Angestellter	white collar worker, salaried employee
Arbeiter	manual worker, wage earner
Arbeitsamt (pl. Arbeitsämter)	labour exchange
Arbeitsdirektor	labour director
Arbeitsgemeinschaft der öffentlich–rechtlichen Rundfunkanstalten Deutschlands	Association of Public Broadcasting Corporations in Germany
Arbeitsgemeinschaft Industrieller Forschungsvereinigungen	Confederation of Industrial Research Associations
Arbeitsgericht	labour court
Arbeitslosenversicherung	unemployment insurance
Assistent	junior lecturer
Aufbauzug (pl. Aufbauzüge)	extension or promotion course
Aufsichtsrat	supervisory board of directors
Ausschuss (pl. Ausschüsse)	committee
Autobahn	motorway
Bad	spa
Bausparkasse	building and loan association
Bayerische Staatsbibliothek	Bavarian State Library
Beamter (pl. Beamte)	civil servant
Bereitschaftspolizei	police reserve
Berufsaufbauschule	voluntary extension school
Berufsfachschule	full-time vocational school
Berufsgenossenschaft	occupational self-governing industrial injuries institution
Berufsschule	part-time vocational school
Bezirk	district
Betriebsrat	works council
Betriebsverfassungsgesetz	Industrial Constitution Act
Bildungsgesamtplan	Comprehensive Education Development Plan
Bizone	economically fused British and American occupation zones
Börse	stock exchange
Bund	federation
Bundesamt für Verfassungsschutz	Federal Office for the Protection of the Constitution

Bundesanstalt für Arbeit	Federal Labour Office
Bundesausbildungsförderungsgesetz	Federal Education Grants Act
Bundesbahn	Federal Railways
Bundesbank	Federal Bank
Bundesbeamtengesetz	Federal Civil Service Act
Bundesgericht	Supreme Federal Court
Bundesgesetzblatt	Federal Gazette
Bundesgrenzschutz	frontier police
Bundeskanzler	Federal Chancellor (Prime Minister)
Bundeskartellamt	Federal Cartel Office
Bundeskriminalamt	Federal Criminal Office
Bundesliga	Federal Football League
Bundesminister der Finanzen	Federal Minister of Finance
Bundesminister für Arbeit und Sozialordnung	Federal Minister of Labour and Social Order
Bundesminister für Wirtschaft	Federal Minister of Economics
Bundesministerium für Bildung und Wissenschaft	Federal Ministry of Education and Arts and Sciences
Bundesnachrichtendienst	Federal Information Service
Bundespost	Federal Post Office
Bundespräsident	Federal President
Bundesrat	upper house of the federal parliament
Bundesratpräsident	Speaker of the upper house of the federal parliament
Bundesrepublik Deutschland (BRD)	Federal Republic of Germany (West Germany)
Bundesrechnungshof	Federal Auditor General
Bundesregierung	federal government
Bundesstrasse	federal road (A-road)
Bundestag	lower house of the federal parliament
Bundestagspräsident	Speaker of the lower house of the federal parliament
Bundesverband der Deutschen Industrie	Confederation of German Industry
Bundesverfassungsgericht	Federal Constitutional Court
Bundesvereinigung der Arbeitgeberverbände	Confederation of German Employers Associations
Bundesversammlung	assembly to elect the Federal President
Bundeswahlgesetz	federal electoral law
Bundeswehr	federal armed forces
Bund–Länder–Kommission für Bildungsplanung	Federation–States Committee for Educational Planning
Bürgerliches Gesetzbuch	Civil Code
Bürgermeister	mayor
Chancengleichheit	equality of opportunity
Christlich-Demokratische Union (CDU)	Christian Democratic Union
Christlicher Gewerkschaftsbund	Christian Trade Union Association
Christlich-Soziale Union (CSU)	Christian Social Union
Deutsche Angestelltengewerkschaft (DAG)	German Salaried Employees Union
Deutsche Bibliothek	German Library
Deutsche Bundesbahn	German Federal Railways

Deutsche Demokratische Republik (DDR)	German Democratic Republic (East Germany)
Deutsche Forschungsgemeinschaft	German Research Association
Deutsche Kommunistische Partei (DKP)	German Communist Party
Deutsche Mark (DM)	West German monetary unit
Deutsche Presseagentur (dpa)	German Press Agency
Deutsche Partei (DP)	German Party
Deutscher Bauernverband	German Farmers' Association
Deutscher Beamtenbund (DBB)	German Civil Service Federation
Deutscher Bildungsrat	German Education Council
Deutscher Gewerkschaftsbund (DGB)	Federation of German Trade Unions
Deutscher Presserat	German Press Council
Deutscher Sportbund	German Sports Federation
Deutsches Fernsehen	German Television
Deutsches Museum	German Museum for Science and Technology
Deutsches Reich	German Empire, German state
Deutschlandvertrag	Germany Treaty
Diplom	first university degree in certain subjects
Donau	Danube
Dorf	village
Drittes Reich	Third Empire
einfaches Gesetz	bill not requiring the approval of the *Bundesrat*
Einkommensteuer	income tax
Erbschaftssteuer	estate duty
Ersatz	artificial
Ersatzkasse (pl. Ersatzkassen)	institutions for the refund of medical expenses
Erzgebirge	Ore Mountains
Europäische Wirtschafts- gemeinschaft (EWG)	European Economic Community (E.E.C.)
Evangelische Kirche in Deutschland	Evangelical Church in Germany
Fachhochschule	advanced technical college
Fachschule	specialised college
Fachschulreife	leaving certificate of *Berufsaufbauschule*
Fernsehen	television
Fernsehrat	television council
Feuilleton	arts page in a newspaper
Finanzbericht	financial report
Finanzgericht	finance court
Flurbereinigung	consolidation of holdings
Forschung und Technologie	research and technology
Fraktion	parliamentary party
Fraktionsgemeinschaft	joint parliamentary party
Fraktionsvorsitzender	parliamentary party chairman
Fraunhofer–Gesellschaft zur Förderung der Angewandten Forschung	Fraunhofer Society for the Support of Applied Research
Freie Demokratische Partei (FDP)	Free Democratic Party
Freie Marktwirtschaft	Free Market Economy
Freie Universität	Free University
Freiwillige Selbstkontrolle	voluntary self-control
Frühlingsmüdigkeit	tiredness at the onset of spring
Führer	leader

Gastarbeiter	guest worker
Gemeinde	local authority
Gemeinderat	local council
Gemeindeordnung	local government act
Gemeinsamer Ausschuss	joint committee
Gemeinsamer Markt	Common Market
Gemeinschaftsausschuss der deutschen Wirtschaft	Joint Committee of the German Economy
Generalinspekteur	Inspector General
Gesamtdeutscher Block/ Bund der Heimatvertriebenen und Entrechteten (GB/BHE)	All German Bloc/Association of Expellees and Those Deprived of Their Rights
Gesamthochschule	comprehensive university
Gesamtschule	comprehensive school
Gesetz	act of parliament, law
Gewerbesteuer	trade tax
Gewerkschaft	trade union
Graduiert	having obtained *Fachhochschul* diploma
Grosse Koalition	Grand Coalition
Grossforschungseinrichtungen	large science research establishments
Grosstadt	town of more than 100 000 inhabitants
Grundgesetz	Basic Law (the West German constitution)
Grundschule	primary school
Grundvertrag	Basic Treaty (between East and West Germany)
Gymnasium	grammar school
neusprachliches	modern language type
altsprachliches	classical type
mathematisch–naturwissenschaftliches	mathematics and science type
Habilitation	post-doctoral research qualification
Handelsgesetzbuch	Commercial Code
Handelsrecht	commercial and company law
Handwerkskammer	Chamber of Artisans
Hauptschule	upper primary school
Heimatzeitung	local newspaper
Hochschule	institution of higher education
Hochschulrahmengesetz	General Law for Institutions of Higher Education
Höhere Fachschule	a type of technical college
Hypothekenbank	mortgage bank
Industrie- und Handelskammer	Chamber of Industry and Commerce
Innung	guild
Institut für Meeresforschung	Oceanographic Institute
Institut für Zeitgeschichte	Institute of Contemporary History
Intendant	chief executive officer of a radio or television corporation; administrative and artistic director of a theatre or opera house
Jugendgericht	youth court
Jugendherberge	youth hostel
Jungsozialist (pl. Jungsozialisten) Juso	Young Socialist

Kindergarten (pl. Kindergärten)	kindergarten
Kindergeld	family allowance
Kirchentag	mass assembly of members of churches
Kölner Bucht	Cologne Bay
Kommandantura	Allied governing authority for Greater Berlin
Kommunistische Partei Deutschlands (KPD)	Communist Party of Germany
Körperschaftssteuer	corporation tax
Krankenkasse (pl. Krankenkassen)	sickness fund
kreisfreie Stadt	town which is an all-purpose authority, not forming part of a *Kreis*
Kreis	district
Kreisrat	district council
Kriegsopferversorgung	War Victims Relief Fund
Kriminalpolizei	criminal investigation police
Kultusminister	Minister of Education and Cultural Affairs
Kunst-, Musik-, and Sporthochschulen (pl.)	colleges for fine art, drama, music and physical education
Land (pl. Länder)	constituent state of the Federal Republic
Landesbank/Girozentrale	central giro institution of savings banks in one Land
Landeskirche (pl. Landeskirchen)	regional church
Landkreis	rural district
Landgericht	regional court
Landrat	chief executive of the *Kreis*
Landstrassen	roads that are the responsibility of the Länder (B-roads)
Landtag	parliament of a Land
Landwirtschaftskammer	Chamber of Agriculture
Lastenausgleichsgesetz	Equalisation of Burdens Act
Leistungsfähigkeit	educability
Max–Planck–Gesellschaft zur Förderung der Wissenschaften	Max Planck Society for the Advancement of Arts and Sciences
Mehrwertsteuer	value added tax
Ministerpräsident	Prime Minister
Mitbestimmung	co-determination
Mitglied des Bundestages (M.d.B.)	member of the lower house of the federal parliament
Mittelbau	career grade of university lecturer
Mittelgebirge	Central Uplands
Montanunion	European Coal and Steel Community (E.C.S.C.)
München	Munich
Nationaldemokratische Partei Deutschlands (NPD)	National Democratic Party of Germany
Norddeutsche Tiefebene	North German Plain
Nord–Ostsee–Kanal	Kiel Canal
Nordsee	North Sea
numerus clausus	restriction on university admissions

Oberbürgermeister	lord mayor
Oberlandesgericht	court of appeal
Öffentliches Recht	public law
Ostsee	Baltic
Ostpolitik	Eastern Policy
Pädagogische Hochschule	college of education
Parlamentarischer Rat	Parliamentary Council
Parteiengesetz	Act on Political Parties
Patentgericht	patent court
Petersberger Abkommen	Petersberg Agreement (Nov. 1949)
Polizei	police
Privatrecht	private law
Rat	council
Raiffeisenkasse	credit co-operative
Realschule	intermediate school
Rechtsstaat	state based on the rule of law
Rechtsverordnung (pl. Rechtsverordnungen)	delegated legislation
Regierender Bürgermeister	Governing Mayor
Regierung	government
Regierungsbezirk	county
Regierungspräsident	highest official of a *Regierungsbezirk*
Reich	empire, state
Reichsmark (RM)	German currency between 1923 and 1948
Reichstag	lower house of the parliament of the former *Reich*
Reifeprüfung	grammar school leaving examination
Rektor	head of a university
Rente	pension
Rentenversicherung der Arbeiter und Angestellten	pension insurance for manual workers and white collar employees
Richter	judge
Ruhrstatut	Ruhr Statute, agreement to create an international authority for the control of the Ruhr coal and steel production
Rundfunkrat	broadcasting council
Schwarzwald	Black Forest
Schwurgericht	court of first instance for very serious crimes
Sekundarstufe	secondary level
Sonderschule	special school
Sozialbudget	social budget
Sozialdemokratische Partei Deutschlands (SPD)	Social Democratic Party of Germany
Soziale Krankenversicherung	social health insurance
Soziale Marktwirtschaft	social market economy
Sozialgericht	social court
Sozialhilfe	social aid
Sozialistische Reichspartei (SRP)	Socialist Reich Party
Sozialwohnung	flat financed by government grants
Sparkasse	savings bank
Staatsanwalt	public prosecutor
Staatsexamen	state examination (university degree in certain subjects)
Staatssekretär	secretary of state
Staatstheater	state theatre

Stabilitätsgesetz	Act to Promote Stability and Growth of the Economy
Stadtstaat	city state
Stadttheater	municipal theatre
Stadtrat	town council
Ständige Konferenz der Kultusminister der Länder	Standing Conference of the Ministers of Education and Cultural Affairs of the Länder
Shiftung	foundation
Strafgesetzbuch	Criminal Code
Studienseminar	special institute for the professional part of teacher training
Technische Hochschule, Technische Universität	Technical University
Umsatzsteuer	turnover tax
Unfallversicherung	industrial injuries insurance
Universitätspräsident	vice-chancellor
Verband Deutscher Studentenschaften	German National Union of Students
Vermittlungsausschuss	Mediation Committee
Vermögenssteuer	property tax
Vertrag	treaty
Verwaltungsrat	executive council of broadcasting corporation
Verwaltungsgericht	administrative court
Vizepräsident	Deputy Speaker of the lower house of the federal parliament
Volkshochschule	adult education centre
Volkspartei	mass party
Volksschule	*Grundschule* and *Hauptschule* combined
Volkswagen	people's car
Vorstand	board of management
Wahlkreis	constituency
Wahlkreiskommission	constituency boundary commission
Wehrbeauftragter	Parliamentary Defence Commissioner
Wissenschaftsrat	Council for Arts and Sciences
Zentralbankrat	Central Bank Council
Zoll (pl. Zölle)	customs and excise duty
Zollverein	customs union
Zustimmungsgesetz	bill requiring the approval of the *Bundesrat*
Zweites Deutsches Fernsehen	Second German Television

Metric Measures and Equivalents

1 Millimeter (mm)	= 0.0394 inch	1 Liter (1)	= 1.7607 pint
1 Meter (m)	= 3.2809 feet	1 Hektoliter (hl)	= 22.009 gallon
1 Kilometer (km)	= 0.6214 mile	1 Kilogram (kg)	= 2.2046 pound
1 Ar (a)	= 119.6011 sq. yard		(avoirdupois)
1 Hektar (ha)	= 2.4711 acre	1 Tonne (t)	= 0.984 Imperial ton

Index